PRINCIPLES OF GENERATIVE PHONOLOGY

Grover Hudson

AMSTERDAM STUDIES IN THE THEORY AND HISTORY OF LINGUISTIC SCIENCE

General Editor

E.F. KONRAD KOERNER

(Zentrum für Allgemeine Sprachwissenschaft, Typologie
und Universalienforschung, Berlin)

Series IV – CURRENT ISSUES IN LINGUISTIC THEORY

Advisory Editorial Board

Volume 250

John T. Jensen

Principles of Generative Phonology

An introduction

PRINCIPLES OF GENERATIVE PHONOLOGY

AN INTRODUCTION

JOHN T. JENSEN

University of Ottawa

JOHN BENJAMINS PUBLISHING COMPANY
AMSTERDAM/PHILADELPHIA

TM The paper used in this publication meets the minimum requirements of American National Standard for Information Sciences — Permanence of Paper for Printed Library Materials, ANSI Z39.48-1984.

Library of Congress Cataloging-in-Publication Data

Jensen, John T. (John Tillotson)
    Principles of generative phonology : an introduction / John T. Jensen.
        p.   cm. -- (Amsterdam studies in the theory and history of linguistic science. Series IV, Current issues in linguistic theory, ISSN 0304-0763 ; v. 251–250)
    1. Grammar, Comparative and general--Phonology. 2. Generative grammar. I. Title. II. Series.
P217.6.J46 2004
414--dc22   2004048608
ISBN 90 272 4762 5 (Eur.) / 1 58811 513 5 (US) (Hb; alk. paper)
ISBN 90 272 4767 6 (Eur.) / 1 58811 562 3 (US) (Pb; alk. paper)

John Benjamins Publishing Co. • P.O.Box 36224 • 1020 ME Amsterdam • The Netherlands
John Benjamins North America • P.O.Box 27519 • Philadelphia PA 19118-0519 • USA

Contents

31

43

Preface

Principles of Generative Phonology is intended as a basic, thorough introduction to contemporary phonological theory and practice. While the theory is in a constant state of revision and refinement, it is not possible to appreciate recent developments or follow the argumentation involved without a firm foundation in the theory of distinctive features, formal notations for phonological rules, and the theory of rule ordering. In the first six chapters I have essentially followed the theory of *SPE* (Chomsky & Halle 1968) in discussing these concepts, with the exception that I use iterative rules rather than *SPE*'s simultaneous rule schemata for rules with multiple effects, as in vowel harmony.

The first chapter is a review of phonetics. An understanding of phonetics is essential for the study of phonology. The reader unacquainted with phonetics is advised to supplement this chapter with a textbook devoted to the subject, such as MacKay (1987). This chapter also introduces the phonetic symbols used throughout the book, in that I do not strictly follow IPA conventions, for reasons detailed there.

Chapter 2 discusses contrast and distribution, with emphasis on rules as the mechanism for describing distributions. The terms *basic, underlying segment,* and *phoneme* are used more or less interchangeably for the segment that appears in underlying representations at this stage, but problems with the concept of a phoneme as a group of phonetically similar sounds in complementary distribution (or free variation) are also discussed. In anticipation of the discussion of distinctive features, the notion of pattern congruity is also introduced here.

Chapter 3 introduces distinctive features, natural classes, and redundancy. I have adopted strictly binary features, since there does not appear to be any consensus on a replacement set of unary or multivalued features or some combination of these. For similar reasons I have excluded feature geometry, preferring standard unordered feature matrices as the clearest presentation of these concepts at this stage.

Chapter 4 builds on the concept of rules from chapter 2, showing how rules of the same type account for phonological alternations, and introduces additional rule writing conventions.

Chapter 5 demonstrates the use of ordering of rules to achieve maximum generalization, starting with examples of two or three rules and advancing to the nine rules of Yawelmani discussed in Kenstowicz & Kisseberth (1979).

Chapter 6 discusses abstractness and the motivation for abstract underlying representations, as well as the limitations on abstractness.

Chapter 7 discusses some post-*SPE* developments, including autosegmental phonology, metrical and prosodic phonology, underspecification theory, and lexical phonology.

For a number of reasons I have decided not to include Optimality Theory, despite its current popularity. One reason is that it does not really fall under the head of principles of generative phonology, being something of a departure from these principles in rejecting derivations with ordered rules. Second, Optimality Theory has achieved far more success in morphology than in phonology. It has made significant headway in describing infixation and reduplication without resort to unconstrained morphological processes, but encounters difficulties in the description of the opaque phonological interactions that occur constantly in languages and that are most convincingly treated in terms of ordered rules. In order to treat basic principles thoroughly I have thought it best to leave more advanced topics for others to tackle. Indeed there are a number of introductions to Optimality Theory that have recently become available, such as Archangeli & Langendoen (1997) and Kager (1999). Such works are best tackled after mastery has been achieved over the basic ideas underlying generative phonology.

It is my pleasant duty to thank the many colleagues and students who have read, used, and worked with this material in various capacities and provided suggestions for improvement. I am sure that I will regret not having taken their advice on certain matters, but in other cases their input has resulted in significant improvements. Kiyan Azarbar provided extensive comments on the entire manuscript, helped with the spectrograms in chapter 1, and also helped with the Farsi examples. Jon Wood also helped with the spectrograms, providing the graphic versions. Margaret Stong-Jensen read through several versions and offered suggestions at each stage. Leigh-Anne Webster, Natasha Le Blanc, Lisa DiDomenico, Michelle Charette, and Kerry Dockstader made numerous suggestions for improvement and helped with the exercises. Mim Pearse provided the drawings used to illustrate types of rule interaction in chapter 5. Rebecca Silvert read through the entire manuscript in its last stages and helped tremendously with the preparation of the final version. Finally, I am grateful to Konrad Koerner, the editor of the series, and Ms Anke de Looper of Benjamins, for their invaluable assistance. Any remaining errors and inconsistencies have been left as an exercise for the attentive reader to discover.

1   Phonetics

Both phonetics and phonology are concerned with the sounds of language. *Phonetics* can be defined as "[t]he study of the full range of vocal sounds that human beings are capable of making" (Kenstowicz & Kisseberth 1979, 1). This includes sounds like coughs, whistles, and the sound made when blowing out a candle. If we restrict our attention to "[t]he study of sounds human beings employ when speaking a language" (ibid.), we have *linguistic phonetics*. This will be the focus of this chapter. Coughs and whistles do not occur as speech sounds, and are therefore excluded from linguistic phonetics. However, a sound that closely resembles the sound made when blowing out a candle, written with the phonetic symbol [w̥], appears as a speech sound in those North American varieties of English that distinguish the words *witch* [wɪč] and *which* [w̥ɪč] (Sapir 1925). If we further restrict our attention to "the study of the system underlying the selection and use of sounds in the languages of the world" (Kenstowicz & Kisseberth 1979, 1), we are dealing with *phonology*. Sapir emphasizes that candle blowing is functionally quite different from the use of the similar sound in language. Each act of candle blowing is functionally equivalent, whereas the use of the linguistic sound [w̥] in those dialects differs depending on the word in which it appears: *when, whisky, wheel*. Furthermore, the linguistic sound varies, with many speakers using [w] in these words, thus having no distinction between words like *witch* and *which*. Thus, phonology is grounded in linguistic phonetics, and uses much of the terminology of phonetics. The purpose of this chapter is to introduce the phonetic terminology and symbols that will be employed in the remainder of the book.

    In articulatory and acoustic terms, speech is a continuum. In uttering speech, the articulators are constantly in motion, and the acoustic effect is a continuously varying wave. Instrumental investigation allows visual inspection of such a wave or of a sound spectrogram, which analyzes the wave into its component frequencies. Nevertheless, for phonological purposes, we rep-

resent speech as a sequence of discrete units called *segments*. This is known
as a *phonetic representation*. While somewhat more abstract than a pure
record of the articulatory and acoustic events, there are good reasons for
believing that speech is represented this way. One is that speakers can generally agree on the number of sounds in a relatively short utterance of their language: English speakers would say that *cat* has three sounds. Another is the
existence of alphabetic writing systems: the orthographic representation of *cat*
contains three separate symbols. Another is that individual speech sounds
"can be substituted, omitted, transposed or added" in speech errors (Fromkin
1971, 29–30). She cites example of speech errors such as those in (1).

(1)   cu*p* [kəp] of coffee   → cu*ff* [kəf] of coffee   (anticipatory
                                                                  substitution)

       *w*eek [wiyk] long race   → *r*eek [ɹiyk] long race

       *k*eep a *t*ape   → *t*eep a *c*ape   (transposition)
       [kʰiyp ə tʰeyp]   [tʰiyp ə kʰeyp]

       fish g*r*otto   → f*r*ish gotto

       b*r*ake f*l*uid   → b*l*ake f*r*uid

       *s*ou*p* is *s*erved   → *s*er*p* is *s*oo*v*ed [suwvd]

Clearly, it is easier to work with an inventory of discrete segments than to
explain every combination of articulatory events. It is important to realize that
a phonetic transcription is *abstract* in this sense. Phonology necessarily deals
with such abstractions. As we proceed we will find that we need to have representations considerably more abstract than this. However, the abstract representations of phonology are always rooted in phonetics. We will thus begin
our discussion of phonetics by considering the individual sound segments of
which speech is composed.

1.1   Articulatory phonetics

Articulatory phonetics describes the position of the various organs of speech
in the production of different speech sounds. For convenience, the sounds are
divided into two large groups, consonants and vowels, and each group is
described separately, although the same organs are involved in the production
of both. We use square brackets around phonetic symbols to distinguish them
from orthographic symbols. Roughly, vowels are sounds that can function as
syllable peaks, while consonants are sounds that surround such peaks.

THE INTERNATIONAL PHONETIC ALPHABET (revised to 1993, corrected 1996)

CONSONANTS (PULMONIC)

	Bilabial	Labiodental	Dental	Alveolar	Postalveolar	Retroflex	Palatal	Velar	Uvular	Pharyngeal	Glottal
Plosive	p b			t d		ʈ ɖ	c ɟ	k ɡ	q ɢ		ʔ
Nasal	m	ɱ		n		ɳ	ɲ	ŋ	N		
Trill	B			r					R		
Tap or Flap				ɾ		ɽ					
Fricative	ɸ β	f v	θ ð	s z	ʃ ʒ	ʂ ʐ	ç ʝ	x ɣ	χ ʁ	ħ ʕ	h ɦ
Lateral fricative				ɬ ɮ							
Approximant		ʋ		ɹ		ɻ	j	ɰ			
Lateral approximant				l		ɭ	ʎ	L			

Where symbols appear in pairs, the one to the right represents a voiced consonant. Shaded areas denote articulations judged impossible.

CONSONANTS (NON-PULMONIC)

Clicks		Voiced implosives		Ejectives	
ʘ	Bilabial	ɓ	Bilabial	ʼ	Examples:
ǀ	Dental	ɗ	Dental/alveolar		
ǃ	(Post)alveolar	ʄ	Palatal	pʼ	Bilabial
ǂ	Palatoalveolar	ɠ	Velar	tʼ	Dental/alveolar
ǁ	Alveolar lateral	ʛ	Uvular	kʼ	Velar
				sʼ	Alveolar fricative

OTHER SYMBOLS

- ʍ Voiceless labial-velar fricative
- w Voiced labial-velar approximant
- ɥ Voiced labial-palatal approximant
- ʜ Voiceless epiglottal fricative
- ʢ Voiced epiglottal fricative
- ʡ Epiglottal plosive

- ɕ ʑ Alveolo-palatal fricatives
- ɺ Alveolar lateral flap
- ɧ Simultaneous ʃ and x

Affricates and double articulations can be represented by two symbols joined by a tie bar if necessary.

k͡p t͡s

VOWELS

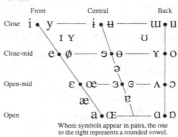

Where symbols appear in pairs, the one to the right represents a rounded vowel.

SUPRASEGMENTALS

ˈ	Primary stress
ˌ	Secondary stress

ˌfoʊnəˈtɪʃən

ː	Long	eː
ˑ	Half-long	eˑ
̆	Extra-short	ĕ
.	Minor (foot) group	
‖	Major (intonation) group	
.	Syllable break	ɹi.ækt
‿	Linking (absence of a break)	

DIACRITICS Diacritics may be placed above a symbol with a descender, e.g. ŋ̊

̥	Voiceless	n̥ d̥		̤	Breathy voiced	b̤ a̤		̪	Dental	t̪ d̪
̬	Voiced	s̬ t̬		̰	Creaky voiced	b̰ a̰		̺	Apical	t̺ d̺
ʰ	Aspirated	tʰ dʰ		̼	Linguolabial	t̼ d̼		̻	Laminal	t̻ d̻
̹	More rounded	ɔ̹		ʷ	Labialized	tʷ dʷ		̃	Nasalized	ẽ
̜	Less rounded	ɔ̜		ʲ	Palatalized	tʲ dʲ		ⁿ	Nasal release	dⁿ
̟	Advanced	u̟		ˠ	Velarized	tˠ dˠ		ˡ	Lateral release	dˡ
̠	Retracted	e̠		ˤ	Pharyngealized	tˤ dˤ		̚	No audible release	d̚
̈	Centralized	ë		̴	Velarized or pharyngealized	ɫ				
̽	Mid-centralized	e̽		̝	Raised	e̝	(ɹ̝ = voiced alveolar fricative)			
̩	Syllabic	n̩		̞	Lowered	e̞	(β̞ = voiced bilabial approximant)			
̯	Non-syllabic	e̯		̘	Advanced Tongue Root	e̘				
˞	Rhoticity	ɚ a˞		̙	Retracted Tongue Root	e̙				

TONES AND WORD ACCENTS

LEVEL			CONTOUR		
e̋ or	˥	Extra high	ě	ˇ	Rising
é	˦	High	ê	ˆ	Falling
ē	˧	Mid	e᷄	ˈ	High rising
è	˨	Low	e᷅	ˌ	Low rising
ȅ	˩	Extra low	e᷈	˜	Rising-falling
↓		Downstep	↗		Global rise
↑		Upstep	↘		Global fall

ɓ = bʰ ?

However, certain consonants, in particular the sonorants [l], [r], [m], and [n] in English, can function as syllable peaks, as in the final sounds of *bottle, butter, bottom,* and *button* [ˈbɒɾl̩], [ˈbəɾɹ̩], [ˈbɒɾm̩], [ˈbəʔn̩]. These words might also be transcribed with a vowel in the second syllable, as [ˈbɒɾəl], [ˈbəɾəɹ], [ˈbɒɾəm], [ˈbəʔən].

A consonant like the glide [w] has basically the same articulatory properties as the vowel [u]. Articulatorily, glides are like vowels, but not functionally. We will follow the usual convention of dividing speech sounds into consonants and vowels in this section, but return to the question of the interplay of consonant and vowel properties in chapter 3.

The symbols used for phonetic segments are essentially arbitrary. For mnemonic convenience the symbols in use are borrowed from various alphabetic writing systems, with the addition of modifications and diacritics of various kinds. To begin the discussion we will refer to the chart of the International Phonetic Alphabet on the previous page. In section 1.3 we will introduce certain modifications to this system to remedy some of its inadequacies. The chart of the organs of speech on page 5 should also facilitate some of this discussion.

1.1.1   Consonants

Consonants are divided into groups along three basic dimensions. First is the manner of articulation, which refers to how the sound is produced. Second is the place of articulation, the position in the mouth of the greatest obstruction. Third is the state of the glottis in the production of the sound. We will start with the manner of articulation.

1.1.1.1 Manner of articulation

Consonants are divided into two broad groups in terms of the manner of their articulation: *obstruents* and *sonorants.* The obstruents are formed by obstructing the passage of air to a degree sufficient to produce a significant pressure increase within the mouth behind the obstruction. Included in this category are the stops (sometimes called "plosives"), fricatives, and affricates. In a stop the airstream is totally blocked for a short period, producing sounds like [tʰ] as in *ten* or [d] as in *den*. In the case of voiceless stops, the acoustic result is a period of silence up to the release of the stop. In fricatives the articulators are partially open, allowing air under pressure to escape and produce a hissing sound,

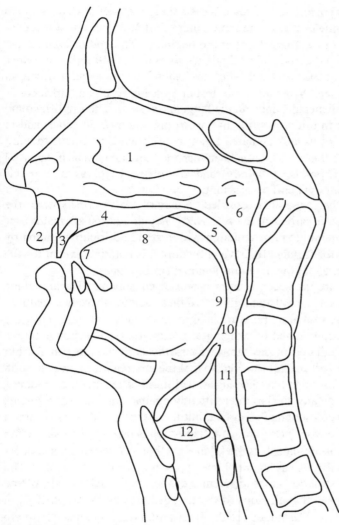

The principal organs of speech

1.	Nasal cavity	7.	Tongue tip (apex)
2.	Lips	8.	Tongue blade
3.	Upper incisor teeth	9.	Tongue root
4.	Hard palate	10.	Oral pharynx
5.	Soft palate (velum)	11.	Laryngeal pharynx
6.	Nasal pharynx	12.	Vocal folds

as in [s] in *sip* or [z] in *zip*. An affricate is essentially a sequence of a stop plus a fricative at the same or nearly the same point of articulation, but considered a single sound, as in the English [č] at the beginning and end of *church*. On the other hand, the [ts] at the end of English *cats* is not an affricate, but rather a *sequence* of [t] plus [s]. Roughly the same sound occurs as an affricate in Russian [t͡sɨ'nɑ] 'price.' Whether or not a sound of this type is an affricate or a stop-fricative sequence depends on the language system. The English sound [ts] does not occur in initial position in a word (as it does in Russian) and in English this sequence usually contains a morpheme boundary (*cats* is the plural of *cat*). In Polish there is a contrast between the sequence [tš] as in *trzy* [tši] 'three' or *wietrzny* [vyɛtšnɨ] 'windy' and the affricate [č] as in *czy* [či] 'whether' or *wieczny* [vyɛčnɨ] 'everlasting.'

The IPA chart lists stops (there called "plosives") in the first row of the consonant chart and fricatives in the fifth row. They do not list affricates separately but recommend the representation with a stop and fricative joined by a tie bar as we did for Russian [t͡s]. We will adopt this notation except for the postalveolar affricates [č] (as in *church*) and [ǰ] (as in *judge*).

The sonorants are the second major group of consonants. These include the nasals, trills, flaps, laterals and glides. In these sounds there is a relatively free air passsage, so that no pressure is built up in the vocal tract. They are most frequently accompanied by voicing at the glottis (see section 1.1.1.3). The nasals are articulated in the same way as the corresponding stops, but have the velum (or soft palate) lowered so that the airstream can pass through the nose. These are sounds like the English [n] in *no*. The trills are produced by allowing an articulator to flap intermittently against another. Such sounds are not used as speech sounds in English, but the alveolar trill [r] is common in Spanish, as in the word *perro* 'dog.' A flap or tap is essentially a single-tap trill; these also occur in Spanish as the [ɾ] in *pero* 'but.' This sound also occurs in North American English as an allophone of /t/[1] in a word like *city* [sɪɾi]. The laterals have an obstruction along the centre of the vocal tract, but allow free air passage along one or both sides of the tongue, such as the English [l] in *leap* or the [ɫ] of *pull*. The glides are the final group of sonorants. These are sometimes called semivowels because of their articulatory and acoustic similarity to vowels. The [w] of *win* has the same articulation as the vowel [u] of

---

[1] Slant lines // enclose *phonemes,* or, more precisely, *underlying representations.* These are further levels of abstraction from phonetic transcription. A single phoneme may have a variety of phonetic realizations, also called *allophones.* This concept is developed in detail in chapters 2 and 4.

boot and the [y] (IPA [j]) of *yes* has the articulation of the vowel [i] in *beet*. French has the glide [ɥ] as in *huit* 'eight,' with the same articulation as the vowel [ü].

The laterals and the glides are sometimes grouped together under the term *approximant*. This term suggests that the articulators are brought close enough together to produce a sound with a recognizable point of articulation, but not close enough to produce the hissing noise associated with fricatives. When this is done with articulators otherwise associated with fricatives, for example both lips, the result is an approximant at the same point of articulation. For example the bilabial approximant [β̞] has roughly the same articulation as the voiced bilabial fricative [β] but lacks the fricative noise of the latter. The approximant is indicated by the diacritic [̞] placed below the corresponding voiced fricative symbol.

The term *rhotic* or *r-sound* is sometimes applied to the phonetically rather heterogeneous group of sounds whose phonetic symbols are varieties of the letter *r*. This group includes the trills [r] and [ʀ], the flaps [ɾ] and [ɽ], the approximants [ɹ] and [ʁ], and the fricatives [ʁ] and sometimes [χ] (also written [ʁ̞]). While phonetically quite distinct, this group of sounds are often functionally similar. We will discuss some examples where some of these sounds stand in an allophonic relation in section 2.1 of chapter 2. The term *liquids* is applied to the group of sounds containing laterals and rhotics.

1.1.1.2 Place of articulation

In describing the place of articulation it is useful to distinguish *passive* articulators and *active* articulators. The active articulators are the lower lip and the tongue, including the tip, the blade, and the body of the tongue. These highly mobile organs are capable of moving in such a way as to vary the shape of the vocal tract and thus give rise to a variety of sounds. The passive articulators are the more stationary parts of the mouth and pharynx, from the lips to the glottis, with reference to which the active articulators move. The place of articulation is the point in this region where the greatest approach of the articulators takes place. Stating the place of articulation as a point along the passive articulators is usually sufficient to identify a unique articulation, since even the active articulator is somewhat limited in its motion. If we state a place of articulation alone, e.g., *dental*, it indicates the passive articulator: this case the articulation is made at the upper teeth. If we want to specif active articulator we use a prefix, e.g., *apicodental* indicates that th articulator is the tip (apex) of the tongue. Such prefixes are not normally necessary. The active articulator for bilabial and labio dental sounds is the lower lip; for dental, alveolar, postalveolar, and retroflex sounds it is the blade of the tongue; and for prepalatal, palatal, and velar sounds the body of the tongue is raised. The current IPA chart recognizes eleven points of articulation: bilabial (instead of labio-labial), labiodental, dental, alveolar, postalveolar, retroflex, palatal, velar, uvular, pharyngeal, and glottal. Earlier IPA charts included an additional point, alveolopalatal (or prepalatal) between the retroflex and the palatal. Because quite a few languages (e.g., Polish) use sounds articulated in this region, we will restore it to our revised chart in section 1.3.

Points of Articulation

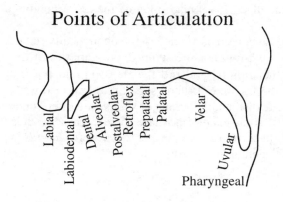

Glottal (at the vocal folds)

1.1.1.3 Glottal state

The state of the glottis varies independently of the articulators involved in consonant production, and thus gives an additional variable. There is, however, some dependency between glottal state and manner of articulation. Vowels, sonorants, and approximants are nearly always voiced, although they can be devoiced under certain conditions. The symbols for these sounds, for example [ɑ], [n], indicate voicing along with the other features of the sound; a diacritic, e.g., [ɑ̥], [n̥] is needed to indicate a voiceless variety of these sounds. Obstruents are often voiceless, since it is difficult to maintain the airflow needed for voicing while making a major obstruction in the airstream. Despite this latter fact many languages contrast voiced and voiceless obstruents. Thus,

obstruents have separate symbols for the voiceless and voiced varieties of
these sounds, e.g., [p] and [b].

Voicing is produced by a regular vibration of the vocal folds, the result of
an aerodynamic process known as the Bernoulli effect. The vocal folds are
brought together, nearly touching along their entire length. The airstream
flowing between them creates a suction that draws them together, rather in the
way that the air flowing over an airplane wing creates a negative pressure
above the wing resulting in a lift. Once the folds come together, the suction
ceases and they are forced apart by the pressure beneath them. Once apart, the
suction reappears, and so the cycle is repeated.

A voiceless sound is characterized by the vocal folds being drawn apart,
so that the vibration characteristic of voicing does not take place. A voiceless
fricative such as [s] has noise produced only at the point of articulation, while
a voiced fricative such as [z] has such noise and, in addition, voicing at the
glottis. Because an obstruent has a major obstruction at the point of articulation, it is more difficult to sustain voicing in an obstruent than in a sonorant.
However, voiced and voiceless obstruents are common enough to have separate symbols, as in our examples [z] and [s]. Voiceless sonorants are rare, so
voicelessness in a sonorant must be indicated by a diacritic, as in [n̥] for a
voiceless alveolar nasal. Such sounds rarely contrast, but Ladefoged (1971,
11) reports contrasting voiced and voiceless nasals and laterals in Burmese, as
in (2).

(2)	mà	'healthy'	nà	'pain'	ŋã	'fish'
	m̥à	'order'	n̥à	'nostril'	ŋ̥ã	'rent'
			lɑ	'moon'		
			l̥á	'beautiful'		

Voiceless vowels also occur, but not contrastively. In Chatino, a language
of Mexico, unstressed vowels are voiceless betweeen voiceless consonants, as
in (3) (Gleason 1955, 62).

(3)

ti'yeʔ	'lime'	t̥ị'hi	'hard'
ki'no	'sandal'	kị'su	'avocado'
su'wi	'clean!'	sụʔ'wa	'you send'
laʔa	'side'	tɑ̣ʔa	'fiesta'
ŋgu'ta	'seed'	kụ'ta	'you will give'
'kiʔ	'fire'	kị'ta	'you will wait'

In classifying a sound as voiced or voiceless, we have so far considered only whether the vocal folds are vibrating during the articulation of the sound. It is also necessary to investigate the dynamic aspect of how this glottal state relates to surrounding sounds. In the case of fricatives, this is clear enough: the period of fricative noise and the period of voicing coincide almost entirely. Stops are more complex, however. Let us consider a single syllable consisting of a stop followed by a vowel. If the vowel is voiced, we may ask when the voicing begins. If voicing occurs throughout the stop closure and continues into the vowel, we say that the stop is fully voiced. The voiced stops of French [b], [d], [g] are usually said to be fully voiced. Another possibility is that voicing begins only at the release of the stop. In this case the stop is, strictly speaking, voiceless, as the French [p], [t], [k]. The voiced stops of English, [b], [d], [g], are often produced in a manner similar to that of the French voiceless stops. A third possiblilty is that voicing begins somewhat later than the stop release; these are then referred to as voiceless *aspirated* stops. The English voiceless stops (at the beginning of a word or a stressed syllable) are usually aspirated, and thus are notated [pʰ], [tʰ], [kʰ] phonetically. In English these are allophones of the plain voiceless stops [p], [t], [k], which occur phonetically after [s] in word-initial position, in words such as *spare, stick, skate*. It is interesting that, if you were to tape record these words and cut the [s] portion from the tape, then play it back, these words would sound like *bare, Dick, gate* rather than *pair, tick, Kate* (MacKay 1987, 95). While aspirated and unaspirated stops do not contrast in English, they do contrast in Thai. Two sounds are said to *contrast* if they can form the minimal distinction between two otherwise identical utterances. The examples of (4) demonstrate this and also show contrasting voiced stops (Ladefoged 1971, 12).

(4)

pʰàɑ	'to split'	tʰam	'to do'	kʰàt	'to interrupt'
pàɑ	'forest'	tam	'to pound'	kat	'to bite'
bàɑ	'shoulder'	dam	'black'		

Aspiration is also possible, but rarer, with fricatives. Aspirated and unaspirated voiceless fricatives contrast in Burmese, as in (5) (Ladefoged 1971, 12).

(5)　zãn　　　'levitation'　　zauŋ　　'edge'

　　　sãn　　　'example'　　　sauŋ　　'harp'

　　　sʰãn　　'rice'　　　　　sʰauŋ　'winter'

Sounds commonly referred to as voiced aspirates occur in languages like Hindi and Gujarati. Ladefoged (1971, 12) characterizes these sounds as having a laryngeal configuration different from both voiced and voiceless sounds, one in which the posterior portion of the vocal folds are held apart while the anterior portion is allowed to vibrate. He refers to this as "murmured"; in the IPA chart the sounds are indicated with a dieresis (‥) below the symbol and are referred to as "breathy voiced." Ladefoged (1971, 13) cites the contrasts in (6) from Gujarati, noting that Pandit (1957) analyzes the murmured (breathy voiced) stops as a voiced stop plus /h/, phonemically, as shown.

(6)　/bar/　　[bɑr]　　'twelve'　　/pɔr/　　[pɔr]　　'last year'

　　　/bhar/　[b̤ɑr]　'burden'　　/phɔdž/　[pʰɔdž]　'army'

Another laryngeal state is creaky voice, indicated by a tilde under the consonant symbol. In this type of phonation, the posterior portion of the vocal folds are held together so that only the anterior portions are able to vibrate. These occur contrastively in Margi (Africa; Ladefoged 1971, 15; 1964; Hoffman 1963), as in (7).

(7)　paɖʊ́　'rain'　　　bábál　'open place'　　b̰àbàl　'hard'

　　　pʷa　'pour in'　　bʷál　'ball'　　　　b̰ʷàb̰ʷà　'cooked'

　　　p͡tə́l　'chief'　　　ɓdàgʊ̀　'valley'　　　ɓd̰əbdʊ̀　'chewed'

　　　tátá　'that one'　dàlmà　'big ax'　　　d̰àd̰áhʊ　'bitter'

　　　w̰àw̰à　'boiled'　kawà　'sorry'　　　w̰áw̰í　'adornment'

　　　çà　'moon'　　　yà　'give birth'　　　ya̰　'thigh'

1.1.1.4 Airstream mechanisms

All the sounds described to this point have been ones produced with an airstream originating in the lungs and pushed outward by the action of the internal intercostal muscles. This is called *pulmonic egressive airstream*. This airstream mechanism characterizes most speech, but other airstream mechanisms are also possible. The glottis initiates the airstream in two types of sounds. *Glottalic egressive* airstream is involved in the production of *ejective* (sometimes called *glottalized*) consonants, mostly stops, with the phonetic symbols [p'], [t'], [k']. For these sounds there is a closure at both the point of articulation of the stop (bilabial, dental or velar) and at the glottis. The upward movement of the closed glottis compresses the air between itself and the point of articulation, which is then released, giving a popping sound. The reverse of this airstream mechanism is known as *glottalic ingressive*. In this type of articulation the glottis is not closed and moves downward during vibration, while there is a closure at some point of articulation, e.g., [ɓ], [ɗ], [ɠ]. These sounds are known as implosives. *Velaric ingressive* airstream is used to produce *clicks*. These involve a closure at the velum and an additional closure further forward in the mouth. The backward and downward movement of the tongue rarifies the air inside the mouth which, when released, produces a sudden inrush of air. A dental or alveolar click is the sound you make as a sign of disapproval written *tsk-tsk* or *tut-tut*. This has the phonetic symbol [ʇ]. In Zulu, this click (dental) appears as a speech sound, as do the lateral click [ʖ] and the retroflex click [ʗ].[2]

1.1.2 Vowels

1.1.2.1 Parameters of vowel articulation

Vowels are described using somewhat different terminology from consonants, since there is no obstruction in their production. The parameters for vowels are the height of the tongue, the position from front to back of the highest portion of the tongue, the rounding of the lips, and tongue root position. The vowel symbols are commonly arranged on a vowel quadrangle whose corners represent extreme vowel positions, such as (8).

---

[2] These symbols have been replaced by others in the recent revision of the IPA. The new symbols are unfortunately virtually identical in some cases to the recommended symbols for certain suprasegmentals, making the older symbols preferable.

(8)

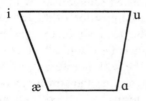

? Not stop?

The high front vowel [i] is the highest possible front vowel; any further raising of the tongue would result in a fricative sound. The low back vowel [ɑ] is the lowest possible back vowel; further retraction of the tongue would result in a pharyngeal fricative. It is similar with the high back (round) vowel [u] and the low front vowel [æ].[3] Daniel Jones (1966) devised a system of cardinal vowels in which these four extreme positions are supplemented by two additional vowels between the highest and lowest position in both the front and back areas. This results in a system with two degrees of backness (i.e., back and front) and three of height (high, mid, and low), with the mid region subdivided into higher mid and lower mid. Of the primary cardinal vowels, [u], [o], and [ɔ] are rounded; that is, the tongue position is accompanied by lip rounding. The other cardinal vowels are unrounded. The IPA distinguishes secondary cardinal vowels where these rounding values are reversed. We give the cardinal vowels in (9).[4]

(9) | Primary cardinal vowels | Secondary cardinal vowels

High	i	u	ü	ɨ
Higher mid	e	o	ö	ʌ
Lower mid	ɛ	ɔ	ő	ə
Low	æ	ɑ	œ	ɒ

One problem with the cardinal vowel system is that it grants special status to the distinction between higher mid and lower mid that is not granted to the high vowels. Put differently, the distinction between higher mid and lower

---

[3] The IPA symbol [a] for this vowel will not be used in this book, for reasons detailed in section 1.3.

[4] The IPA term for high vowels is "close," and for low vowels, "open."

mid is not so much one of height but one of the position of the tongue root. The higher mid vowels have an advanced tongue root while the lower mid vowels have a retracted tongue root. The position of the tongue root can also serve to distinguish high vowels, and to a lesser extent, the low vowels. Advanced tongue root vowels are often called "tense," while retracted tongue root vowels are referred to as "lax." We will therefore use a more symmetrical system, as in (10). This chart also provides the vowel symbols we will use, in preference to those of the IPA. The terms "advanced" and "retracted" in the second column refer to advanced and retracted tongue root, respectively.

(10)

		front		back	
		unround	round	unround	round
high	advanced (tense)	i	ü	ɨ	u
	retracted (lax)	ɪ	ü	ɤ	ʊ
mid	advanced (tense)	e	ö	ʌ	o
	retracted (lax)	ɛ	ɔ̈	ə	ɔ
low	advanced (tense)	æ̧	Œ	ɑ̧	ɒ̧
	retracted (lax)	æ	Œ	ɑ	ɒ

The table in (11) illustrates these sounds with examples from English, where possible, and in other languages, where the abbreviations Fr. is French and Ger. is German. Some vowel sounds are restricted to particular dialects of English, e.g., NYC (New York City). This table must be used with a degree of

(11)

	front		back	
	unround	round	unround	round
high, tense	[i] *bead* (also [iy])	[ü] Fr. *rue* 'street'	[ɨ] Turkish [kɨz] 'girl'	[u] *boot* (also [uw])
high, lax	[ɪ] *bid*	[ü] Ger. *Hütte* 'hut'	[ɤ] ?	[ʊ] *book*
mid tense	[e] Ger. *See* 'lake,' Fr. *été* 'summer'	[ö] Ger. *schön* 'beautiful,' Fr. *peu* 'few'	[ʌ] Shan [kʌʔ] 'salt' Vietnamese [hʌn] 'more'	[o] Ger. *wohl* 'well'
mid lax	[ɛ] *bed*	[ɔ̈] Ger. *zwölf* 'twelve,' Fr. *peur* 'fear'	[ə] *but*	[ɔ] *hot* (British), Ger. *Sonne* 'sun'
low, tense	[æ] *bad* (NYC)	[œ̧] ?	[ɑ̧] *balm*	[ɒ̧] *dog* (Northeast U.S.)
low, lax	[æ] *had*	[œ] ?	[ɑ] *hot* (NAm)	[ɒ] Hungarian *magyar* [mɒɟɒr] 'Hungarian'

caution, since there is much dialectal variation and the values indicated may not correspond to your own pronunciation.

In addition to front and back vowels, the IPA provides a rather rich set of symbols for "central" vowels. However there is little evidence that such vowels ever exist in contrast to back vowels. We will therefore operate without the category of "central" vowels, though some of the IPA's symbols for central vowels will be used for back vowels (such as [ɨ]).

1.1.2.2 Glides and diphthongs

We discussed glides briefly when discussing consonants in section 1.1.1.1, where we noted that glides have vowel articulations but function as consonants. Therefore another notation for glides is a vowel symbol with a nonsyllabic diacritic below it, e.g., [i̯] = [y]. A diphthong is a sequence of two different vowels that are part of a single syllable. Usually one of the vowels is stronger than the other, and is considered the syllabic segment, and the other is written as a glide or with the nonsyllabic diacritic. Still another notation (MacKay 1987) joins two vowel symbols with a ligature below. English has the diphthongs in (12), which illustrate these conventions. For English transcriptions we will prefer the left column of (12). The vowels of English *bead* and *boot* are also often represented as diphthongs; these are shown in the last two lines of (12).

(12)	[ay]	or	[ai̯]	or	[ai̯]	my
	[aw]	or	[au̯]	or	[au̯]	how
	[ɔy]	or	[ɔi̯]	or	[ɔi̯]	boy
	[ey]	or	[ei̯]	or	[ei̯]	bay
	[ow]	or	[ou̯]	or	[ou̯]	low
	[iy]	or	[ii̯]	or	[ii̯]	bead
	[uw]	or	[uu̯]	or	[uu̯]	boot

The diphthongs in (12) are called *falling diphthongs*, since the sonority falls from the first to the second element. The opposite is a *rising diphthong*, in which the sonority rises from the first to the second element. Such diphthongs occur in Spanish, as in [ye] of *hierba* [yɛrba] 'grass.' However, the sequence [yɛ] in the English word *yes* is not a diphthong but simply a consonant plus vowel. Spanish also has triphthongs of rising-falling sonority, as in the final syllable of *Uruguay* [uru'gwɑy].

1.1.3   Suprasegmentals

The term *suprasegmentals* implies phonetic features outside the linear sequence of segments. It includes stress, tone, intonation, and syllable structure. A common indicator of syllable boundary is a period between the syllables, also adopted by the IPA. Syllable boundaries are also shown by the symbol $ or by a period, especially in phonological rules (see section 5.5 in chapter 5). The IPA indicates stress with tick marks before the syllable concerned, so these marks indicate syllable boundaries as well. Primary stress is shown by a tick at the top of the line and secondary stress is shown by a tick at the bottom. Finer degrees of stress cannot be indicated by this method, so another system is sometimes employed using accent marks. The acute accent (´) indicates primary stress, the circumflex (^) indicates secondary stress, the grave accent (`) indicates tertiary stress. The IPA uses these symbols only for tone, so we will not use them for stress. The IPA also uses the tone letters of Chao (1930). Long segments are marked with a following colon, for example [eː]. If a finer distinction is needed, a half-long segment is marked with a single raised dot: [eˑ]. Occasionally, a long vowel is shown by a double vowel symbol [ee], but this would ordinarily represent two syllables, which can be made explicit with a boundary symbol: [e.e]. Long consonants are generally indicated by the double symbol method (e.g., Italian [fɑt.to] 'made'), since such a long consonant (or *geminate*) ordinarily spans two syllables, unlike long vowels, which are normally part of a single syllable. A long consonant confined to a single syllable (e.g., Estonian [linː.tu] 'bird, partitive singular') can be indicated by the colon, as with vowels.

The representation of suprasegmentals is clearly bound up with prosodic structure and is not easily represented in a linear string. We will therefore defer further discussion until we introduce syllable structure in section 7.2.1 of chapter 7 and metrical structure in sections 7.2.2 and 7.2.3.

1.1.4   Broad and narrow transcription

Because speech is a continuum, a transcription can indicate only a limited amount of articulatory detail. In effect we strive to transcribe the most important aspects of an utterance, omitting details considered less important. What counts as important may be somewhat subjective. A transcription that is limited to expressing only the contrastive sounds of a given language is termed a *broad transcription*. A broad transcription of English utterances, for example, would write /p/ for [p] and [pʰ], since the distinction between aspirated and unaspirated stops is not contrastive in English, as discussed in section 1.1.1.3. A broad transcription of Thai would represent this distinction, however, since these sounds contrast in Thai. A *narrow transcription* includes more phonetic detail, such as aspiration in English, information regarding the exact point of articulation of consonants and vowels, various degrees of length, etc. The same utterance can be transcribed in a range of ways, from very broad to quite narrow and detailed, depending on the purpose of the transcription. In this book most transcriptions are moderately narrow, enough so to make the point at issue without being overly detailed, which could be distracting.

1.2 Acoustic phonetics

Acoustics is the branch of physics that deals with sound. Acoustic phonetics is therefore the study of the physics of speech sounds. Our discussion of articulatory phonetics has concentrated on individual speech sounds and their properties, but articulation in continuous speech is actually in constant motion, and steady-state articulations are rarely achieved. This constant change in the speech stream is quite evident in acoustic records of speech, for example in sound spectrograms. A major result of modern linguistics is that the *perception* of speech is *categorial,* despite the continuous nature of speech production and of the acoustic signal. We *think* of language as composed of discrete units, such as the sound units discussed in section 1.1. Further such discrete units involved in language use are morphemes, words, and phrases. In addition, speech is *encoded* in a rather special way that is revealed by a study of acoustics. Sequences, say of a stop followed by a vowel, are present simultaneously in a speech event in such a way that it is impossible to isolate a single portion of the signal that corresponds just to the stop without any trace of the vowel. It is this encoding that makes speech a particularly efficient medium of communication. Lieberman (1984, 139) points out that speech can be produced and understood at a rate of about 150 words per minute. He contrasts this with Morse code, a system with a one-to-one relation between the code and the units of the message (letters of the alphabet), which has a maximum transmission rate of 50 words per minute. Even at that rather slow rate, a Morse code operator does not remember the message transmitted, and must rest after an hour or two of transmitting due to fatigue. Spoken messages, in contrast, are better remembered and not particularly fatiguing. As Lieberman puts it, speech is a *special* communicative mechanism, that has evolved along with the human organism. Human language is characterized by a wide range of distinguishable sounds, wider than the range possessed by most other animals. This range of sounds is made possible by a lengthened vocal tract, which evolved in humans with a lowering of the larynx, giving the vocal tract a right-angle bend. This lowered larynx also interferes with swallowing and increases the chance of choking. Similarly, the larynx has evolved in a way that allows fine variation in pitch and efficient phonation, but interferes with rapid, deep breathing. While in one sense the human speech apparatus is overlaid on structures originally evolved for more basic purposes (eating, breathing), the evolutionary value of speech must have outweighed the decreased efficiency of these basic functions in the changes in the organs involved.

The simplest type of sound is a sine wave. Such a sound is produced by a tuning fork in the absence of friction that started sounding at the beginning of time (real tuning forks have to be struck to start sounding and slowly fade due to friction). A sine wave is illustrated in (13). It can be considered as having two independent dimensions. The first is *amplitude,* measured as the height of the peak of the wave, measured, in the case of soundwaves travelling in air, in units of pressure. The second dimension is *frequency,* the number of times the wave is repeated in one second, for which the unit is Hertz (Hz) or cycles per second. A diagram like (13) might be produced by dragging a vibrating tuning fork with a pen attached to one of the prongs across a sheet of paper at a uniform rate.

(13)

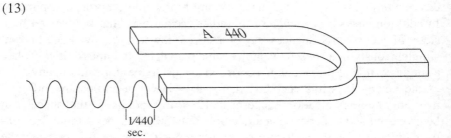

An extremely important result, known as Fourier's theorem (from the French mathematician Jean Fourier, who discovered it), is that any complex wave can be represented as the sum of a number (perhaps infinite) of sine waves, each with its own amplitude and frequency. The spectrographic analysis of speech consists of determining the component sine waves of a given speech signal. Acoustic phonetics is also concerned with the vocal tract configurations that give rise to various acoustic effects.

For acoustic purposes, the vocal tract can be considered a tube from the vocal folds to the lips. The 90° bend at the velum can be ignored. The length of the tube varies considerably with the individual; the average for adult males is approximately 17.6 cm, less for women and children. A tube has certain natural resonance frequencies that depend on the length of the tube and whether the ends are open or closed. The term *standing wave* is applied to a wave confined to a tube, since it is simply present in the tube and not propagating from the source. The vocal tract in the production of a vowel can be regarded as a tube open at the lip end and closed at the glottal end. (The glottis is also vibrating during the production of voiced sounds; we will return to the function of the glottis in the production of these sounds.) A tube open at one end and closed at the other can accommodate various standing waves, the longest of which is such that 1/4 wave length is within the tube. This is because the closed end of the tube must be a *node* of the vibrating wave,[5] where the motion of vibration is zero, and the open end must be an *antinode* or *loop,* where the motion of vibration is greatest. The frequency of such a standing wave is given by the formula (14), where c is the speed of sound in air and L is the length of the tube.

(14) $f = \dfrac{c}{4L}$

The speed of sound in air varies with the temperature and is 331.5 m/sec (1087 ft/sec) at 0°C and 344 m/sec (1130 ft/sec) at 20°C. The lowest frequency standing wave in a tube 17 cm long at 20°C is therefore given by the calculation in (15)

(15) $f = \dfrac{c}{4L} = \dfrac{344 \text{ m/sec}}{4(0.17\text{m})} = 505.88 \text{ sec}^{-1} \text{ (Hz)}$

---

[5] More precisely, it is a displacement node. The wave also consists of varying pressure, such that a displacement node corresponds to a pressure antinode and a displacement antinode corresponds to a pressure node. For simplicity and ease of presentation, we will refer only to displacement nodes and antinodes in this discussion.

For ease of working with round numbers (since both vocal tract length and air temperature vary) let us say 500 Hz is the lowest frequency standing wave in a typical vocal tract with a relatively uniform cross section along its length, as it would roughly be in the production of the vowel [ə].

The 17 cm tube can accommodate additional standing waves whose frequencies are odd-numbered multiples of 500, namely 1500, 2500, and so on. This is because the same tube can accommodate a 3⁄4 wave length, a 5⁄4 wave length, and so on, all of which have a node at the closed end and a loop at the open end. The first three standing waves in a 17 cm tube are shown in (16).

(16)

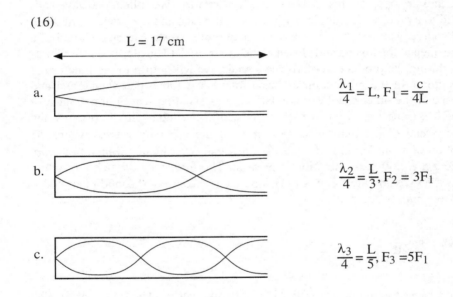

$$\frac{\lambda_1}{4} = L, \ F_1 = \frac{c}{4L}$$

$$\frac{\lambda_2}{4} = \frac{L}{3}, \ F_2 = 3F_1$$

$$\frac{\lambda_3}{4} = \frac{L}{5}, \ F_3 = 5F_1$$

First three vibration modes of a tube open at one end and closed at the other (based on Backus 1969, 64. l = wave length, L = length of the tube, F = formant frequency).

These frequencies are the resonance frequencies of the tube, commonly known as *formants*. The lowest formant is commonly designated F_1 (here, 500 Hz), the next formant is designated F_2 (here 1500 Hz), and so forth. In a musical instrument such as a clarinet, which is also a tube closed at one end (the reed end) and open at the other, the lowest resonance frequency corresponds to a musical note, with the higher resonances produced simultaneously adding a certain tone colour to the note. The human vocal tract produces an additional sound frequency of great importance, the vibration of the vocal folds described in section 1.1.1.3. The vocal folds do not vibrate in a simple sine wave. The lowest vibration frequency of the vocal folds is the *fundamental frequency,* designated F_0. In addition to F_0, the vocal folds vibrate at many whole-number multiples of the fundamental frequency, with generally decreasing amplitudes. These multiples are known as *harmonics.* If F_0 is fairly low, say on the order of 100 Hz, there will be a number of harmonics at or near the formant frequencies of the vocal tract, which then *filter* the harmonics, so that the harmonics that are near a formant frequency are transmitted well and make a large contribution to the overall sound, while the harmonics away from the formant frequencies are reduced in amplitude and make little or no contribution to the overall sound. This is known as the *source-filter theory of speech production,* and is illustrated in (17), on the next page, based on the discussion in Lieberman (1984, 151 and 153) and MacKay (1987, 14). The diagram in (17a) represents spectrum of a glottal source with a fundamental frequency of 100 Hz, corresponding to a rather low bass note (the closest

musical note is G_2, written on the lowest line of the bass clef, with a frequency of 97.999 Hz). This spectrum contains the fundamental frequency of 100 Hz plus all multiples of this, i.e., 200 Hz, 300 Hz, etc., in decreasing amplitudes. The diagram in (17b) represents the formant structure of the vowel [i]. The diagram in (17c) represents the result of filtering this spectrum through the formant structure of the vowel [i]; note that the formant structure is readily apparent in this spectrum. If the glottal source has a higher fre

quency, say 500 Hz, a middle range soprano note (close to B_4, written on the middle line of the treble clef, with a frequency of 493.88 Hz), with a spectrum represented in (17d), the result of filtering through the formant structure of the same vowel [i] is that shown in the (17e). In this case there is actually no acoustic energy at the formant frequencies, represented by the dots in the diagram.

The formant frequencies of 500, 1500, 2500, and so on that we calculated above were based on a tube of uniform cross section. The highly mobile nature of the tongue and lips make it possible to vary the shape of the vocal

(17)

a. Glottal source with F_0
    at 100 Hz.

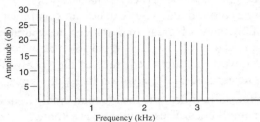

b. Vocal tract transfer
    function (resonances)
    for the vowel [i].

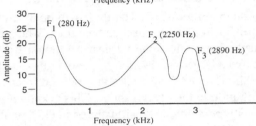

c. Result of filtering the
    the glottal spectrum (a)
    through the formant
    structure of the vowel
    [i].

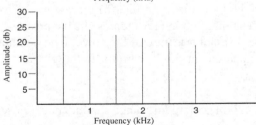

d. Glottal source with F_0
    at 500 Hz.

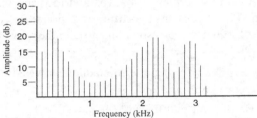

e. Result of filtering the
    glottal spectrum (d)
    through the formant
    structure of the vowel
    [i]. Black dots represent
    the formants; no actual
    acoustic energy appears
    at these frequencies.

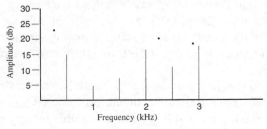

tract considerably, and this has an effect on the formant frequencies. Exactly how this comes about is not entirely clear. One prevailing theory (Chiba & Kajiyama 1941, cited in Kenstowicz 1994, 178) explains the change in resonance as the result of the rule in (18).

(18)   When the cross-sectional area of the tube is reduced at or near a loop, the frequency of the corresponding resonance is lowered; when the cross-sectional area of the tube is reduced at or near a node, the frequency of the corresponding resonance is raised.

The vowel [u] is produced with a narrowing of the tube at the lip end, which is a loop for all resonances. This implies lower resonance frequencies for this vowel than for the uniform tube, and indeed [u] has a first formant of about 300 Hz and a second formant of about 870 Hz. In addition, the high back tongue position may be near a loop for the second resonance, contributing to a further lowering of F_2. On the other hand, with the vowel [i], there is a radical constriction at approximately 1/3 the distance from the lips, corresponding to a node of the second resonance, resulting in a relatively high (around 2290 Hz) F_2 for [i]. In (19) we list the first three formant values for eight vowels of American English (Ladefoged 2001, 172).

(19)

	[i]	[ɪ]	[ɛ]	[æ]	[ɑ]	[ɒ]	[ʊ]	[u]
F_3	2890	2560	2490	2490	2540	2540	2380	2250
F_2	2250	1920	1770	1660	1100	880	1030	870
F_1	280	400	550	690	710	590	450	310

Another view of vowel formants (MacKay 1987, 268) holds that the point of greatest constriction in the production of a vowel effectively divides the vocal tract into two parts, the resonance frequencies of which correspond to the first two formants. Whichever theory turns out to be correct (and they may both be true to a certain extent), it is clear that different vowels are associated with different resonance frequencies, though of course the exact frequencies will vary considerably from one speaker to another. It is possible to demonstrate the first two formants by pronouncing the sequence of vowels in slightly artificial ways. If the sequence of vowels in (19) is pronounced in a whisper, the sound heard corresponds to the frequency of F_2. If pronounced in a creaky voice, the rising then falling pitch of F_1 is readily heard.

As we have stated, vocal tract size is highly variable over individuals. Fundamental frequencies are also highly variable. A speaker's intonation varies over a considerable range and each speaker has his or her own particular range. The source-filter effect illustrated in (17) with a fundamental frequency of 100 Hz actually represents a rather deep bass voice. Many women and some men have fundamental frequencies above 400 Hz, and children under 6 years old typically have fundamental frequencies above 500 Hz (Lieberman 1984, 153). Even though the fundamental frequency may be well above the lowest formant frequency, vowel quality, say of the vowel [i], may still be perceived. Lieberman calls this process *formant frequency extraction*. Lieberman also notes that formant frequencies also vary with the length of the vocal tract, and that vocal tract length tends to correlate with larynx size, so that a lower fundamental frequency correlates with a longer vocal tract. There is thus a considerable overlap in formant frequencies from one speaker to another, yet vowel quality is clearly perceived by what Lieberman calls *vocal tract normalization*. He speculates that the vowel [i] shows the least such overlap; as a result of identifying a speaker's [i], a listener is able to extrapolate to the formant values for other vowels produced by that speaker.

The encoding of speech is best illustrated with a sequence of a (voiced) stop and a vowel. A reasonable approximation to such sequences can be produced synthetically using cues such as those in (20), on the next page. These are recognizable as the sequences shown with only the first two formants; a third formant adds some degree of naturalness to these cues.

It can be observed that there is no acoustic constant corresponding to the stop [b] as we read across the top series of synthetic utterances. The closest we can come to a constant cue for [b] is a rising value for both formants. In fact, it is only the rise in the second formant that characterizes [b] as opposed to the other stops, as a comparison to the other two lines shows. In all three sequences, the transistion in the first formant is identical; the behaviour of the second formant distinguishes the three stops from each other.

The acoustic explanation for this phenomenon is the following. For a labial stop the vocal tract is closed at both ends. No actual sound is emitted from such a tube, but it has resonance frequencies all the same. Since it is closed at both ends, any standing wave within it necessarily has a node at both ends and the longest wave it can contain is one with a half wave length of 17 cm, with a frequency of 1000 Hz. It can also contain a full wave length with a frequency of 2000 Hz and so on, all multiples of 1000 Hz (or even multiples of 500 Hz). In fact, a theoretical resonance at 0 Hz is also present. With the

(20)

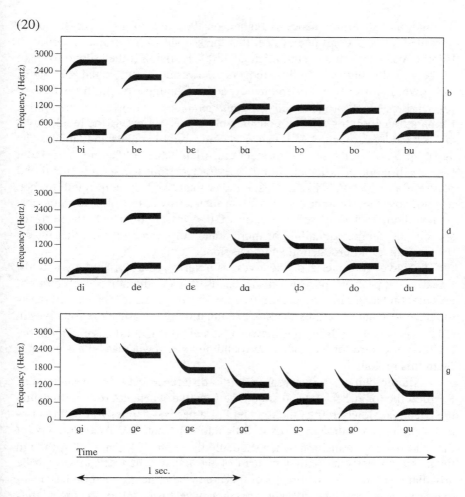

Stylized spectrograms of CV syllables, showing steady-state vowels
(constant in columns) and formant transitions corresponding to
voiced stops. The perceived stop is constant across the rows, but
the formant transitions vary depending on the following vowel.

release of the stop, the articulators move toward the steady-state vowel configuration and the formant frequencies exhibit a transition, from 0 Hz for the
first formant and from 1000 Hz for the second formant. For a dental or alveolar point of articulation, the cavity behind the constriction is shorter than for

a labial, and so its frequency is higher, on the order of 1800 Hz. It can be observed in the second line of (20) that the second formant in a sequence of [d] plus vowel appears to start at about 1800 Hz, rising if the second formant of the vowel is higher than this frequency, lowering if the second formant of the vowel is lower than this frequency, and remaining straight in the case of [ε], whose second formant is close to this frequency. The origin of the second formant transition for velars is considerably higher, reflecting the much short-er back cavity associated with velars as compared to dentals and labials. The apparent origin of the second formant transition is the only common element to a given point of articulation, but if extracted from the speech signal and played alone, it sounds like a whistle rather than like a speech sound. In fact, it is not possible to cut the cues in (20) in such a way as to isolate the stop por-tion without including some portion of the vowel. It is this encoding of speech, the parallel signalling of more than one sound at a time, that makes possible the rapid production and understanding of speech.

We have characterized fricatives as relatively noisy, hissing sounds. Fricatives appear on spectrograms as bands of aperiodic noise, each point of articulation having its own pattern (see the spectrograms in 21). Yet fricatives too have formant structures. A close examination of the voiceless fricatives in (21) reveals that the difference between [s] and [š] is that [š] has energy in the region of the third formant of the surrounding vowels whereas [s] has no ener-gy in this region.

A simple demonstration can show the difference between these sounds. Position the tongue for [s] and sound the fricative. Then, continuing to sound the fricative, slowly retract the tongue. For a period of time, you will contin-ue to hear [s], even though the exact articulation is changing. At a certain point there is an abrupt transition, when suddenly the sound is [š], not [s]. Although there is apparently a continuous area of the palate where fricatives can be articulated, there is a broad range of this area where the articulation has a sin-gle acoustic effect. The speaker does not have to hit an exact target, thus allowing for faster articulation. In addition this shows once again that speech is categorial. Over a broad continuous articulatory area we find just two cate-gorially distinct speech sounds, [s] and [š].

1.3   Phonetic alphabets

There is obviously a great advantage to having an internationally recognized standard phonetic alphabet for transcribing the sounds of various languages. The standard orthography of no single language is adequate for the task, since

(21)

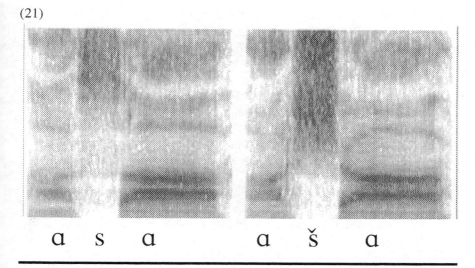

a s a   a š a

no single language possesses all the required sounds, and the writing system of each language is uniquely adapted to its own system. The English writing system would be especially poorly adapted for phonetic purposes, since it has multiple phonetic values for certain letters (e.g., <a> has the value [ɑ] in *father,* [ey] in *mate,* and [æ] in *mat*), silent letters as in *though,* and other well known idiosyncrasies. The English writing system is basically well suited to writing English, since it tends to write each morpheme with the same letters, even if the sound changes by the operation of certain rules, so that *sane* and *sanity* both spell the root morpheme with the letter <a> although the sound varies from [ey] to [æ]. Unfortunately, several distinct phonetic alphabets have been devised, each with slightly different conventions. The International Phonetic Alphabet (or the alphabet of the International Phonetic Association) is the best known and most widespread of the phonetic alphabets.

1.3.1 The IPA

The International Phonetic Association was founded in 1886 by the French phonetician Paul Passy. The original name of the association was The Phonetic Teachers' Association, which began publication of a journal, *Dhi Fonètik Tîtcer,* printed entirely in phonetic transcription. Their symbols were not yet those of the IPA, as can be guessed from the title of the journal. It was not until 1888 that the first version of the International Phonetic Alphabet was published in ðə fonetik tîtcər. It was based on six principles, listed in (22) (*The Principles of the International Phonetic Association* 1949).

(22)   1. There should be a separate letter for each distinctive sound; that, for each sound which, being used instead of another, in the same language, can change the meaning of a word.

        2. When any sound is found in several languages, the same sign should be used in all. This applies also to very similar shades of sound.

        3. The alphabet should consist as much as possible of the ordinary letters of the roman alphabet, as few new letters as possible being used.

        4. In assigning values to the roman letters, international usage should decide.

        5. The new letters should be suggestive of the sounds they represent, by their resemblance to the old ones.

        6. Diacritic marks should be avoided, being trying for the eyes and troublesome to write.

When criteria 3 and 6 were in conflict, the IPA chose to create new letters rather than to employ diacritics, thus [ʃ] instead of [š] for the voiceless postalveolar fricative, etc. The IPA has undergone only minor revisions since then, most recently at a convention of the Association in 1989 in Kiel, Germany (see Ladefoged 1990). It is basically this revision that appears in the chart on page 3.

   A somewhat different system of phonetic transcription developed in North America. Because this tradition was often used under field conditions, using specially designed typewriters, the diacritic solution was preferred over the invention of new symbols. By and large, however, the rival systems agree on the majority of symbols, and even in many cases where different symbols are employed, such as [ʃ] and [š], there is little chance of confusion. Certain symbols with varying usage, such as [y] and [c], require special attention.

The diacritic approach has certain advantages beyond the design of type-writers. One is that the total number of symbols is reduced. Another is that using a particular diacritic for a natural class of sounds makes the relation among those sounds clearer. For example, the haček diacritic is used for all the postalveolar sounds in the system we use in this book (i.e., [š, ž, č, ǰ]), thus bringing out the common point of articulation among these sounds better than the use of a plethora of separate symbols, as in IPA [ʃ, ʒ, ʧ, ʤ]. Similarly, in our vowel chart in (9), front rounded vowels are indicated by an umlaut dia-critic (¨) over the corresponding back vowel, rather than the unrelated set of symbols [y, ø, œ] preferred in the IPA.

1.3.2   Problems with the IPA

The IPA suffers from a number of problems beside the ones already mentioned at the end of the last section. Outside the "cardinal" vowels, the IPA approach to vowel symbols is rather unsystematic, having a number of symbols scattered in seemingly random places on the vowel quadrangle. A phonological vowel system needs to be more systematic, as we have indicated in our chart in (10).

A special problem with the IPA vowel system is its provision of a full set of symbols for "central" vowels, despite there being little or no evidence that these ever need to be distinguished from back vowels of the same height and rounding, in contravention of IPA principle 1. Our vowel system (10) eliminates this category, reassigning some of the symbols to back vowel function when this seems indicated.

A related problem concerns the IPA symbol [a] for the low front unround cardinal vowel, which we designate [æ]. The IPA also uses the symbol [æ], but for a slightly higher articulation. The IPA handbook of 1949 notes the problems with these symbols as follows:

> The Association's treatment of **a** and **ɑ** as different letters denoting different sounds has not met with the success originally hoped for. In practice it is found that authors and printers still generally regard the two forms as variants of the same letter. The difficulty might be solved by altering the value of **æ** and assigning this letter to cardinal vowel No. 4…

Up until the 1989 revision, the IPA had not followed through on this suggestion, and still recommends [a] for cardinal vowel No. 4, i.e., our [æ]. In actual usage, the value assigned to [a] can be a front vowel, a back vowel, a central vowel, or a vowel whose position on the front-back axis is not specified
or does not matter. In the light of this ambiguity, we have thought it best to
avoid the symbol [a] altogether and to use [æ] for the low nonround front
vowel and [ɑ] for the low nonround back vowel. The ambiguity of the symbol [a] must be borne in mind when reading other works on phonology.

With regard to the consonants, the 1989 revision of the IPA has omitted
the alveolo-palatal (prepalatal) consonants from the main chart. They include
symbols for a voiced and a voiceless fricative at this point of articulation only
under the list of "other symbols." We have reinstated this point of articulation
in the main chart, with symbols for the affricates as well as the fricatives.

The 1989 revision has replaced the earlier symbols for clicks with ones
that in two cases are nearly identical to newly proposed symbols for supraseg-
mentals (i.e., [|] for dental click *or* minor (foot) group; [‖] for alveolar lat-
eral click *or* major (intonation) group). Although we will not discuss clicks
much in this book, where they do occur (e.g., exercise 2.10 of chapter 2) we
will use the older symbols, since these are less confusing.

Pullum & Ladusaw (1986) is an excellent guide to phonetic symbols from
both the IPA and American traditions, as well as some other usages.
Unfortunately, it was published before the 1989 revision of the IPA

1.3.3   Compromise adopted in this book

The system we will use in this book is a compromise. While retaining the bulk
of the IPA conventions, we have tried to remedy some of its most serious defi-
ciencies. Further improvements could no doubt be made, but because the
focus of this book is phonology, not phonetics, we need not consider this problem further. One obvious difficulty remaining is the lack of a unitary symbol
for most of the affricates. While we have [č] and [ǰ] for the postalveolar
affricates, the others all require a digraph. Some traditions use [c] for a dental
(or alveolar) affricate, which makes a nice parallelism with the corresponding
fricatives [s] and [š], but then another symbol would be required for the voiceless palatal stop. We thus use digraphs (with a tie, indicating unitary sounds)
for affricates other than the postalveolar ones in our compromise. Our consonant system is given in (23). As in the IPA chart, shaded areas indicate articulations judged impossible. In the prepalatal column, we have adopted the

Apical (handwritten)

(23)

	Bilabial	Labiodental	Dental	Alveolar	Postalveolar	Retroflex	Pre-palatal (Alveolopalatal)	Palatal	Velar	Uvular	Pharyngeal	Glottal
Plosive (Oral) stop	p b		ṭ ḍ	t d		ṭ ḍ		c ɟ	k g	q ɢ		ʔ
Ejective or glottalized stop	p'		ṭ'	t'		ṭ'		c'	k'	q'		
Implosive	ɓ		ḍ	ɗ					ɠ	ʛ		
Nasal	m	ɱ	n̪	n	ň	ṇ	ń	ɲ	ŋ	N		
Trill				r		ṛ				R		
Tap, flap				ɾ		ɽ						
Nonstrident fricative	ɸ β		θ ð					ç ʝ	x ɣ		ħ ʕ	h ɦ
Strident fricative		f v	ṣ ẓ	s z	š ž	ṣ ẓ	ś ź			χ ʁ		
Nonstrident affricate			t͡θ d͡ð									
Strident affricate		p͡f b͡v		t͡s d͡z	č ǰ		ć ĵ					
Lateral fricative (strident)				ɬ ɮ								
Lateral affricate (strident)				t͡ɬ d͡ɮ								
Approximant	β̞	ʋ	ð̞	ɹ		ɻ		j	ɰ	ʁ̞		
Lateral approximant				l		ɭ		ʎ				

glides   ω (handwritten)

notation of an acute accent, thereby grouping the prepalatals together. In the retroflex column, we adopt the notation with the diacritic dot underneath, as in *ṭ*.

   In the dental column, in the case of fricatives, we distinguish the inter-dentals, with the symbols [θ, ð], from the dentals [ṣ, ẓ]. Fricatives and affricates can be distinguished in terms of stridency, as shown in the table. We will use the consonant symbols in (23) and the vowel symbols in (10) consistently in this book, replacing symbols in data from other sources where necessary. We have avoided ad hoc symbols, though these will be often encountered in other sources, often reflecting typographic limitations of the time they were first used. For example, *SPE* uses [D] for the flap [ɾ], as well as certain other capital letters. Certain phonetic symbols are expressed as small caps, such as [ɢ], but full caps are not properly used as phonetic characters. They may be used for *archisegments,* or a natural class of segments, a topic addressed further in chapters 3 and 7. For example /I/ may be used to express the class of high vowels in Turkish, {i, ü, ɨ, u}, where the backness and round-ness of the vowel is determined by the process of vowel harmony.

To supplement the phonetic symbols introduced so far, we use the diacrit-

(24)   Diacritics

̥	Voiceless	n̥ l̥	W	Labialized	tW dW
ʰ	Aspirated	tʰ dʰ	ʸ	Palatalized	tʸ dʸ
̪	Dental	t̪ s̪	̩	Syllabic	ɹ̩ n̩ l̩
ˎ	Lowered; approximant	e̞ β̞	˕	Raised	e̝
				ATR	a̘
̃	Nasalized	ẽ	̯	Nonsyllabic	e̯
̈	breathy voiced	b̤, a̤	̰	creaky voiced	b̰, a̰
ˈ	Primary stress		˞	Unreleased	t̚
ˌ	Secondary stress			Example of stresses:	
ː	long	eː		ˌfownəˈtʃ šən	

Tones		Diacritic	Tone letters
́	High tone	é	˥
̄	Mid tone	ē	˧
̀	Low tone	è	˩
̌	Rising tone	ě	˨˦
̂	Falling tone	ê	˦˨
̃	Rising-falling tone	ẽ	˧˥˧
̃	Falling-rising tone	ẽ	˧˩˧

Other symbols

w̥	Voiceless labial-velar fricative	glide corresponding to voiceless vowel [u̥]
w	Voiced labial-velar approximant	glide corresponding to vowel [u]
ɥ	Voiced labial-palatal approximant	glide corresponding to vowel [ü]
ǀ	Dental click (Zulu *c*)	
ǁ	Lateral click (Zulu *x*)	
ʗ	Retroflex click (Zulu *q*)	

ics and other symbols in (24), on the previous page and this. For the most part the diacritics are self-explanatory. The voiceless diacritic is used to indicate voicelessness in sounds that would normally be voiced, such as vowels and sonorant consonants. The dental diacritic is placed under symbols that otherwise indicate alveolar sounds. The syllabic diacritic indicates that the consonant symbol that bears it is a syllable peak; conversely, the nonsyllabic diacritic signifies a vowel used in a nonsyllabic function. The unreleased diacritic is used with stop consonants to show that either phonation ceases prior to release of the stop articulation or that there is no audible break before the next sound.

1.4   Exercises

1.1   Give the phonetic symbol for each sound.
  a. Voiced uvular stop ɢ
  b. Mid back tense round vowel o
  c. Velar nasal ŋ
  d. Low front tense unround vowel æ
  e. Voiceless dental stop t̪

1.2   Give a phonetic description for each symbol.
  a. [ʌ]
  b. [ʊ]
  c. [o̞]
  d. [ɛ]
  e. [χ]

1.3   Several phonetic symbols fit into each category. List as many as are
       appropriate for each description.

       a.   Voiceless stop
       b.   Back rounded vowel
       c.   Voiced uvular
       d.   High tense vowel
       e.   Voiceless bilabial

stressed?

In exercises 1.4 and 1.5, use the following conventions for English transcription. The vowel of *but* should be transcribed as [ə], in accordance with the
vowel chart in (10). While some books use the symbol [ʌ] for this vowel, we
reserve this symbol for the tense (advanced tongue root) correspondent of [ə].
See section 3.3 of Chapter 3 and especially the chart in (13) of that chapter,
for a demonstration that the vowel of *but* should be considered lax in English.
Use the left column of (12) for the English diphthongs. Transcribe according
to your own dialect, but bear in mind that some transcriptions may represent
a dialect other than your own. Some of the words for detranscription in exercise 1.4 are not strictly speaking English words, and the errors in exercise 1.5
are not related to dialect but simply to misuse of phonetic symbols.

1.4	Transcribe	De-transcribe (i.e., write in ordinary English spelling)
1.	judge	['yuwz]
2.	house	['myuwl]
3.	debt	['how]
4.	nation	['šəv]
5.	right	['saykɪk] ['səykɪk]
6.	them	['ærəm] *ATOM*
7.	thin	['kʰlowz]
8.	chuck	['bɑx]
9.	singer	['ʔəʔow]
10.	amaze	['pʰiytsə]
11.	thumb	['pʰiyrəɹ'pʰəypəɹ'pʰɪktə'pʰɛkə'pʰɪkl̩ d'pʰɛpəɹz]
12.	thistle	['meyɹziyɾ'owtsn̩'dowziyɾ'owtsn̩'lɪɾl̩ 'læmziyɾ'ɑyvi]

1.5   Some of the following English words have been incorrectly tran-
       scribed. Make appropriate corrections.

acquisition	[ˌæ¢kwɪˈzɪšən]
disappeared	[ˌdɪsəˈpʰeɑɪd]
mythological	[ˌmyt͡ʰəˈlɒjɪkəl]
designation	[ˌdɛsɪgˈneyʧ́ón]
consequences	[ˈ¢ɒnsɪˌḓensɪs] −ʒ
innocuous	[ɪˈnn̩ɒkyʊəs] ɑ
quietness	[ˈkwɑyətɛ$s] ɳ
naturalize	[ˈnæčʊɪəˌlɑyzȩ] ɪ
Egyptian	[Iˈjɪpšən] ɪ
mixture	[ˈmɪxčʊɪ] kʃ
writer	[ˈyɪɹ́əyɹəɪ] ɑ

2 Contrast and Distribution

In chapter 1 we surveyed the sounds that are used in various languages, in isolation from the use that individual languages make of these sounds. We can say that phonetics is about sounds, while phonology is about the organization of sounds in a linguistic system. But phonology is based on phonetics and uses the same terminology and symbols. The purpose of this chapter is to investigate the distribution of sounds in various languages and to see how languages use sounds to distinguish utterances and so to convey distinct meanings.

Languages differ both in the individual sounds they use and in the way these sounds are distributed in utterances. For example, French and German use the front rounded vowels [ü] and [ö] as distinctive sounds while English does not. On the other hand, English uses interdental fricatives [θ] and [ð] which are absent from both French and German. In terms of distribution of sounds, we will see in sections 2.1 and 2.2 that both English and Hindi make use of aspirated and unaspirated voiceless stops. In Hindi these sounds are contrastive, whereas in English they are not.

The first task in analyzing a language phonologically is to obtain a list of all the sounds used in utterances of that language, perhaps by phonetically transcribing a reasonably long text in the language spoken by a native speaker. The next task is to classify these sounds and to describe the sound pattern of the language. A useful first step is to determine which sounds play a crucial role in distinguishing utterances and which are variants of other, phonetically similar sounds in the language.

2.1 Complementary distribution

Two sounds are said to be in *complementary distribution* if they never appear in exactly the same environment. The *environment* is the class of surrounding sounds and certain boundaries, such as the word boundary. Two sounds in complementary distribution can never serve to contrast two utterances. If two such sounds are phonetically similar, they may be grouped together as a single sound unit of the language. The term *phoneme*[1] is used either to refer to the group of sounds or to the *basic* sound of the group, while the other souds of the group are referred to as *allophones* of this basic sound. Each phoneme is in contrast with other such units. For example, in English the phoneme /p/ contrasts with /b/ and with /t/. The term *phonetically similar* is somewhat vague, but basically refers to sharing a number of phonetic features, a concept to be clarified in chapter 3. Let us consider an example from English. In (1a) we give examples of words with aspirated *p* [pʰ], while in (1b) we have examples of unaspirated [p].

(1)   a. [pʰ]   b. [p]

pin	['pʰɪn]	spin	['spɪn]
parade	[pʰə'ɹeyd]	aspire	[ə'spɑyɹ]
appear	[ə'pʰiyɹ]	aspirate	['æspɪˌɹeyt]
topaz	['tʰowˌpʰæz]	happy	['hæpi]
play	['pʰ̥ley]	opera	['ɒpəɹə]

In analyzing a set of data such as (1) we start from the assumption that the forms given are representative of the language as a whole. In working with an unknown language it is always possible that we have missed some crucial data, and even in English we may have occasion to revise our analysis on the basis of additional data (see section 2.4). For now, let us make the following observations. In (1a), aspirated [pʰ] appears at the beginning of a word regardless of whether a vowel or a consonant follows, and regardless of the stress of the initial syllable (*pin, parade, play*), and at the beginning of a stressed syllable internal to a word, whether the stress is primary or secondary (*appear, topaz*). In (1b), unaspirated [p] appears after [s], regardless of stress (*spirit, aspirate*), and word internally at the beginning of a stressless syllable (*happy*). Let us set out these observations regarding [p] and [pʰ] in tabular form, as in (2). In this table # indicates a word boundary, V́ indicates a stressed vowel, V̊ indicates a stressless vowel, and the underscore represents the position where the sound in question (here [p] or [pʰ]) appears.

---

[1] This method of determining phonemes is not foolproof, as we will see in later chapters. We will discuss some problems with this concept in section 2.8.

(2)

	#____	s____	V___V́	V___V̊
[p]		s*p*in		ha*pp*y
[pʰ]	*p*in		a*pp*ear	

In reading downward for each environment, we find that only one of the sounds in question appears in that environment. They are thus in complementary distribution. The sounds [p] and [pʰ] are also phonetically similar, in that both are voiceless bilabial stops, differing only in terms of aspiration. Therefore, we can group these sounds together as one phoneme. We then say that [p] and [pʰ] are *allophones* of the phoneme /p/, using slashes // instead of brackets [] to show that we have a phoneme rather than a phonetic entity here. We use curly braces {} to enclose a set of elements; in the case of a phoneme we can say /p/ = {[p], [pʰ]}. In designating phonemes we use the same phonetic symbols that we use for sounds, to emphasize the fact that, although the phoneme is a more abstract entity than a speech sound, it is still composed of phonetic properties. The distribution in (2) is governed by a *rule:* the appearance of the phonetic property of aspiration is determined by the context, and so is not a contrastive property of voiceless stops in English. It is common to represent phonemes by a diagram such as (3), with the basic sound at the top.

(3)   /p/   (phoneme)

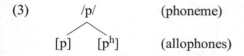

      [p]   [pʰ]   (allophones)

Not every case of two segments in complementary distribution can be analyzed as a single phoneme, however. In English, the velar nasal [ŋ] and the glottal fricative [h] are in complementary distribution as shown by the table in (4).

(4)

	#____	____#	V___V́	V___V̊	____{g, k}
[ŋ]		si*ng*		si*ng*er	a*ng*er, i*n*k
[h]	*h*appy		a*h*ead		

The two sounds are in complementary distribution, but they are not phonetically similar. Put another way, no rule relates these two sounds, unlike the case of complementary distribution of [p] and [pʰ] in (2). Therefore we do not count these as a case of one phoneme.

For another example of sounds in complementary distribution that do form a single phoneme, consider the data from French in (5) (based on Carr 1993, 14). The symbol [ʁ] represents a voiced uvular fricative, the symbol [χ] its voiceless counterpart, and the symbol [ʁ̞] represents a voiced uvular approximant (refer to the chart of phonetic symbols for consonants in chapter 1, page 31).

(5) | *phonetic* | *orthographic* | *gloss* |
|---|---|---|
| ['ʁyɛ̃] | rien | 'nothing' |
| [ʁɑ'tɔ̃] | raton | 'baby rat' |
| [mu'ʁiʁ̞] | mourir | 'to die' |
| [mɑ'ʁi] | mari | 'husband' |
| ['pχɛ̃s] | prince | 'prince' |
| ['tχɛ̃] | train | 'train' |
| [kχi'e] | crier | 'to shout' |
| [fχɛ'ne] | freiner | 'to brake' |
| ['bʁi] | brie | 'brie' |
| ['dʁol] | drôle | 'funny' |
| ['gʁɑ̃] | grand | 'large' |
| [ü ʁ̞'le] | hurler | 'to howl' |
| ['buʁ̞s] | bourse | 'purse' |
| ['fɛʁ̞] | faire | 'to do' |
| ['mɛʁ̞] | mère | 'mother' |

An examination of the data reveals that the voiceless uvular fricative [χ] occurs after a voiceless sound, the voiced uvular approximant occurs before another consonant or at the end of a word, while the voiced uvular fricative appears in other environments, i.e., at the beginning of a word, between vowels, or after a voiced consonant. As before, we can set out the results in tabular form, as in (6).

(6)

	Voiceless____	____C, ____#	#____, V____V, voiced C____
voiced uvular fricative [ʁ]			['ʁ̃ỹẽ], [mu'ʁiʁ̥], ['bʁi]
voiceless uvular fricative [χ]	['pχẽs]		
voiced uvular approximant [ʁ̥]		[üʁ̥'le], ['feʁ̥]	

Once again, if we read down the columns for each environment, we find that no two of these sounds occur in the same environment, and, because they are phonetically similar,[2] we can group these three sounds together as one phoneme. We can represent this as in (7).

(7)

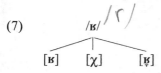

One question that naturally arises at this point is how to choose the *basic* form of the sounds in (3) and (7). This can usually be answered by looking at the types of environments in which each allophone appears. In our French example, the voiceless uvular fricative [χ] and the voiced uvular approximant [ʁ̥] each occurs in a rather specific environment: the first after voiceless sounds and the second before consonants and at word end. In contrast the voiced uvular fricative [ʁ] occurs in a rather miscellaneous set of environments: word initial, between vowels, and after a voiced consonant. It is generally best to choose the allophone that appears in the greatest range of environments as the basic one, and to state rules that derive the others from this. In this way the rules can be stated in the simplest form, as we will discuss in section 2.6. We assume that the basic (or *underlying*) form of the sound appears unless some rule requires some other allophone in a specific environment.

A somewhat similar example comes from the Lowland Scots dialect of English (based on Carr 1993, 14). Consider the data in (8).

---

[2] They are phonetically similar in the sense that they are all *rhotics,* as defined at the end of section 1.1.1.1 of chapter 1. The term 'phonetically similar' is unfortunately somewhat vague. The theory of distinctive features developed in chapter 3 and the theory of phonological rules will help to clarify the situation.

(8) *phonetic* *orthography*
     and gloss

[ˈɹod]	road
[ˈɹɑm]	ram
[ˈhəɹe]	hurry
[ˈmæɹe]	marry
[ˈpɾ̥uf]	proof
[ˈtɾɪk]	trick
[ˈkɾ̥ip]	creep
[ˈfɹi]	free
[ˈbrɪŋ]	bring
[ˈdrɪp]	drip
[ˈɡrɪp]	grip
[ˈhɑɹt]	heart
[ˈfiːɹ]	fear
[ˈheːɹ]	hair

As before, we can construct a diagram of the environments in which each of the rhotics in Scots appears, as in (9).

(9)

		voiced consonant___V	voiceless stop___V	beginning, end of words, before consonants, after fricatives, between vowels (i.e., elsewhere)
voiced tap	[ɾ]	[ˈbrɪŋ]		
voiceless tap	[ɾ̥]		[ˈpɾ̥uf]	
approximant	[ɹ]			[ˈɹod]

The voiced tap [ɾ], the voiceless tap [ɾ̥], and the approximant [ɹ] are all in complementary distribution, and are phonetically similar, and so can be grouped together as a single phoneme. It should also be clear that the approximant [ɹ] occurs in the widest range of environments, and so should be considered basic. We can then make the diagram in (10).

(10)   /ɹ/

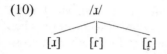

[ɹ]   [r]   [ɾ̥]

Another way of illustrating complementary distribution is by means of Venn diagrams, which are used in set theory to show the relations of sets. In the Venn diagram in (11), the large box represents all possible environments in Lowland Scots, and each circle represents the environments in which each of the rhotic allophones of the language appears. The environments do not overlap, which is the defining characteristic of complementary distribution.

(11)

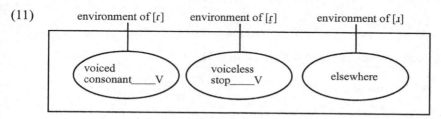

environment of [r]   environment of [ɾ̥]   environment of [ɹ]

voiced consonant___V   voiceless stop___V   elsewhere

A similar example comes from Farsi, the principal language of Iran. Consider the data in (12).[3]

(12)

voiced flap [ɾ]		voiceless trill [r̥]		voiced trill [r]	
[bi'ræn]	'pale'	['mɛtr̥]	'metre'	[fɑr'si]	'Persian'
[širi'ni]	'pastry'	['čætr̥]	'umbrella'	['rɑh]	'road'
[ɑhɑ'ri]	'starched'	['ætr̥]	'perfume'	['ræŋ]	'paint'
[dɑ'rid]	'you have'	['omr̥]	'life'	['bærg]	'leaf'
[bo'ros]	'hairbrush'	['æbr̥]	'cloud'	['ruz]	'day'
[do'rost]	'correct'	['tæmbr̥]	'stamp'	['šir]	'lion'
[bæ'rɑ]	'for'	[sæbr̥]	'wait'	[bærɑ'dær]	'brother'
[b'irun]	'outside'	[ʔæsr̥]	'evening'	['čɑhɑr]	'four'
[pæræn'dɛ]	'bird'			[beh'tær]	'better'
[pæri'ruz]	'day before yesterday'			[tor'moz]	'break'
[pɑrɑ'mɛtr̥]	'parameter'				

---

[3] I am grateful to Kiyan Azarbar for discussion of the Farsi data.

The three sounds [r], [ɾ], [r̥] represent a single phoneme in Farsi. The flap [ɾ] occurs between vowels, the voiceless trill occurs in word-final position when preceded by a consonant, and the voiced trill [r] occurs in all other environments. Note that [pɑrɑmɛtr̥] contains two allophones. As before, we make a chart of these observations, in (13).

(13)	V____V	C____#	elsewhere
[r]			[fɑrˈsi]
[ɾ]	[biˈræŋ]		
[r̥]		[ˈčætr̥]	

We can give the phonemic diagram in (14).

(14)   /r/

             [r]   [ɾ]   [r̥]

Here again we have taken the allophone that occurs in the widest range of environments, here the voiced trill, as the basic form of the phoneme. In chart (12) we state its environment simply as *elsewhere,* that is everywhere except where a specific environment requires one of the other allophones.

2.2   Coincident distribution

The situation in the English distribution of aspirated and unaspirated /p/ in (1)–(3) may be usefully contrasted with Hindi, as in (15) (Ladefoged 2001, 130).

(15)	pɑl	'take care of'	pʰɑl	'knife blade'
	ṭɑl	'beat'	ṭʰɑl	'plate'
	ṭɑl	'postpone'	ṭɑl	'wood shop'
	kɑn	'ear'	kʰɑn	'mine'

In Hindi, in contrast to English, unaspirated [p] and aspirated [pʰ] occur in identical environments in the words *pal* and *pʰal.* This can be called *coincident distribution* (Bloch 1953). These two words together constitute a *minimal pair,* that is, a pair of utterances that differ only in one respect. This respect is the phonemic difference. Such a minimal difference is often used to demonstrate that some linguistic feature is *contrastive,* that is, that it differentiates utterances. Another way of stating this is to say that there is no *rule* that relates unaspirated and aspirated voiceless stops in Hindi. The *list* of Hindi morphemes must include information regarding whether voiceless stops are aspirated or not, whereas this information is absent from the list in English.

We can represent coincident distribution with the Venn diagram in (16). While only a single oval appears, there are really two that overlap completely. We illustrate with the bilabial; the other points of articulation have the same picture.

(16) environment of [p] environment of [pʰ]

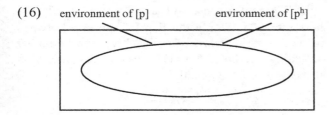

In Hindi, the feature of aspiration is contrastive, not only in labial stops, but in dental, retroflex, and velar stops as well, as shown in (15), whereas in English it is allophonic, that is, not contrastive. Therefore, while two languages may use the same sounds, they may differ in the distribution of these sounds.

2.3   Overlapping distribution

A similar point can be illustrated by comparing the Farsi data in (12) with the European Spanish data in (17).

(17)   *phonetic*   *orthographic* *gloss*

     ['roxo]   rojo   'red'

     [ra'θon̪]   razón   'reason'

     ['onra]   honra   'honour'

     [alreðe'ðor]   alrededor   'about'

     ['foro]   forro   'lining'

     ['foro]   foro   'forum'

['pɛɾo]	pero	'but'
['pɛro]	perro	'dog'
['pɾaðo]	prado	'meadow'
[kɾɛ'θɛɾ]	crecer	'to grow'
[d̥aɾ]	dar	'to give'
['pɛɾla]	perla	'pearl'

The distribution here is a little more complicated (Navarro 1967; Harris 1983). At the beginning of a word and at the beginning of a syllable after a consonant within a word only the trill [r] appears. Finally in a word, within a word at the end of a syllable before a consonant, and within a word after another consonant in the same syllable only the flap [ɾ] appears. Between vowels within a word, however, both sounds appear. We observe two minimal pairs in the data of (17). Setting out the table in (18) makes the distribution clear.[4] The symbol $ represents a syllable boundary.

(18)	#___	___#	V___V	C$___	___$C, $C___
voiced tap [ɾ]		[d̥aɾ]	[foɾo]		[pɛɾla], [pɾaðo]
voiced trill [r]	[roxo]		[foro]	['onra]	

If we read down the environments of this chart, we find that the environment V____V may contain either [ɾ] or [r]. This means that we cannot consider these sounds to be members of a single phoneme in Spanish, although they do represent a single phoneme in Farsi. Since they contrast in the environment V____V, they must be separate phonemes. However, unlike the Hindi aspirated and unaspirated stops, the flap and trill in Spanish do not contrast in all environments. In word-initial position only the trill appears; in word-final and in medial position adjacent to another consonant only the flap appears. This then is a case of *overlapping distribution,* which can be represented graphically in the Venn diagram in (19).

---

[4] We will return to these facts in section 5.5 of chapter 5 and give a somewhat different analysis. I am indebted to Leigh-Anne Webster for discussion of the Spanish facts.

overlapping allophones

(19)   environment of [ɾ]   environment of [r]

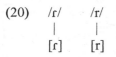

$C____
____#

V____V

C$____
#____

As before, the ovals for the two sounds correspond to their environments of occurrence. The area where the two ovals overlap represents the environment V____V, i.e., between vowels. The area of the /ɾ/ outside this overlap represents the environments where only the flap appears, that is, word-internally after a consonant and word-finally. The area of /r/ outside the overlap represents the environments where only /r/ appears, that is, word initially. A phonemic diagram shows two separate phonemes, as in (20).

(20)   /ɾ/   /r/
        | |
       [ɾ]   [r]

[r]

[ɾ] /r/
     /ɾ/

[ɾ]

[ɾ]

Even though there are some environments where only one of these sounds appears, the fact that they contrast in the environment V____V shows that they have to be analyzed as two separate phonemes. This does not preclude the possibility of rules governing the environments where these sounds do not contrast, as developed further in section 5.5 of chapter 5.

2.4   Pattern congruity

In the Hindi data of (15), we observed that aspirated stops contrast with unaspirated ones at four points of articulation. Thus there is a *pattern* of contrast in that the constrast in one feature (aspiration) affects items that contrast in another feature (point of articulation). Such patterns can also be observed in cases of complementary distribution. An example is English aspiration. So far, in discussing English aspiration, we have considered only the labials, but English has aspirated stops at other points of articulation as well. The data in (21) show this for velars.

which phoneme in env. of neutralization

(21)   a.   [kʰ]   b.   [k]

           kin   [ˈkʰɪn]   skin   [ˈskɪn]

           cat   [ˈkʰæt]   askance   [əˈskæns]

           canoe   [kʰəˈnu]   scurry   [ˈskəɹi]

           account   [əˈkʰæwnt]   escalate   [ˈɛskəˌleyt]

           raccoon   [ˌɹæˈkʰun]   wicked   [ˈwɪkɪd]

The distribution of aspirated and unaspirated *k* in English is completely parallel to that of *p*. Aspirated [kʰ] appears at the beginning of a word and at the
beginning of a stressed syllable internal to a word, while unaspirated [k]
appears after [s] and word internally at the beginning of a stressless syllable.
We can set this out in tabular form (22), as we did for /p/ in (2), and conclude
that [kʰ] and [k] form a single phoneme, as in (23).

(22)

	#____	s____	V__V́	V__V̊
[k]		*s*kin		wi*ck*ed
[kʰ]	*k*in			a*cc*ount

(23)   /k/   (phoneme)

          [k]   [kʰ]   (allophones)

This parallelism in the distribution of the allophones of /p/ and of /k/ is called
pattern congruity. We have two classes of sounds both of which contain voiceless stops. That is, /p/ represents the class of sounds {[p], [pʰ]} while /k/ represents the class {[k], [kʰ]}. Within each class there is an unaspirated member
with a distribution identical to that of the unaspirated member of the other;
likewise the aspirated member of each class has the same distribution as the
aspirated member of the other. These two classes of sounds behave in a parallel fashion. The two classes contrast with each other, as shown by minimal
pairs like *pin* and *kin, spin* and *skin*. The aspirated and unaspirated stops of
Hindi likewise show pattern congruity, only in Hindi the aspirated and unaspirated stops contrast with each other at each point of articulation.

    There is pattern congruity in the alveolar stops of English as well, but with
a slight wrinkle. In North American dialects, /t/ has an additional allophone:
the flap [ɾ]. Consider the data in (24).

(24) a. [tʰ]   b. [t]   c. [ɾ]

    tin   stone   city
    ['tʰɪn]   ['stown]   ['sɪɾi]

    topaz   starry   butter
    ['tʰow,pʰæz]   ['staɹi]   ['bəɾɹ]

    attire   astonish   attic
    [ə'tʰayɹ]   [ə'stɒnɪš]   ['æɾɪk]

    tradition   estimate   sanity
    [tʰɹə'dɪšən]   ['ɛstɪ,meyt]   ['sænɪɾi]

    tenacious   industry   attitude
    [tʰɪ'neyšəs]   ['ɪndəstṛi]   ['æɾɪ,tyuwd]

Once again we can set out the distribution in a table, as in (25).

(25)

	#_____	s_____	V___V́	V___V̊
[t]		s*t*one		
[tʰ]	*t*in		at*t*ire	
[ɾ]				ci*t*y

We find that the alveolar stops pattern similarly to the labials and velars, but not quite identically. As with the labials and velars we find the aspirated allophone in word-initial position and word internally after a vowel before a stressed vowel, and we find the unaspirated allophone after [s]. But, whereas with the velars and labials we also found the unaspirated allophone word internally before an unstressed vowel, in the case of the alveolar we find the flap allophone in that position. We can still call this pattern congruity, but the pattern is not completely parallel. Actually, we will have to modify our analysis of English voiceless stops again slightly in section 2.5.

For another example of pattern congruity, consider the data in (26) from Spanish.

(26) [b]   [d̪]   [g]

    ['baɲo] 'bathroom'   ['d̪aɲo] 'damage'   ['gaɲo] 'I howl'

    ['mambo] 'mambo'   ['man̪d̪o] 'I send'   ['maŋgo] 'mango'

    [a'blað̞o] 'spoken'

[β̞]		[ð̞]		[ɣ̞]	
[aˈβ̞ɛɾ]	'to have'	[ˈn̩að̞a]	'nothing'	[luˈɣ̞aɾ]	'place'
[roˈβ̞ar]	'to rob'	[roˈð̞ar]	'to roll'	[roˈɣ̞ar]	'to beg'
		[aˈblað̞o]	'spoken'	[ˈaɣ̞wa]	'water'
		[ˈlað̞o]	'side'	[ˈlaɣ̞o]	'lake'

In these data we see that voiced stops [b], [d̪], and [g] occur at the beginning of a word and word internally after a nasal consonant or before a consonant (except a glide). The corresponding approximants [β̞], [ð̞], and [ɣ̞] occur between vowels or between a vowel and a glide. This illustrates perfect pattern congruity because all three voiced stops have the same relation to their corresponding approximant, in that the approximant occurs between vowels (or between a vowel and a glide) while the stop occurs in other positions.

2.5   Free variation

In the discussion of the Hindi data in (15), and of the Spanish data in (17), we observed that distinct sounds may occur in the same phonological environment where they serve to contrast utterances. It may happen that distinct, phonetically similar sounds may appear in the same phonological environment yet not contrast utterances. Let us consider a slightly expanded set of examples containing the voiceless bilabial stop in English in (27).

(27)   [p]   [pʰ]   [p̚]

spin	[ˈspɪn]	pin	[ˈpʰɪn]	elapse	[ɪˈlæp̚s]
aspire	[əˈspayɹ]	parade	[pʰəˈɹeyd]	apt	[ˈæp̚t]
aspirate	[ˈæspɪˌɹeyt]	appear	[əˈpʰiyɹ]	slipped	[ˈslˌɪp̚t]
happy	[ˈhæpi]	topaz	[ˈtʰowˌpʰæz]	cape	[ˈkʰeyp̚]
opera	[ˈɒpərə]	play	[ˈpʰlˌey]	captain	[ˈkæp̚tɪn]
trip	[ˈtʰɹ̥ɪp]	trip	[tʰɹ̥ɪpʰ]	trip	[tʰɹ̥ɪp̚]

To the two allophones we considered in (1) we have added a third, the unrealeased stop [p̚]. (See the table of diacritics on page 32 after the phonetic chart of consonants.) We find the unrealeased allophone in word-final position and before another consonant. If we now construct a chart of the occurrences of the three allophones, we obtain (28).

(28)	#___	___#	s___	___C	V___V́	V___V̊
[p]		tri*p*	s*p*in			ha*pp*y
[pʰ]	*p*in	tri*p*			a*pp*ear	
[p˺]		tri*p*		a*p*t		

If we read down the environment columns in (28), we find that all three allo-phones occur in the word-final environment. This resembles the situation we found in (18) in Spanish, where, reading down the column representing the intervocalic environment, we found that both the trill [r] and the flap [ɾ] occur in that context. However, in the Spanish case, the two words are entirely different: [foro] means 'forum' and [foɾo] means 'lining.' In contrast, reading down the word-final column in (28) reveals three occurrences of the *same* word: *trip* always means 'trip,' whether the final stop is pronounced with a normal [p], an aspirated [pʰ] or with an unreleased [p˺]. This is known as *free variation*. Care must be taken in interpreting charts such as (18) and (28). The discovery of two or more entries in a single column (representing a particular environment) reveals a contrast only if the entries are different words. If they are variants of the same word it represents free variation. We still say that the three allophones whose distribution is shown in (28) form a single phoneme whose members are in complementary distribution in most environments but in free variation in word-final position.

Because of pattern congruity, we expect to find a similar situation with the alveolar and velar stops in English, as indeed we do. Consider an expanded data set for the velar stops in (29).

(29)

[k]		[kʰ]		[k˺]	
skin	['skɪn]	kin	['kʰɪn]	act	['æk˺t]
askance	[ə'skæns]	cat	['kæt]	ax	['æk˺s]
scurry	['skəɹi]	canoe	[kʰə'nuw]	picked	['pɪk˺t]
escalate	['ɛskə,leyt]	account	[ə'kʰæwnt]	peak	['piyk˺]
wicked	['wɪkɪd]	raccoon	[ˌræ'kʰuwn]	accent	['æk˺sɪnt]
back	['bæk]	back	['bækʰ]	back	['bæk˺]

The chart for the distribution of the allophones in (29), given in (30), is similar to the chart for the labial stops.

(30)

	#____	____#	s____	____C	V___V́	V___V̊
[k]		back	skin			wicked
[kʰ]	cat	back			account	
[k˺]		back		act		

Once again we find that the three allophones of /k/ are either in complementary distribution or, in the case of word-final position, in free variation, and so form one phoneme.

In the case of the alveolar stop, we considered three allophones in (24) and (25). We can now consider two more. The five allophones of /t/ are illustrated in (31).

(31)

[t]	[tʰ]	[t˺]	[ɾ]	[ʔ]
stone	tin	sits	butter	button
starry	topaz	cats	attic	butler
astonish	attire		water	cats
estimate	tradition		sanity	kitten
industry	tenacious		attitude	atlas
cat	cat	cat	cattle	cat

As with the labials and velars we have added the unreleased [t˺] to the data set. The fifth allophone is the glottal stop [ʔ], which appears before syllabic [n̩] or before [l] and a vowel. The table in (32) shows this distribution.

(32)

	#____	____#	s____	____C	V___V́	V___V̊	V___n̩, ____lV
[t]		cat	stone				
[tʰ]	tip	cat			attempt		
[t˺]		cat		cats			
[ɾ]						butter	
[ʔ]		cat		cats			button, butler

The alveolar stop has a more complex distribution than the labial and the velar, as before. Here we have two environments where more than one allophone appears: four allophones are found in word-final position and two are found before a consonant. But in each case there is free variation rather than contrast in these environments. We can still safely analyze /t/ as a single phoneme, now with five allophones in complementary distribution and free variation.

2.6   Phonological rules and notations

The most common format for phonological rules is given schematically in (33).

(33) $A \rightarrow B / P\_\_\_\_Q$

This is read "A becomes B in the environment of a preceding P and a follow-ing Q." A and B must each be a single segment or a class of segments defined by distinctive features, as developed later in chapter 3. P and Q can be any segment or boundary or a sequence of segments and boundaries. Either P or Q or both may be left unspecified, in which case the rule applies regardless of what material, if any, appears to the left (if P is unspecified) or right (if Q is unspecified) of A. Term A is referred to as the *input,* term B is the *structural change,* and the expression P____Q is the *environment.* To illustrate, let us see how we can write phonological rules to account for some of the allophones we have discussed so far in this chapter.

For example, in Farsi we took the voiced trill /r/ as the basic form and said that it appears as a voiceless trill in word-final position after a consonant (see the data in 12). The statement that the basic form is /r/ is equivalent to stating that /r/ appears in *all* environments in basic or *underlying* representations of the language, and that the phonetic form of this phoneme is determined by context. This takes the form of a rule that can be stated as in (34).

(34)   r-*Devoicing (Farsi)*
        $r \rightarrow \underset{\circ}{r} / C\_\_\_\_\#$

Given rule (34), we can assume that a word like 'čætr̥ 'umbrella' has the underlying phonological representation /čætr/, with a final voiced /r/. We can then *derive* the phonetic form by applying the rule. This works as shown in (35). (Stress is also predictable, although we have not given the rule. It is always on the final syllable in (12). Hence we show it in the phonetic repre-sentation but not in the underlying representation.)

(35)   /#čætr#/   underlying representation
       ŗ   Rule (33)
       [#ˈčætŗ#]   Phonetic representation

A display such as that in (35) is known as a *derivation*. The first line shows the underlying representation. The succeeding lines show the results of applying one or more rules to this representation, allotting one line to each rule;[5] conventionally, only the item(s) changed by each rule are shown on such lines. The final line shows the phonetic representation, after the application of all relevant rules.

The other allophone of /r/ in Farsi is the voiced flap [ɾ], which appears in the environment between vowels. This requires the rule in (36).

(36)   r-*Flapping (Farsi)*
       r → ɾ / V____V

We can now take the underlying representation of *širiˈni* 'pastry' as /širini/ and derive the phonetic form in the derivation (37).

(37)   /#širini#/   Underlying representation
       ɾ   Rule (35)
       [#širiˈni#]   Phonetic representation

Let us now consider the form *pæræˈmetŗ* 'parameter.' This form needs to have *both* rules (34) and (36) apply. The derivation is given in (38).

(38)   /#parametr#/   Underlying representation
                ŗ   Rule (34)
       ɾ   Rule (36)
       [#paɾaˈmetŗ#]   Phonetic representation

In the derivation (38), the two rules could apply in either order; the results are the same. In subsequent chapters we will see examples where the order of application makes a difference to the outcome.

---

[5] In complex derivations involving several rules, each line between the underlying and phonetic representations shows the result of applying the rule of that line to the line immediately above, which may have resulted from the application of previous rules. We will return to this question in chapters 4 and 5.

2.7 Common types of phonological processes

Some phonological processes occur commonly enough to have acquired descriptive names. In analyzing the exercises it is always best to look for such processes first before proposing a rule of a completely different nature. We discuss some of these processes in this section.

2.7.1 Assimilation

In *assimilation*, a sound changes to become more like a nearby sound. For example, in the French data of (5), the uvular fricative is realized as a voiceless [χ] following a voiceless sound. A similar example occurs with the English plural morpheme, which is pronounced [z] in words like *dogs* and *cows*. In the word *cats*, the plural morpheme has been devoiced to [s], in assimilation to the voiceless [t] which precedes it. In both the French and English cases, we say that a sound assimilates in voicing to what precedes. For more examples, see exercises 2.6, 2.9, 2.10, 2.13, 2.15, and 2.16.

The assimilation need not be to an *immediately* adjacent sound. A very common type of assimilation is *vowel harmony*, by which a vowel takes on some characteristics of a nearby vowel regardless of intervening consonants. For example, in Hungarian the suffix meaning 'from beside' has two forms: [toːl], which appears after words with back vowels, e.g., *haːstoːl* 'from beside the house' and [töːl], which appears after words with front vowels, e.g., *köɲvtöːl* 'from beside the book.' The vowel of the suffix assimilates to the preceding stem vowel in terms of backness. (See exercises 2.9, 4.9, and 6.1.)

2.7.2 Dissimilation

Dissimilation is the opposite of assimilation. In dissimilation, a sound becomes *less* like a neighbouring sound. For example, in Modern Greek, the aorist passive suffix *-θik,* (as in (39a) becomes *-tik* after a fricative, as shown in (39b) (Sofroniou 1962; K. Harris 1976).[6]

(39)	a.	[aɣaˈp-o]	'I love'	[aɣaˈp-i-θik-ɛ]	'he was loved'
		[ˈfɛr-o]	'I bring'	[ˈfɛr-θik-ɛ]	'it was brought'
		[ˈstɛl-o]	'I send'	[ˈstal-θik-ɛ]	'it was sent'
		[siŋ-kiˈno]	'I move'	[siŋ-kin-iˈθik-ɛ]	'it was moved'

---

[6] The form [ˈkrif-tik-ɛ] also illustrates voicing assimilation: the basic [v] seen in [ˈkriv-o] is devoiced in assimilation to the following voiceless [t].

b. [aˈku-o]   'I hear'   [aˈku-s-tik-ɛ]   'he was heard'

    [ˈðɛx-o-mɛ]   'I receive'   [ˈdɛx-tik-ɛ]   'it was received'

    [ˈɣraf-o]   'I write'   [ɣraf-tik-ɛ]   'it was written'

    [ˈkriv-o]   'I hide'   [ˈkrif-tik-ɛ]   'he hid himself'

2.7.3 Lenition

Lenition literally means weakening. It generally refers to a reduction in the degree of stricture in a sound, roughly along the scales of (40) (Spencer 1996, 62). The scale in (40a) varies by manner of articulation, while that in (40b) involves glottal state.

(40)   a.   stops > flaps > fricatives > approximants > Ø
       b.   voiceless aspirated > plain voiceless > voiced

An example is the Spanish change illustrated in (26), where voiced stops become approximants between vowels. This can be seen as a type of assimilation, where the stop assimilates to degree of stricture of surrounding vowels.

Another example is a process in Japanese known as Rendaku, by which a voiceless obstruent at the beginning of a word is voiced when that word is joined into a compound with a preceding vowel-final word. We give some examples in (41) (Itô & Mester 1986).

(41)   [ori]   'fold'

       [kami]   'paper'

       [tana]   'shelf'

       [t͡sukuri]   'make'

       [origami]   'origami (paper folding)'

       [origamidana]   'origami shelf'

       [origamidanad͡zukuri]   'origami shelf making'

Another example is the flapped allophone of English /t/ illustrated in (31). Here a voiceless stop becomes a voiced flap, thus advancing along both scales in (40).

2.7.4 Fortition

The opposite of lenition is *fortition,* by which a sound is strengthened by moving to the left along the scales of (40). An example is the aspiration of English voiceless stops in word-initial position and before stressed vowels observed in (1), (21), and (24). Another example occurs in some dialects of Spanish, such as Argentinian, where the glide /y/ is pronounced [ž] at the beginning of a syllable, in such words as *yo* [žo] 'I,' *ayer* [ɑ.žɛɾ] 'yesterday,' *leyes* [lɛ.žɛs] 'laws' (compare *ley* [lɛy] 'law'), *creyendo* [kɾɛˈžɛn.do] 'believing,' (compare *comiendo* [koˈmyɛn.do] 'eating,' etc. (Harris 1983, 57–61).

2.7.5 Insertions

Insertion or *epenthesis* is the addition of a segment, often to facilitate pronunciation. The productive morpheme for 'plural' in English is phonologically /-z/ in words like *dogs* and *cows.* As we saw in section 2.7.1, this morpheme undergoes assimilation in words like *cats.* In words like *horses, buzzes, bushes, churches, judges,* an insertion of [ɪ] takes place, so that the plural morpheme has the shape [ɪz]. Because it is difficult to pronounce sequences like [sz], a vowel is inserted between these segments to make it easier and to ensure that the plural morpheme is clearly understood. The insertion of a vowel here affects the syllable structure, in fact adding a syllable to the word. An insertion is given a formal expression in terms of a phonological rule in the form of (33) with term A = Ø.

2.7.6 Deletions

The opposite of insertion is *deletion.* In French, many word-final consonants are dropped if the following word begins with a consonant or at the end of a phrase. The word-final consonant is retained before a vowel. Examples of all three types are found in (42) (Schane 1973, 53). Deletion is another way of dealing with difficult clusters of consonants. These are written in the format of (33) with term B = Ø.

(42)	*before vowel*	*before consonant*	*phrase final*
	[pətit æˈmi]	[pəti gaʁˈsɔ̃]	[il ɛ pəˈti]
	'little friend'	'little boy'	'he is little'

[gʁoz æ'mi]   [gʁo gaʁ'sɔ̃]   [il ɛ 'gʁo]
'big friend'   'big boy'   'he is big'

[tχop e'tχwa]   [tχo 'laʁžə]   [sɛ 'tχo]
'too narrow'   'too wide'   'it's too much'

[tχɛz e'tχwa]   [tχɛ 'laʁžə]   ['tχɛ]
'very narrow'   'very wide'   'very'

In some cases there may be both deletion and insertion of the same segment. In some dialects of English, notably southern British RP and Eastern New England, /ɹ/ does not appear word finally or before another consonant in the same word, as shown in (43).

(43)   bar   ['bɑː]   barring   ['bɑːɹɪŋ]

        soar   ['sɔə̯]   soaring   ['sɔə̯ɹɪŋ]

        fear   ['fɪə̯]   fearing   ['fɪə̯ɹɪŋ]

        park   [pɑːk]

        Homer   ['howmə]   Homeric   [ˌhow'mɛɹɪk]

The data in (43) could be used to justify a rule deleting /ɹ/ in the environments ____# and ____C. Other data of a similar sort suggests that /ɹ/ may be inserted in some cases like (44).

(44)   saw   ['sɔə̯]   sawing   ['sɔə̯ɹɪŋ]

        law   ['lɔə̯]   law and order ['lɔə̯ɹən'ɔdə]

Therefore this dialect would appear to need both insertion and deletion to account for these very similar phenomena. For some discussion of the complexities involved, see McCarthy (1993) and Halle & Idsardi (1997).

2.7.7 Lengthening

In Russian, vowel length is allophonic. Stressed vowels are longer than unstressed vowels. For example the stressed [u] of *rúki* 'hands' is longer than the unstressed [u] of *rukí* 'of a hand' while the stressed [i] of the latter is longer than the unstressed [i] of the former. Lengthening may also affect phonemic vowel length. Vowel length is phonemic in Latin, as shown by the pairs in (45).

(45) [oːs]   'mouth   [os]   'bone'
      [hiːk]   'here'   [hik]   'this (masculine)'
      [portaː]   'gate (ablative)'   [porta]   'gate (nominative)'

Nevertheless, vowels are lengthened in certain environments, such as before the sequences *ns* and *nf.* Compare the short vowel of the prefix *in-* 'not' in the left column of (46) with the lengthened vowel of the same prefix in the right column.

(46) [inhuːmaːnus] 'inhuman'   [iːnsaːnus]   'mad'
      [inimiːkus]   'unfriendly' [iːnfeːliks] 'unhappy'

2.7.8 Compensatory lengthening

A special form of lengthening is known as *compensatory lengthening,* which often results from deletion of a consonant. The lengthenings in (47) occurred historically in Latin (Hayes 1989, 260). The vowel is lengthened in compensation for the loss of the [s] that originally followed it.

(47) [kasnus] > [kaːnus]   'grey'
      [kosmis] > [koːmis]   'courteous'
      [fideslia] > [fideːlia] 'pot'

2.7.9 Shortening

Shortening is the opposite of lengthening. While the vowels of English *bee, bead* have roughly the same length, the vowel of *beat* is shorter. In general a vowel is shorter before a voiceless consonant than it is either word finally or before a voiced consonant. With the diphthongs [ay] and [aw] the vowel is noticeably raised (to a mid vowel [ə]) as well. Compare the examples in (48).

(48) write   ['ɹəyt]   ride   ['ɹɑːyd]
      writer ['ɹəyɾəɹ]   rider   ['ɹɑːyɾəɹ]

Notice that the raised and shortened version of the diphthong appears in *writer* as well as in *write,* even though the following segment is the (voiced) flap [ɾ] allophone of /t/. We will return to this question in section 2.8.1.

2.8   Problems with phonemic analysis

2.8.1   Neutralization

The theory of phonological analysis that divides language sounds into contrasting groups is known as *taxonomic phonemics,* since it provides a taxono-
my of the sounds of the language. While this theory can offer considerable
insight into the phonological structure of a language, it has inherent limitations. These limitations can be overcome only by a more sophisticated form
of analysis, known as *generative phonology,* discussed starting in chapter 4.
One type of limitation in this theory occurs in overlapping distribution, illustrated in the Spanish distribution of the trill [r] and the flap [ɾ] in the data of
(17) and diagrammed in (19). Because these segments contrast in the intervocalic environment, phonemic theory assigns them to separate phonemes. Once
this assignment is made, phonemic theory does not countenance rules governing their distribution. Rules in phonemic theory can only state the distribution of the allophones of a phoneme. They cannot substitute one phoneme
for another. Nevertheless, the occurrence of the trill [r] in word-initial position, to the exclusion of the flap [ɾ], appears to be a rule-governed phenomenon. However, the phonemic slogan "once a phoneme, always a phoneme"
disallows a rule expressing this fact. See section 5.5 of chapter 5 for an analysis of Spanish *r*-sounds.
      A second serious limitation of phonemic theory is its inability to deal
insightfully with the very common phenomenon of neutralization.
Neutralization occurs whenever two or more distinct underlying segments
have the same realization in a particular environment. In discussing the allophones of English /t/ in (24) and (31) we noted that one of the allophones of
/t/ is the flap [ɾ]. But the flap [ɾ] is also an allophone of the voiced stop /d/. As
in the case of Spanish trill [r] and flap [ɾ], there are environments in which [t]
and [d] contrast, for example at the end of a word, as in *heat* and *heed.* But if
a participial suffix is added to each of these, as in *heating* and *heeding,* the
words are pronounced the same, since the alveolar stop is converted to a flap
in both cases. While phonemic theory commonly employs a branching diagram such as the one we gave in (3) (repeated here as 49) to illustrate allophones, where a phonemic unit branches into two or more phonetic units, it
does not allow diagrams in which a single phonetic unit is connected to two
or more phonemes, as in (50).[7]

---

[7] Such a diagram is legitimate in a theory based on rules, however.

(49)   /p/   (phoneme)

        [p]   [pʰ]   (allophones)

(50)   /t/   /d/

... [t]   ([ɾ])   [d] ...   Non-overlap

(where the ellipsis indicates other allophones of /t/, /d/)

This is because phonemic analysis starts from the bottom up: it begins with phonetic material and groups phonetically similar elements into phonemes if they are in complementary distribution (or free variation). But a diagram like (50) implies that a phonetic [ɾ] could sometimes be assigned to /t/ and sometimes to /d/; the analysis would be indeterminate. There are two possible solutions within phonemic theory. One is to assign [ɾ] always to one or the other phoneme, which would be arbitrary. Let us suppose that [ɾ] is assigned to the /d/ phoneme on the grounds that the flap is more phonetically similar to /d/ than to /t/. Then we would say that *heat* has two arbitrary *allomorphs,*[8] phonemically /hit/ that appears in *heat,* and /hid/, that appears in *heating.* These two allomorphs cannot be related by phonological rules. They may be given a single representation on a morphological level, a representation that has been called *morphophonemic.* This might be represented as //hiT//, where the *morphophoneme* //T// is realized as either the phoneme /t/ or the phoneme /d/, depending on its environment. This view commits us to setting up three levels of representation: the morphophonemic, the phonemic, and the phonetic, as in (51). We temporarily introduce the notation of a double slant line (e.g., //T//) to represent morphophonemes and the morphophonemic level. A rule is required to replace the morphophoneme //T// by the phoneme /d/ in the environment V____ V̌ (compare the allophonic distribution in 31).

No!

(51) Morphophonemic

level	//hiyT//	//hiyT+ɪŋ//	//hiyd//	//hiyd+ɪŋ//
Phonemic level	/hiyt/	/hiyd+ɪŋ/	/hiyd/	/hiyd+ɪŋ/
Phonetic level	[hiyt]	[hiyɾɪŋ]	[hiyd]	[hiyɾɪŋ]
	'heat'	'heating'	'heed'	'heeding'

---

[8] The term "allomorph," as used in this book, refers to different forms of a morpheme that are not phonologically predictable (Aronoff 1976). Phonologically predictable forms of a morpheme are referred to as "alternants," discussed in chapter 4.

It should be emphasized that the only motivation for setting up the phonemic level is to maintain a single level where all and only the contrastive sounds of the language appear. Because /t/ and /d/ contrast in some environments, for instance in 'heat' and 'heed,' they must be represented as such *phonemically* everywhere they contrast, even where the apparent contrast is completely predictable, as in 'heat' and 'heating.'

The second solution within phonemic theory would be to give /ɾ/ phonemic status on its own. This would have the same unfortunate consequences as assigning this sound arbitrarily to one of the sounds which it realizes, and moreover it would require the inclusion of an additional phoneme in the system whose appearance is always predictable. In fact, this solution would require *both* 'heat' and 'heed' to have arbitrary allomorphs, as in (52). The rule required in this solution is that the morphophonemes //t// and //d// are replaced by the phoneme /ɾ/ in the environment V____ V̆.

(52)   Morphophonemic
       level   //hiyt//   //hiyt+ɪŋ//   //hiyd//   //hiyd+ɪŋ//

       Phonemic level   /hiyt/   /hiyɾ+ɪŋ/   /hiyd/   /hiyɾ+ɪŋ/

       Phonetic level   [hiyt]   [hiyɾɪŋ]   [hiyd]   [hiyɾɪŋ]
                          'heat'   'heating'   'heed'   'heeding'

This solution does not require the morphophoneme //T//, but like the solution illustrated in (50) it requires that the neutralization take place between the morphophonemic and the phonemic levels. Generative phonology, as detailed in chapter 4, eliminates the necessity of setting up extra levels and extra elements (morphophonemes like //T// or phonemes like /ɾ/) simply by dropping the requirement that the grammar provide a level where all and only the contrastive elements appear.

The difficulties posed by neutralization for taxonomic phonemic theory become more acute when two or more processes are involved. For example, in (48), the shortened diphthong [əy] (in *writer*) contrasts with the regular diphthong [aːy] (in *rider*). They must therefore both be present on the phonemic level, despite the fact that they are mostly predictable (as in the difference between *write* and *ride*). Generative phonology easily accounts for this case with phonemes /t/, /d/, and /aːy/ and two ordered rules. We will return to this example in section 6.7.6 of chapter 6. Malécot (1960) discusses a similar example of this type in many dialects of English, where the words *cat* [kæt] and *can't* [kæ̃t] differ just in that the first has an oral vowel and the second has a nasal vowel, suggesting that nasal vowels are phonemic in these dialects. Again, generative phonology can propose a phonemic distinction between /kæt/ and /kænt/, where the difference resides in the absence versus the presence of a nasal consonant, and the phonetic difference is derived by applying rules that first nasalize the vowel and then delete the nasal consonant. The generative solution is clearly more in line with native speakers' intuitions.

Generative phonology also does not make a distinction between a morphophonemic level and a phonemic level, and so can dispense with the double slant notation (//T//). In generative phonology the input to the phonological rules is known as the *systematic phonemic* level, and is enclosed in single slants, as shown in derivations like (37). While there may be intermediate stages in a derivation after the operation of each rule, none of the intermediate stages has the theoretical significance to require a specific name. The result of applying all the phonological rules is known as the *systematic phonetic* level.

2.8.2 Pattern congruity

Pattern congruity provides another ground for arguing against phonemic theory. One of the most celebrated examples comes from Halle (1959). Most Russian obstruents have distinctive voicing, that is, there is a voiced and a voiceless consonant that are otherwise identical in place and manner of articulation that contrast, as shown by the minimal pairs in (53).

(53) [pɑˈkɑ]   'while'   [bɑˈkɑ]   'sides'

　　 ['tom]   'volume'   ['dom]   'house'

　　 ['sloy]   'layer'   ['zloy]   'bad'

　　 ['šɑr]   'sphere'   ['žɑr]   'heat'

　　 ['klup]   'club'   ['glup]   'stupid'

But three Russian voiceless obstruents, /x, č, t͡s/ have no contrastive (phonemic) counterparts. But the corresponding voiced obstruents, [ɣ, ǰ, d͡z] are found *phonetically* in Russian. Russian has a rule of voicing assimilation by which an obstruent takes on the voicing of an immediately following obstruent. That is, an obstruent becomes voiced if the immediately following obstruent is voiced and becomes voiceless if the immediately following obstruent is voiceless. We illustrate this process in (54).

(54)   ['mok li]   'whether he soaked'   ['mog bɨ]   'were he to soak'
        ['žeč li]   'whether he burned'   ['žeǰ bɨ]   'were he to burn'

The replacement of //k// by /g/ in the first line of (54) must be a matter of morphophonemics, since, as we saw in (53), the sounds /k/ and /g/ are contrastive
in Russian and thus separate phonemes. However, in the second line of (54),
the replacement of //č// by [ǰ] is allophonic, since these sounds do not contrast.
Thus phonemic theory requires two separate voicing assimilation rules for
Russian, one morphophonemic and one allophonic, which misses the generalization that a single, unified process is involved. Generative phonology solves
this problem once again by not requiring there to be a single level where all
and only the contrastive segments are represented. There can then be a single
rule, which does not care whether assimilation produces an otherwise distinctive segment or not.

In fact, there seems to be a major contradiction in taxonomic phonemic
theory. In order to determine the pattern of contrasting and allophonic segments in a language, an analysis is made on the basis of a phonetic transcription. But, once the allophones have been determined, the rules responsible for
their distribution must operate on phonemic representations. For many of the
examples in this chapter this causes no problems, but in the cases discussed in
this section, where rules interact with each other, problems can arise. This is
because there is no way to ensure, on the basis of the phonetic forms alone,
that the appropriate conditions for a particular rule will be present in the
phonemic representation. In more complex cases, it is possible to start the
analysis in the manner described in this chapter, but ultimately recourse must
be had to other information about the sound patterns of the language, such as
alternations, discussed in chapter 4.

2.9   Summary

Our focus in this chapter has been on the distribution of language sounds. The
grammar of a language must contain a *list* of morphemes, each specified with
the unpredictable phonological information on the pronunciation of that morpheme, as well as with syntactic and semantic information that allows the
speaker to use that morpheme correctly. The phonological information for
each morpheme is given in terms of *contrastive* sound units, the *underlying*

representation of that morpheme, omitting predictable aspects of pronunciation. Predictable aspects of pronunciation are the result of applying *rules* to the underlying representation. A major aspect of phonological analysis consists in determining which aspects of pronunciation are unpredictable, and therefore part of the underlying representations of the morphemes of that language, and which aspects are predictable, and establishing the rules that predict these aspects. Aspects of pronunciation assigned to the underlying representations of morphemes are peculiar to those morphemes, whereas rules are general, applying, where relevant, throughout the language. The English rule that aspirates word-initial voiceless stops applies to every word that has an intial voiceless stop in its underlying representation. But the fact that a word like *pin* begins with a voiceless bilabial stop is unpredictable, hence listed. On the other hand, Hindi contrasts aspirated and unaspirated stops, so this information must be listed for Hindi, unlike English.

We can distinguish two broad categories of rules. *Allophonic* rules result in segments which are never contrastive in the language, such as aspiration in English. Such rules are generally easy to discover.[9] *Neutralizing* rules have the effect of merging segments in a particular environment that are contrastive in other environments. In English, voiced and voiceless alveolar stops generally contrast, as in words like *tin* versus *din, heat* versus *heed,* but in the environment V____ V̌, both are realized phonetically as the voiced flap [ɾ]. In such cases of overlapping distribution we need a rule to account for the neutralization in one environment, while allowing both /t/ and /d/ in underlying representations. Such rules may be more difficult to find, because they often require access to morphological information as well as purely phonetic information. But the rules are still stated in phonological terms, not morphological ones. We take up this question in more detail in chapter 4, which is concerned with alternations. Prior to that, however, we will develop the theory of distinctive features in the next chapter, as the fundamental units of which language utterances are composed.

---

[9] While allophonic rules do not merge distinct representations, they may still be involved in alternations, such as *atom* ['ærəm] and *atomic* [ətʰɒmɪk]. They may even, under certain circumstances, produce minimal phonetic distinctions, as in the pair *saw Ted* [ˌsɒˈtʰɛd] and *sought Ed* [ˌsɒˈrɛd].

2.10 Exercises

The exercises in this chapter ask you to determine the distribution of certain sounds in various languages. Except in exercise 2.9, all examples are single words. Word boundaries are not explicitly represented in the data, but may be required as conditioning environments.

2.1 Turkish (Underhill 1976). Determine the phonemic status of [r] (voiced) and [r̥] (voiceless). If they are allophones, state the rule that determines their distribution. If they contrast, give pairs where they occur in similar or identical environments.

[ke're]	'time'	['vɑr]	'there is'
[kɑ'rɑ]	'black'	['bir̥]	'one'
[ku'ru]	'dry'	['gör̥]	'see'
[siv'ri]	'pointed'	['hɑyɨr̥]	'no'
[gɨrt'lɑk]	'throat'	[odɑ'lɑr̥]	'rooms'
['reŋk]	'colour'	[hɑ'zɨr̥]	'ready'

2.2. English /l/ has three allophones. State the distribution in the dialect shown. If your dialect differs, state the distribution in your dialect also.

'clear' l		'dark' l (velarized)		syllabic (velarized) l	
[l]		[ɫ]		[l̩]	
leap	['liyp]	pillow	['pʰɪɫow]	syllable	['sɪɫ-əbl̩]
low	['low]	mallet	['mæɫɪt]	muddle	['mədl̩]
allow	[ə'law]	malt	['mɒɫt]	axolotl	['ɒæksə,lɒtl̩]
align	[ə'layn]	velar	['viyɫəɹ]	sickle	['sɪkl̩]
sleek	['sliyk]	rail	['ɹeyɫ]	animal	['ænɪml̩]
clear	['kliyɹ]	real	['ɹiyɫ]	carnival	['kaɹnɪvl̩]

2.3. Georgian (Robins & Waterson 1952).

The two laterals, [l], a clear l, and its velarized counterpart [ɫ], are in complementary distribution. Determine the distribution and state the rule; state also why you choose one over the other as the underlying representation.

[ɬamɑzɑd]	'prettily'	[zɑɹɑli]	'loss'
[leɬo]	'goal'	[k'ɑɬa]	'tin'
[sɑxʧ̌i]	'at home'	[p'ep'eɬa]	'butterfly'
[ɬxenɑ]	'joy'	[k'lebɑ]	'reduce'
[k'biɬs]	'tooth (dative)'	[eɹtʰxeɬ]	'once'
[k'ɑk'ɑli]	'nut'	[k'iɬo]	'dialect'
[d͡zɑɬa]	'strength'	[p'olit'ik'a]	'politics'
[xeli]	'hand'	[xoɬo]	'however'
[t͡sʰet͡sʰxli]	'fire'	[vxlečʰ]	'I split'
[t͡sʰoli]	'wife'	[t͡s'it͡s'iɬa]	'chicken'
[t'ɹiɑli]	'turn (noun)'	[ɑɬq'a]	'siege'

2.4 Canadian French (Walker 1984). Determine the phonemic status of three pairs of high vowels. Each pair consists of a tense vowel and its lax correspondent. If the tense and its lax correspopndent are contrastive, state the environment of contrast. If they are not contrastive, state a rule governing the distribution. Comment on whether or not these examples illustrate pattern congruity. Thanks to Linda Legault and Marie-Hélène Côté for discussion of the data for this problem.

	[i] vs [ɪ]			[ü] vs [ö]	
pipe	['pɪp]	'pipe'	jupe	['žöp]	'skirt'
vite	['vɪt]	'quickly'	butte	['böt]	'knoll'
électrique	[elɛk'tχɪk]	'electric'	tuque	['t͡sök]	'tuque'
libre	['lɪb]	'free'	tube	['t͡söb]	'tube'
vide	['vɪd]	'empty'	rude	['ʁöd]	'uncouth'
ligue	['lɪg]	'league'	fugue	['fög]	'fugue'
vif	['vɪf]	'live'	buffle	['böf]	'buffalo'
vis	['vɪs]	'screw'	juste	['žös]	'just'
riche	['ʁɪš]	'rich'	cruche	['kχöš]	'jug'

(Continued)

rime	['ʁɪm]	'rhyme'	plume	['plɔ̈m]	'feather'
racine	['ʁæsɪn]	'root'	lune	['lɔ̈n]	'moon'
signe	['sɪɲ]	'sign'			
ville	['vɪl]	'city'	nul	['nɔ̈l]	'none'
fille	['fɪy]	'girl'			
poli	[pɔ'li]	'polished'	cru	['kχü]	'raw'
finesse	[fi'nɛs]	'fineness'	brutal	[bʁü'tæl]	'brutal'
vie	['vi]	'life'	jus	['žü]	'juice'
petit	[pö'tsi]	'small'			

[u] vs [ʊ]

coupe	['kʊp]	'cut'	pousse	['pʊs]	'growth'
croûte	['kχʊt]	'crust'	touche	['tʊš]	'touch'
bouc	['bʊk]	'goat'	boum	['bʊm]	'bang!'
j'adoube	[žæ'dʊb]	'I dub'	pitoune	[pi'tʊn]	'floating log'
soude	['sʊd]	'soda'	foule	['fʊl]	'crowd'
joug	['žʊg]	'yoke'	grenouille	[gʁö'nʊy]	'frog'
touffe	['tʊf]	'tuft'	clou	['klu]	'nail'
clouter	[klu'te]	'to stud'	vous	['vu]	'you'

2.5. Sierra Popoluca (Elson 1947). Aspiration of consonants is predictable. Determine the distribution and state the rule.

['pikʰši?]	'bow'	['mičpa?]	'he is playing'
['?iškuy]	'eye'	['kɛkʰpa?]	'it flies'
['pokʰ]	'gourd water jug'	[kɛk'gakʰpa?]	'it flies again'
['nɨkʰpa?]	'he goes'	[?an'tikʰ]	'my house'
['koːbakʰ]	'head'	['makʰti?]	'ghost'
['hoːppa?]	'it rolls'	['tiːttitʰ]	'mestizo'
['pɛtʰpa?]	'he sweeps'	[?ik'ka?]	'he killed it'
['?aŋki?]	'yard'	[?i'hɨkʰpa?]	'he pulls it'

(Continued)

[ʔaŋ'kɨʔ]	'my hand'	[wicʰpaʔ]	'he walks'
['iškuypɨkʰ]	'of the eye'	[nuːts'nɛʔ]	'he is serious'
[ʔiš'kuypɨkʰ]	'eyebrow'	['tsaːɲ]	'snake'
[ʔi'čič]	'he jerked it'	['tofs]	'tongue'

Word-final ɛ before a stop (handwritten margin note)

2.6 Greenlandic Eskimo (Kleinschmidt 1851). There are five phonetic vowels but only three underlying (phonemic) vowels. Determine the distribution of the vowels and the rules that govern it.

a.

ilumut	'truly'	qaqaq	'mountain'
tamaʀmik	'all'	issika	'my eyes'
inuk	'person'	sava	'sheep'
igdluk	'two houses'	kamik	'boot'
uyaʀak	'stone'	maʀdluk	'two'
nuna	'land'	umiaq	'woman's boat'

i u / e o / a (handwritten margin note)

b.

nano	'bear'	ike	'wound'
igdlo	'house'	mato	'lid'
mike	'small'	neqe	'meat'
isse	'eye'	iso	'end'
ine	'dwelling'	nio	'leg'
ikane	'there'	tuŋo	'juice'
siko	'ice'	puto	'hole'
nipe	'voice'	time	'body'

e, i / o, u / o, e word-fin / o, e / — uvula (handwritten margin notes)

c.

qeqeʀtaq	'island'	neʀdleq	'goose'
amaʀoq	'wolf'	qoʀoq	'valley'
meʀdleʀtut	'children'	aleq	'harpoon strap'
kiŋoʀná	'afterwards'	meʀqut	'sewing needle'
ayoq	'bad'	mikivoq	'he is small'
oʀpik	'tree'	qeʀltoq	'wild duck'
eʀneq	'son'	ayoʀpoq	'he is bad'

2.7. Mohawk (Postal 1968). Vowel length is predictable. State the rule, taking stress and the distribution of consonants into consideration.

['katshe?]	'bottle, can'	['geːzɑks]	'I look for it'
['dzʌthos]	'you plant it'	[ro'yo?de?]	'he works'
['isrɑks]	'he eats it again'	['iːrɑks]	'he eats it'
[rɑ'geːdɑs]	'he scrapes it'	[niga'nuhzɑgeh]	'houses'
[wa'giːdɑ?s]	'I sleep'	[wɑho'yo?dʌ?]	'he worked'
['rɑːgʌs]	'he sees her'	[ra'nuːwe?s]	'he likes it'

V →Vːl _ CV

2.8. Sierra Miwok (Freeland 1951). The location of stress is predictable. Formulate a rule, taking vowel length and the distribution of consonants into consideration. Thanks to Natasha LeBlanc for discussion of the data for this problem.

stress leftmost CC
Vl — ːi
(strong syl.)

stress on first syllable		*stress on second syllable*	
['leppanaː]	'he finished'	[wa'kaːlɨ?]	'creek'
['?immu?oːk]	'from there'	[?o'noššo?]	'old woman'
['yaːyaːli?]	'giant'	[ta'yišmu?]	'jay'
['ṭaːči?]	'elder brother'	[pa'laṭṭata?]	'woodpecker'
['wakkaːli?]	'rattlesnake'	[?ɨ'wɨːšakṭe?]	'I, eating'
['huššeːpi?]	'water spirit'	[ka'wɨːlɨːṭ]	'throughout the night'
['šukkumi?]	'owl'	[ši'yaːšit]	'with my cane'
['howwotu?]	'beads'	[we'lɨːša?]	'a seeker'
['haːna?]	'gambling bones'	[le'miːɳa?]	'a hunter'
['čaːmayɨːš]	'with a seed basket'	[hi'?eːma?]	'sun, day'
['uːču?]	'house'	[pu'lissa?]	'drinking basket'
['paːpa?]	'grandfather'	[hi'šoːṭa?]	'eastern'

2.9. Hungarian (Vago 1980). Determine the conditions under which the labiodental nasal [ɱ] and the velar nasal [ŋ] occur.

[m]		[n]	
[harɔm]	'three'	[veːn]	'old'
[menni]	'to go'	[neɟ]	'four'

(Continued)

[meleg]	'warm'	[nɒɟ]	'big'
[vɒlɒmi]	'something'	[vɔnɒt]	'train'
[ɛmbɛr]	'person'	[mindig]	'always'

[ɱ]		[ŋ]	
[hɒɱvɒd]	'smoulder'	[veːŋ kucɒ]	'old dog'
[sɛɱvɛd]	'suffer'	[laːŋg]	'flame'
[yɔbbɒɱ vɒn]	'it is better'	[ɒŋgɔl]	'English'
[harɔɱ viraːg]	'three flowers'	[iŋkaːbb]	'rather'
[harɔɱ fɒrkɒš]	'three volves'	[muŋkaːš]	'worker'

2.10 Zulu (Doke 1926). Determine the phonemic status of two pairs of mid vowels that differ in tenseness: [ɔ] vs [o] and [ɛ] vs [e]. If they are contrastive, state the environment(s) in which they contrast. If they are not contrastive, state the rule governing their distribution. Clicks are represented by the symbols [ǀ] (dental click), [ǁ] (lateral click), and [ǃ] (retroflex click), but the clicks are not a crucial environment for determining the phonemic status of these pairs of sounds.

[ɔ]		[o]	
[ˈɓːɔna]	'see'	[ɓoˈniːsa]	'show'
[iˈsiːlɔ]	'leopard'	[uˈɓoːvu]	'puss'
[iŋˈkʼɔːmɔ]	'head of cattle'	[noˈmuːtʰi]	'and the tree'
[iˈxɔːxɔ]	'small of back'	[ˌoːɓiˈsiːni]	'in the milk'
[ˌiːtʼitʼiˈfiɔːyɛ]	'lapwing'	[ˌoːkʰuˈniːni]	'on the piece of firewood'
[uˈkʼɔːkʼɔ]	'ancestor'	[ˌuɓuˈkʰoːsi]	'chieftainship'
[ˈlɔːwɔ]	'that'	[ǁoˈɓiːsa]	'worry'
[ˈɓɔːpʰa]	'tie'	[moˈɲuːla]	'pull out nail'

[ɛ]		[e]	
[ˈǃeːda]	'finish'	[ˈleːli]	'this'
[iːˈɓeːlɛ]	'corn'	[ˌnentɬʼiˈziːyɔ]	'with heart'
[sɛˈkeːza]	'enclose'	[ˌaɓeˈluːsi]	'herdsmen'

(Continued)

[iː'ʒɛːlɔ]	'pasture ground'	[p'e'uːka]	'fall over'
[tʰu'mɛːla]	'send for'	['neːŋʰi]	'with contradiction'
[uːˈkʰɛːzɔ]	'spoon'	['k'weːtʰu]	'at our home'
[ɛ'yɑːkʰɛ]	'his'	[iːˈk'eːu]	'duck'
[pʰɛ'ʃɛːya]	'on the other side'	['neːzwi]	'and the word'

2.11 Canadian French (Walker 1984). Determine the phonemic status of the dental affricates; i.e., whether they are variants of the corresponding stops or in contrast with the latter. Comment on whether these examples illustrate pattern congruity. Thanks to Linda Legault and Marie-Hélène Côté for discussion of the data for this problem.

	[t] vs [t͡s]			[d] vs [d͡z]	
tigre	['t͡sɪg]	'tiger'	dîner	[d͡zi'ne]	'dinner'
type	['t͡sɪp]	'type'	dire	['d͡zɪʁ]	'to say'
petit	[pö't͡si]	'small'	indigne	[ɛ̃'d͡zɪɲ]	'unworthy'
attirer	[æt͡si'ʁe]	'to attract'	crocodile	[kχoko'd͡zɪl]	
					'crocodile'
témoin	[te'mwɛ̃]	'witness'	débat	[de'ba]	'debate'
thé	['te]	'tea'	défi	[de'fi]	'challenge'
tête	['tɛːt]	'head'	dette	['dɛt]	'debt'
terre	['tɛʁ]	'world'	destin	[dɛs'tɛ̃]	'fate'
table	['tæb]	'table'	dame	['dæm]	'lady'
timbre	['tɛ̃ỹm]	'stamp'	dinde	['dɛ̃ːd]	'turkey'
tant	['tɑ̃]	'so much'	danse	['dɑ̃s]	'dance'
tube	['t͡süb]	'tube'	dupe	['d͡zöp]	'dupe'
tunnel	[t͡sü'nɛl]	'tunnel'	rendu	[ʁɑ̃'d͡zü]	'arrived'
coutume	[ku't͡sʏm]	'custom'	dur	['d͡zöʁ]	'hard'
battu	[bæ't͡sü]	'beaten'	pendule	[pɑ̃'d͡zöl]	'pendulum'
teuton	[tö't͡ɔ̃]	'Germanic'	deux	[dö]	'two'
tien	['t͡syɛ̃]	'yours'	indien	[ɛ̃'d͡zyɛ̃]	'Indian'

(Continued)

tiède	[ˈt͡sych	'tepid'	diable	[ˈd͡zyab]	'devil'

tiède   [ˈt͡syɛd]   'tepid'   diable   [ˈd͡zyab]   'devil'
tuer   [ˈt͡sɥe]   'to kill'   conduire   [kɔ̃ˈd͡zɥiʁ]   'to drive'
tuile   [ˈt͡sɥɪl]   'tile'   aujourd'hui   [oʒuʁˈd͡zɥi]   'today'
toueur   [ˈtwɔʁ]   'tugboat'   douane   [ˈdwæn]   'customs'
train   [ˈt͡χɛ̃]   'train'   drap   [ˈdʁɑ]   'cloth'

2.12   Cree (Wolfart & Carroll 1973). Determine the phonemic status of the four pairs of voiceless and voiced obstruents. If a voiceless and voiced sound are contrastive, state the environment of contrast. If not contrastive, state a rule governing the distribution.

a. [p] vs [b]

[pɑhki]   'partly'
[waːbameːw]   'he sees him'
[niːsosap]   'twelve'
[aːbihtaw]   'half'
[naːbeːw]   'man'
[taːnispiː]   'at what time'
[nibimohtaːn]   'I walk'
[pimibɑhtaːw]   'he runs'

b. [t] vs [d]

[tɑhki]   'all the time'
[meːdaweːw]   'he plays'
[miht͡seːt]   'many'
[nisto]   'three'
[ɑdim]   'dog'
[nisit]   'my foot'
[oːdeːnaw]   'town'
[nidabin]   'I sit'

c. [t͡s] vs [d͡z]

[t͡siːgɑhigan]   'axe'
[miːd͡ziwin]   'food'
[meːgwaːt͡s]   'in the meantime'
[wiːd͡ziheːw]   'he helps him'
[kod͡ziːw]   'he tries'
[t͡siːmaːn]   'boat'
[taːbiskoːt͡s]   'like'
[od͡ziːmaːn]   'his boat'

d. [k] vs [g]

[kiːba]   'soon'
[maːga]   'but'
[kodak]   'another'
[sagaːw]   'it is bush'
[maskisin]   'shoe'
[kiːsigaːw]   'it is day'
[maskeːk]   'swamp'
[wiːgihk]   'in his house'

2.13 Brazilian Portuguese (Ipola & de Ras 1962). Determine the phonemic
      status of the two pairs of dental stop and corresponding palatal stop. If
      contrastive, state the environment of contrast; if not, state the rule gov-
      erning the distribution.

	[t] vs [c]	
estudo	[es'tudu]	'study'
centro	['sẽɲtɾu]	'centre'
todo	['todu]	'all'
também	[tãm'bẽỹɲ]	'also'
eqüestre	[e'kwɛstɾi]	'equestrian'
toca	['tɔka]	'touches'
tango	['tãŋgu]	'tango'
manteiga	[mãŋ'teyga]	'butter'
tia	['cia]	'aunt'
noite	['noyci]	'night'
imediatamente	[imeɟiata'mẽɲci]	'immediately'
gente	['žẽɲci]	'people'
leite	['leyci]	'milk'
partir	[paɾ'ciɾ]	'to leave'
fonético	[fon'ɛciku]	'phonetic'
antigo	[ãŋ'cigu]	'ancient'

	[d] vs [ɟ]	
mundo	['mũŋdu]	'world'
ducha	['duša]	'douche'
quadro	['kwadɾu]	'square'
cadeira	[ka'deyɾa]	'chair'
dez	['dɛz]	'ten'
corda	['kɔɾda]	'rope'
doutor	[dow'toɾ]	'doctor'
dona	['dona]	'lady'

(Continued)

dia	['ɹia]	'day'
tarde	['taɾʝi]	'afternoon'
desde	['dezʝi]	'since'
discreto	[ʝis'kɾɛtu]	'discrete'
tempestade	[tẽmpes'taʝi]	'storm'
sêde	['seʝi]	'thirst'
ódio	['ɔʝiu]	'hatred'
diferença	[ʝife'rẽ̄ŋsa]	'difference'

2.14 Brazilian Portuguese (Ipola & de Ras 1962). Determine the phonemic status of three pairs of vowels.

[o] vs [ɔ]

gôta	['gota]	'drop'	goza	['gɔza]	'enjoys'
fôrça	['foɾsa]	'force'	xarope	[ša'rɔpi]	'syrup'
goma	['goma]	'gum'	nota	['nɔta]	'note'
môsca	['moska]	'fly'	sola	['sɔla]	'leather'
pôr	['poɾ]	'to put'	cofre	['kɔfri]	'chest'
cebola	[se'bola]	'onion'	bossa	['bɔsa]	'lump'
homem	['omẽ̄ỹɲ]	'man'	forma	['fɔrma]	'form'
hoje	['oži]	'today'	dor	['dɔɾ]	'pain'

[e] vs [ɛ]

cêra	['sera]	'wax'	mulher	[mu'ʎɛɾ]	'woman'
apêlo	[a'pelu]	'appeal'	belo	['bɛlu]	'beautiful'
letra	['letra]	'letter'	fera	['fɛra]	'wild beast'
gêlo	['želu]	'ice'	pele	['pɛli]	'skin'
dedo	['dedu]	'finger'	gesto	['žɛstu]	'gesture'
começo	[ko'mesu]	'beginning'	reta	['rɛta]	'straight line'
fresco	['fresku]	'fresh'	neto	['nɛtu]	'grandson'
beber	[be'beɾ]	'to drink'	convés	[kõɱ'vɛs]	'deck'

(Continued)

[ɑ] vs [ə]

gato	[ˈgɑtu]	'cat'	pano	[ˈpənu]	'cloth'
casa	[ˈkazɑ]	'house'	cama	[ˈkəmɑ]	'bed'
chapa	[ˈšapɑ]	'plate'	lama	[ˈləmɑ]	'mud'
chave	[ˈšavi]	'key'	cana	[ˈkənɑ]	'reed'
jarra	[ˈžɑrɑ]	'vase'	manha	[ˈməɲɑ]	'craft'
sala	[ˈsɑlɑ]	'room'	dama	[ˈdəmɑ]	'lady'
baga	[ˈbɑgɑ]	'berry'	vamos	[ˈvəmus]	'we go'
cara	[ˈkɑrɑ]	'face'	gerânio	[žeˈrəniu]	'geranium'

2.15   Lumasaaba (Brown 1972). Determine the phonemic status of [k], [c], [g], and [ɟ]. Determine the phonemic status of [ŋ] and [ɲ].

[kɑtemu]	'a small snake'	[kucinɑ]	'to dance'
[kunilɑ]	'to wince'	[iŋkɑːfu]	'a cow'
[kubululukɑ]	'to fly'	[cinɑgɑ]	'a pipe'
[cisiɟe]	'an eyebrow'	[lusece]	'a straw'
[iɲcese]	'a sheep'	[kɑcese]	'a small sheep'
[mugundɑ]	'a farm'	[iɲɟegɑ]	'I mix'
[umuɟelemɑ]	'a wife'	[liːɟi]	'an egg'

2.16   Japanese (Tsujimura 1996). Determine the phonemic status of [t], [t͡s], and [č]. Write the phonological (phonemic, underlying) representation for each word.

[ita]	'song'	[t͡sɨkai]	'use'
[kita]	'came'	[tat͡sɨ]	'stand'
[heta]	'unskilful'	[tet͡sɨdai]	'help'
[oto]	'sound'	[kat͡sɨ]	'win'
[koto]	'thing'	it͡sɨsɨ	'reflect'
[tokeː]	'clock'	[it͡sɨ]	'when'
[setomono]	'pottery'	[it͡sɨ]	'hit'

(Continued)

[tateri]	'build'	[čikaki]	'near'
[tabete]	'eating'	[očiri]	'fall'
		[keči]	'stingy'
		[iči]	'house'
		[akiči]	'empty hand'
		[moči]	'rice cake'
		[kači]	'value'

3 Distinctive features

3.1   Features as smallest building blocks

While in chapter 2 we concentrated on the distribution of individual segments, much of our discussion involved a recognition of more basic building blocks of phonological analysis. Indeed, phonetic analysis implicitly recognizes a number of phonetic features that distinguish broad classes of elements. For example, consonants fall into two major classes, those that are voiced and those that are voiceless. This in turn implies a binary distinctive feature [±voice], defined so that voiced consonants carry the feature [+voice] while voiceless consonants carry the feature [−voice]. Our goal in this chapter is to extend this notion of distinctive features to all possible distinctive phonological opposition. These features serve two purposes. One is to provide a unique set of feature values for each distinctive sound unit in human languages. The other is to have a natural way of identifying classes of sounds that function together in phonological operations. For example, in chapter 2 we observed that voiced stops in Spanish become approximants in the intervocalic environment. We need a way of referring to the set of voiced stops as a natural class.

3.2   Binary distinctions

Many phonological distinctions are naturally binary, in the sense that some physiological gesture is either present in or absent from any given phonological element. The feature [±voice], introduced in section 3.1, refers to vocal fold vibration. If the vocal folds are vibrating periodically during the production of some sound, we say that the sound is [+voice]; otherwise it is [−voice]. Some other phonological distinctions may seem to be continuous, rather than binary in this sense, such as consonant point of articulation. However, even here we will see that the relevant classes can be distinguished by using several binary features. We will thus take the strong position that all phonological

ɛ = [-bk, -lo, -hi, -tns]

features are binary.[1]

As we have seen, a single binary feature distinguishes between two classes of sounds. If we have two independent binary features, we can distinguish a total of four classes. The features are said to be *independent* if the values of one are completely independent of the values of the other. In this case we say that the features *cross classify* the segments. If we then add a third feature, we double the number of classes to eight, assuming all the features are independent. In general, with any number *n* of independent binary features, we can distinguish 2^n classes of elements.

A real example of three independent binary features is provided by the system of Turkish vowels. An important feature for vowels is [±high].[2] We define the feature [+high] as involving the raising of the body of the tongue above the neutral position, which is defined as the tongue position present in the articulation of the vowel [ɛ]. A [–high] vowel is articulated without such a gesture. Turkish has four [+high] vowels and four [–high] vowels, as in (1). The feature notation to the left represents the class, while the phonetic symbols in the curly braces to the right of the equal sign designate the sounds included in that class. Notice that the class of [–high] vowels includes vowels traditionally classified as mid (e, ö, o) and low (a).

(1)   a.   [+high] = {i, ü, ɨ, u}
       b.   [–high] = {e, ö, a, o}

A second vowel feature is [±back]. The feature [+back] is defined as involving a retraction of the body of the tongue behind the neutral position (the position of [ɛ]). Turkish has four [+back] vowels and four [–back] vowels, as in (2).

(2)   a.   [+back] = {ɨ, u, a, o}
       b.   [–back] = {i, ü, e, ö}

These features *cross classify* as shown in (3). In each cell are the segments that share the features at the head of the column and at the left of the row defining that cell.

---

[1] *SPE* suggests that features are no longer binary at the level of fine phonetic detail, that is, they may assume multiple values. For classificatory, phonological, distinctive purposes, however, they are binary.

[2] To designate a feature without specifying a value we write the feature with a preceding plus or minus (±) sign, or simply with no sign: [high].

(3)

	−back	+back
+high	i, ü	ɨ, u
−high	e, ö	ɑ, o

A third feature is [±round]. A sound is [+round] if its articulation involves a narrowing of the lip orifice; otherwise it is [−round]. The set of [+round] vowels includes {ü, u, ö, o}; the [−round] set includes {i, ɨ, e, ɑ}. We give the complete cross classification of these eight vowels (2^3) in terms of three features in (4).

(4)

	−back		+back	
	−round	+round	−round	+round
+high	i	ü	ɨ	u
−high	e	ö	ɑ	o

The analysis of Turkish vowels in (4) fulfills the two goals of distinctive feature theory stated in section 3.1. First, each vowel of Turkish has a unique identification in terms of these three features, where each feature carries either a plus or a minus value. For example, [ö] is identified as [−back, −high, +round].[3] Second, we can identify natural classes of sounds by specifying only one or two features. For example, in (1a) we identified the natural class of [+high] vowels in Turkish. A capital letter is sometimes used to designate such a class, or archiphoneme, for example /I/ can be used to represent the class in (1a), that is, [+syllabic, +high]. In general, any single feature specification designates a class of four vowels in Turkish. Two features together designates a class of two vowels, for example [+back, −round] = {ɨ, ɑ}. However, not all classes of four vowels can be represented by a single feature specification, for example {i, ü, ɑ, o} is not a natural class. The only way to identify this class is by a disjunction, i.e., as those vowels that are either [−back, +high] ({i, ü}) or [+back, −high] ({ɑ, o}). Nor is it possible to designate a set of three Turkish vowels by a simple feature specification. For example, The

---

[3] One or more features representing a sound or a class of sounds are enclosed in square brackets. The order in which the features are listed makes no difference in the class designated by such a feature matrix. In running text the features are listed as here, separated by commas, while in rules the same matrix can be given in a vertical orientation as in (i).

(i)
$$\begin{bmatrix} -\text{back} \\ -\text{high} \\ +\text{round} \end{bmatrix}$$

set {i, ü, ɨ} is not a natural class. Although it includes only [+high] vowels, the class cannot simply be designated by the feature [+high], since the class defined by this feature necessarily includes [u] also. The set {i, ü, ɨ} requires a disjunction also: [+high {[–round], [–back]}] (i.e., the set of high vowels which are either [–round] or [–back] (or both)). We define the concept of natural class in (5).   *= make distinct*

(5)   A *natural class* is a class of sounds that can be designated by fewer features than are required to designate any one of its members.

Since any single vowel of Turkish can be designated by three features, a class like {ɨ, a} counts as a natural class because it can be designated by fewer than three features, in this case two: [+back, –round]. The class {i, ü, a, o} requires four features and thus is not a natural class by the definition in (5).

The natural classes of Turkish vowels are important for an adequate description of the pervasive process of vowel harmony in the language. Consider the data in (6), from Clements & Sezer 1982, 216).

a fact not revealed in phonemic analysis.

(6)

	gloss	nom sg.	gen.sg.	nom.pl.	gen.pl.
1.	'rope'	ip	ipin	ipler	iplerin
2.	'girl'	kɨz	kɨzɨn	kɨzlar	kɨzlarɨn
3.	'face'	yüz	yüzün	yüzler	yüzlerin
4.	'stamp'	pul	pulun	pullar	pullarɨn
5.	'hand'	el	elin	eller	ellerin
6.	'stalk'	sap	sapɨn	saplar	saplarɨn
7.	'village'	köy	köyün	köyler	köylerin
8.	'end'	son	sonun	sonlar	sonlarɨn

The nominative singular form of each noun is the simple root. The genitive singular is formed by adding a suffix, which has four alternants, that is, phonologically determined variants: -in, -ɨn, -ün, and -un. These consist of a [+high] vowel followed by n. There is no reason to regard one of these alternants as basic. The suffix can be represented as having the underlying representation -In, where the symbol /I/ represents the natural class of high vowels, [+syllabic, +high], as suggested earlier. The remaining features of the vowel in this suffix are completely determined by the immediately preceding vowel. That is, if the preceding vowel is [–back], the suffix vowel is [–back]. If the preceding vowel is [+back], the suffix vowel is [+back]. Similarly with [round]: the suffix vowel has the same value, plus or minus, as the preceding vowel. The suffix vowel is not necessarily an identical copy of the preceding vowel: it is always [+high], but assimilates to the values of [back] and [round] of the preceding vowel.

The plural suffix works a little differently. It has two phonological alternants: *-lar* and *-ler*. Its vowel is [–high, –round] and it assimilates to the feature [back] of the preceding vowel. It could be represented as -lAr, where /A/ represents the archiphoneme [+syllabic, –high, –round]. The genitive plural is formed by adding both suffixes to the root: the plural and then the genitive. The suffix vowels assimilate by the rules already given, but note that the vowel of the genitive suffix assimilates to the immediately preceding vowel, which in the genitive plural is the vowel of the plural suffix, not the root vowel. Since the plural always has a [–round] vowel, the genitive suffix in the genitive plural always has a [–round] vowel. In the most general form, we can state the rules for Turkish vowel harmony as in (7).

(7)   Turkish vowel harmony
        Any suffix vowel agrees with the immediately preceding vowel in
        [back].
        A [+high] suffix vowel agrees with the immediately preceding
        vowel in [round].

It is only by appealing to ~~natural classes of sounds, as expressed by~~ distinctive features, that we are able to state the rules for this alternation in full generality. In chapter 4 we will introduce some formal notations for expressing these rules more compactly.

Let us consider the concept of a natural class in a slightly different light. The set of Turkish vowels contains eight members. In set theory it is shown that any set of n elements has a total of 2^n subsets, including the null set and the entire set. That is, a set of 8 elements has $2^8 = 256$ subsets. But only a small fraction of these subsets are natural classes, as defined in (5). There are in fact 20 natural classes of the Turkish vowels, defined in terms of the three features [high], [back], and [round]. These are given in (8).

(8)   a. Six classes defined in terms of a single feature
            [+high]   =   {i, ü, ɨ, u}
            [–high]   =   {e, ö, a, o}

$$[+back] \quad = \quad \{i, ü, a, o\}$$
$$[-back] \quad = \quad \{i, ü, e, ö\}$$
$$[+round] \quad = \quad \{ü, ö, u, o\}$$
$$[-round] \quad = \quad \{i, e, i, a\}$$

b. Twelve classes defined in terms of two features

$$\begin{bmatrix} +high \\ +back \end{bmatrix} \quad = \quad \{i, u\}$$

$$\begin{bmatrix} +high \\ -back \end{bmatrix} \quad = \quad \{i, ü\}$$

$$\begin{bmatrix} -high \\ +back \end{bmatrix} \quad = \quad \{a, o\}$$

$$\begin{bmatrix} -high \\ -back \end{bmatrix} \quad = \quad \{e, ö\}$$

$$\begin{bmatrix} +high \\ +round \end{bmatrix} \quad = \quad \{u, ü\}$$

$$\begin{bmatrix} +high \\ -round \end{bmatrix} \quad = \quad \{i, i\}$$

$$\begin{bmatrix} -high \\ +round \end{bmatrix} \quad = \quad \{ö, o\}$$

$$\begin{bmatrix} -high \\ -round \end{bmatrix} \quad = \quad \{e, a\}$$

$$\begin{bmatrix} +back \\ +round \end{bmatrix} \quad = \quad \{u, o\}$$

$$\begin{bmatrix} +back \\ -round \end{bmatrix} \quad = \quad \{i, a\}$$

$$\begin{bmatrix} -back \\ +round \end{bmatrix} \quad = \quad \{ü, ö\}$$

$$\begin{bmatrix} -back \\ -round \end{bmatrix} \quad = \quad \{i, e\}$$

c. Eight classes defined in terms of three features (each containing a single vowel), as in (4)).[4]

d. The null set plus the entire set.

---

[4] A class consisting of a single segment is not really a natural class according to (5), since it is defined by the same number of features as its only member. So these are not counted in the total of 20.

We therefore see that the number, 20, of natural classes of sounds designated by three features (excluding the classes of a single vowel each in 8c) is considerably less than the total number of classes, 256, of these sounds. The claim that phonological rules operate in terms of natural classes, rather than arbitrary ones, is therefore not a trivial one.

3.3   Further vowel features

The next feature we add for the description of vowels is [low]. A sound is [+low] if it involves lowering the body of the tongue below the neutral position. Unlike the features discussed to this point, [low] is not completely independent of the other features. With the two features [high] and [low] you might expect four classes, but in fact only three classes can be distinguished by these two features, because the combination *[+low, +high] is excluded.[5] This follows from the definitions of these features. We have defined the neutral position of the tongue is its position in pronouncing the vowel [ε]. A vowel is designated [+high] if its articulation involves raising the tongue above the neutral position. A vowel is designated [+low] if its articulation involves lowering the tongue below the neutral position. Since the tongue cannot simultaneously be raised and lowered with respect to the neutral position, no segment can contain the features *[+low, +high]. Therefore we add only four more contrasts to the Turkish eight vowels system, not another eight, bringing the number of possible contrasts to twelve. These are shown in (9). The vowel *a* of Turkish is [+low], even though we did not count [low] among the distinctive features of Turkish vowels. Since this is the only [+low] vowel in the system, and because no other vowel of Turkish is [–high, +back, –round], we say that [+low] is a nondistinctive feature of the Turkish system. We will have more to say about nondistinctive features in section 3.8.

(9)

	−back		+back	
	−round	+round	−round	+round
+high, (−low)	i	ü	ɨ	u
−high, −low	e	ö	ʌ	o
(−high,) +low	æ	œ	ɑ	ɒ

Because of the limitation on the features [high] and [low], this feature analy-

---

[5] We use the asterisk to designate any excluded item, here a feature combination, and for ungrammatical linguistic forms, following standard practice.

sis of vowels is incompatible with the IPA, with its four vowel heights, based on Daniel Jones's cardinal vowels. The cardinal vowels seem to be based on the vowel distinctions of French, where there are eleven distinct vowel qualities arranged in four heights, distinguishing back and front at each height, and a rounding distinction for nonlow vowels, as in (10).[6] (The lower mid vowels show a marginal length distinction in addition.)

(10) high   si   [i]   lune   [ü]   tout   [u]
      (IPA close)

      higher mid   thé,   [e]   peu,   [ö]   beau   [o]
      (IPA close mid)

      lower mid   mettre   [ɛ]   œuf   [ɔ̃]   port   [ɔ]
      (IPA open mid)

                      maître   [ɛː]   veuve   [ɔ̃ː]   fort   [ɔː]

      low   patte; pas   [æ]   pâle   [ɑː]
      (IPA open)

However, there is good phonological evidence that the division into three heights is correct. Kenstowicz & Kisseberth (1979, 246) note that each of the four natural classes designated by values of [high] and [low] play a role in the phonologies of various languages, as follows.

[+high]: in Japanese *t* is affricated before the high vowels *i, ɨ,* but not before mid *e, o,* or the low *a.* (Exercise 2.16). In Turkish [+high] suffix vowels assimilate in round to a preceding vowel but nonhigh vowels do not (cf. 6).

[–high]: In Russian, nonhigh vowels *e, o, a* undergo vowel reduction in unstressed position; high vowels *i, u* do not.

[+low]: Chamorro (Exercise 5.4 in chapter 5) Low vowels *æ* and *a* are reduced to schwa ([ə]) in unstressed position.

[–low] Chamorro high and mid vowels reduce in unstressed position as fol-

---

[6] The low front unrounded vowel is designated [a] in the IPA and in the French phonetic tradition. We have discussed our reasons for not using this symbol in chapter 1, section 1.3.2.

lows: nonback *i, e* reduce to [ɪ]; back u, o reduce to [ʊ].

[−high, −low]: in Lamba (Exercise 5.6 in chapter 5), *i* is lowered to *e* after the mid vowels *e, o,* but not after the high vowels *i, u* or the low *a.*

Nevertheless, it is obviously necessary for our feature system to be able to distinguish between the higher mid and lower mid vowels of French and other languages that make such a distinction. The evidence is clearly on the side of an additional vowel feature that further subdivides the vowel categories of (9). This feature is called [ATR] (for Advanced Tongue Root), or sometimes [tense]. For example, many African languages, such as Akan and Yoruba, have vowel harmony in [ATR] (compare the vowel harmony in [back] and [round] in Turkish in (6)). Consider the Akan forms in (11).

(11)   ɔ-bɛsɪ   'he will say'   o-besi   'he will build'

       ɔ-ɥɪn   'he weaves'   o-bisɑ   'he asks'

As Kenstowicz & Kisseberth (1979, 247) point out, if height were the relevant factor, why should /ɔ/ raise to [o] before /e/ and /i/ but not before /ɪ/? It is more correct to group the vowels {ɔ, ɛ, ɪ} from the left column of (11) as [−ATR] and the vowels {o, e, i} from the right column of (11) as [+ATR]. The vowel [ɑ], although [−ATR], has no [+ATR] counterpart in Akan, and so can cooccur with both [+ATR] and [−ATR] vowels in the same word. When we add [ATR] to the set of vowel features, we obtain the chart in (12), our final vowel system.

(12)

		−back		+back	
		−round	+round	−round	+round
+high	+ATR	i	ü	ɨ	u
(−low)	−ATR	ɪ	ü̈	ɤ	ʊ
−high	+ATR	e	ö	ʌ	o
−low	−ATR	ɛ	ɔ̈	ə	ɔ
(−high)	+ATR	æ̧	œ̧	ɑ̧	ɒ̧
+low	−ATR	æ	œ	ɑ	ɒ

We distinguish the [+ATR] low vowels by adding the diacritic ̭. Otherwise the [−ATR] vowels have distinct symbols from their [+ATR] counterparts, as discussed in chapter 1.

Besides vowel harmony, as in Akan, distributional facts from certain languages such as English argue for [ATR] as the distinguishing factor between such pairs of vowels as *i* and *ι, e* and *ε*. Monosyllabic words of major lexical categories in English (nouns, verbs, and adjectives) may contain [+ATR] or [−ATR] vowels, but, if the vowel is [−ATR], the vowel must be followed by a consonant, as in (13). (In addition, the [−low, +ATR] vowels are diphthongized.)

(13)	beet	[biyt]	bee	[biy]	boot	[buwt]	true	[truw]
	bit	[bɪt]		*[bɪ]	book	[bʊk]		*[bʊ]
	bait	[beyt]	bay	[bey]	boat	[bowt]	tow	[tow]
	bet	[bɛt]		*[bɛ]	but	[bət]		*[bə]
	bad (NYC)	[bæ̭d]	yeah	[yæ̭]	walk	[wɒk]	law	[lɒ]
	bat	[bæt]		*[bæ]	lot	[lɒt]		*[lɒ]

So far we have justified our feature system on the basis of evidence from within the language system, what is sometimes called *internal* or *corpus-internal* evidence. Linguists often seek additional evidence from various aspects of language use, such as speech errors, poetic language, language games, and so forth. This is sometimes called *external* or *corpus-external* evidence. We consider this in more detail in section 6.7 of chapter 6. One striking piece of external evidence for the vowel features comes from German rhyming poetry. As in English, German rhymes require identity of a primary stressed vowel and the remainder of the word, so that in English pairs of words like *lake* and *take* rhyme, as do *linger* and *finger*. In German the stressed vowels must be identical except that they may differ in the feature [round], but in no other respect. That is, they must agree in [high], [low], [back], and [ATR]. Consider the rhyming lines in (14). The vowels that rhyme are in bold italics, with its phonetic transcription at the end of each line. In each case, the rhyming vowels differ only by the feature [round].

(14)   a.   Hat sie dich gesch*i*ckt   [ι]
              Oder hast mich ber*ü*ckt   [ü]
              'has she sent you/or have you deceived me'

b. Der Bach, der ist des Müllers Freund   [ɒy]
   Und hellblau Liebchens Auge scheint   [ay]
   'the brook that is the miller's friend
   /and light blue the dear one's eye shines'

c. Lustig in die Welt hinaus
   Gegen Wind und Wetter!   [ɛ]
   Will kein Gott auf Erden sein
   Sind wir selber Götter!   [ɔ̃]
   'gaily out into the world/against wind and weather
   If no god wants to be here on earth/We'll be gods ourselves!'

The rhyming scheme that requires identity of vowels, except only that [round] can be different, is possible only if segments are decomposed into smaller units, i.e., features. A simple listing of arbitrary pairs that can be considered rhymes would allow many other pairs to be considered rhymes, which does not occur, and would totally miss the generalization that the rhyming pairs in (14) differ in [round] but in no other feature.

3.4 Major classes: major class features

Intuitively, the major division of language sound segments is between consonants and vowels. In continuous speech there is a constant rising and falling of sonority, with the points of highest sonority identified as syllable peaks, separated by periods of lower sonority at the margins of syllables. In fact, we want to be able to distinguish a somewhat finer division of major classes of segments. In this section we will consider how these major classes of segments are distinguished in terms of features. We presupposed such features in section 3.3, where we discussed features of vowels. Vowels are the basic segments that constitute syllable peaks in language utterances. We will use the feature [syllabic] to designate these classes. A segment is [+syllabic] if it functions as a syllable peak; otherwise, it is [−syllabic]. The glides [y] and [w] are nonsyllabic counterparts of the lax high vowels [ɪ] and [ʊ], respectively.

Although syllable peaks are most often vowels, other segments can have this function as well. In English, for example, sonorant consonants (the nasals and liquids) can be syllabic, as in the examples of (15), where the vertical tick below a segment in the transcription denotes a syllabic consonant.

(15)   a.   button   [bətn̩], [bət{n̩}], [bəʔn̩]

       b.   bottom   [bɒtm̩], bɒɾm̩]

       c.   bottle   [bɒtl̩], [bɒɾl̩]

       d.   butter   [bətɹ̩], [bəɾɹ̩]

In some languages, a wider range of consonants can function as [+syllabic] segments. In Imdlawn Tashlhiyt Berber (Dell & Elmedlaoui 1985, 1988, 1989, Prince & Smolensky 1993), any consonant can be a syllable peak, as the examples in (16) show.[7]

(16)   a.   ratkti   [rɑtḵti]   'she will remember'

       b.   txznt   [tx̱zn̩t]   'you stored'

       c.   bddl   [bḍdl̩]   'exchange!'

In English, syllabic obstruents may be observed in an interjection like *pst,* which may be considered *paralinguistic* (outside the linguistic system proper).

     A second feature distinguishing among major classes of segments is [sonorant].[8] A [+sonorant] sound is produced with a minimal constriction in the vocal tract, such that the air pressure is roughly equal inside and outside of the vocal tract. Thus, [+sonorant] includes nasals, liquids, glides, and vowels. The [−sonorant] sounds are produced with a greater constriction in the vocal tract, such that the air pressure is higher inside the vocal tract than outside. The [−sonorant] sounds are thus the (oral) stops, fricatives, and affricates.

     The third major class feature is [consonantal]. A [+consonantal] sound is characterized by a radical constriction in the central region of the mouth at any point from the upper lip along the roof of the mouth onto the pharynx. *SPE* (p. 302) refers to this area as the midsagittal region of the vocal tract.[9] Thus, the oral obstruents, nasals, and liquids are [+consonantal], while the vowels, non-

---

[7] This analysis incorporating syllabic obstruents has been challenged, for example by Shaw (1995).

[8] The feature [obstruent] is sometimes encountered. It is defined such that [+sonorant] = [−obstruent] and [−sonorant] = [+obstruent]. It would therefore be completely redundant to use both. We will use [sonorant] rather than [obstruent] in this book.

[9] In anatomy the median sagittal plane is a vertical plane dividing the body into a left and right half when the body is standing in the anatomical position. It passes approximately through the sagittal suture of the skull between the left and right parietal bones.

lateral approximants, and glides are [–consonantal].[10] By this definition, nasals are [+consonantal] since they have an obstruction (equivalent to that of a stop) in the mouth, even though the nasal passage is open, and laterals are also [+consonantal] by virtue of having an obstruction in the centre of the mouth, even if they permit air passage along the side of the tongue.

The three major class features cross classify, and we would expect eight categories to be defined by these features. Some categories are rather rare, however. The complete set of possibilities is given in (17).

(17) *Major class features*

syllabic	consonantal	sonorant	
+	+	+	syllabic nasals, flaps, and trills
+	+	–	syllabic obstruents *(pst)*, Berber (15)
+	–	+	vowels
+	–	–	syllabic [h], [ʔ][11]
–	+	+	nasals, laterals, flaps, and trills
–	+	–	obstruents
–	–	+	(oral) glides [y], [w]; approximants (except laterals)
–	–	–	[h], [ʔ]

3.5 Features of consonants

As we discussed in chapter 1, consonants are distinguished in terms of three parameters: place of articulation, manner of articulation, and voicing. It is perhaps easiest to consider the features for these parameters in the opposite order.

---

[10] The tap [ɾ] and the trill [r] are thus [+consonantal] while the postalveolar approximant [ɹ] that represents the most common r-sound in English is [–consonantal].

[11] This possibility is included for completeness only. Syllabic laryngeals are apparently unattested in any language.

3.5.1 Voicing and aspiration

Voicing in consonants is straightforwardly represented as a feature [±voice]. A segment is [+voice] if it involves regular vibration of the vocal folds; otherwise it is [−voice]. Voicing is normally contrastive only for obstruents, as [p] [−voice] vs [b] [+voice]. Vowels and sonorant consonants are normally [+voice], but may occur [−voice] by assimilation. For example, in Chatino, a language of Mexico, unstressed vowels are voiceless between voiceless consonants (Gleason 1955, 62).

(18)   ti'yeʔ   'lime'   ti̥'hi   'hard'

        ki'no   'sandal'   ki̥'su   'avocado'

        su'wi   'clean!'   su̥ʔ'wɑ   'you send'

        lɑʔɑ   'side'   tɑ̥ʔɑ   'fiesta'

        ŋgu'tɑ   'seed'   ku̥'tɑ   'you will give'

        'kiʔ   'fire'   ki̥'tɑ   'you will wait'

Consider a CV syllable, where the consonant is a voiceless stop and the vowel is voiced. As discussed in chapter 1, the dividing line between the segments is not sharp. One aspect of the pronunciation that can vary is the timing between the release of the stop and the beginning of voicing. If the voicing is delayed for some time after the release of the stop, the stop is said to be aspirated. If the voicing begins at about the same time as the stop release, the stop is nonaspirated. *SPE* suggests the feature [heightened subglottal pressure] (abbreviated [HSP]) to express this distinction. This difference is allophonic in English, but distinctive in Hindi, as we saw in chapter 2. Voicing and aspiration cross classify in Hindi, Gujarati, and other languages, although the sounds classified as [+voice, +HSP] are phonetically rather different, as discussed in chapter 1, section 1.1.1.3. Thus these languages have sounds that can be transcribed [b, bʰ, p, pʰ]. The symbol [bʰ] can also be expressed as [b]. as we did in (24) of chapter 1. Halle & Stevens (1971) have proposed a set of features to account for these glottal states, as well as other features such as tone. Their feature system is given in (19). In this table, the symbol [p*] represents a moderately aspirated stop, found in Korean, as opposed to the fully aspirated stop [pʰ]. The symbol [ʔ] represents a voiced glottal stop, apparently attested in Jingpho.[12] The symbol [b₁] represents a lax voiceless stop, as in

---

[12] The symbol [ʔ] in IPA is used for an epiglottal stop (Ladefoged & Maddieson 1996).

Danish. The symbol [ʔb] represents a preglottalized [b], though Halle & Stevens provide no examples of this sound. Although this feature set represents a greater range of contrasts than is possible with the features [voice] and [HSP], for the purposes of this book, the latter features are usually sufficient.

3.5.2 Manner of articulation

The major distinction among obstruents is between stops and fricatives. The feature [continuant] makes this distinction: stops are [–continuant] while fricatives are [+continuant]. This much is fairly clear. The application of this feature to other classes of sounds is somewhat controversial. We will adopt the definition that a [+continuant] sound is produced with an opening in the oral tract allowing airflow to pass through the mouth. Thus the [+continuant] sounds are the fricatives, liquids, glides, and vowels. In contrast, a [–continuant] sound is produced with a complete closure of the oral tract, resulting either in complete interruption in the airflow (oral stops) or redirecting the airflow through the nose (nasal consonants). Thus the nasal consonants are classified along with the oral stops as [–continuant]. Affricates are also classified as [–continuant] since they involve a complete interruption in the airflow for the initial period of their articulation.

Classifying the liquids as [+continuant] causes some problems with the trilled and tapped varieties of /r/ and with the lateral [l]. The trills involve an intermittent closure of the oral vocal tract which resembles a stop articulation; the taps involve a single such closure. However, the closure in the trill and tap is not produced by the deliberate gesture that characterizes a stop articulation. Rather, the trill and the tap result from a ballistic movement of the tongue that is essentially the same as that which produces voicing in the vocal folds—the Bernoulli effect. Consequently the trills and taps are normally considered [+continuant]. *SPE* (p. 318) suggests that the feature [HSP], the same feature responsible for aspiration, is also the feature that distinguishes trills from taps: trilled [r] is [+HSP] while the tap [ɾ] is [–HSP].

The lateral [l] is produced by a radical constriction in the midsagittal region of the vocal tract, thus making it [+consonantal], but allowing air to escape along the sides of the tongue, thus making it [+continuant] according to our definition. This is reasonable in view of the existence of the lateral fricatives [ɬ] (voiceless) and [ɮ] (voiced); these are [–sonorant] as distinguished from [l], which is [+sonorant]. Chipewyan provides an example of

(19)   *Distinctive features for glottal state*

	1	2	3	4	5	6	7	8	9
obstruents	b_1	b	p	p*	$b^h = \underset{\cdot}{b}$	p^h	ɓ	ʔb	p'
glides	w, y				ɦ	h, $\underset{\circ}{w}$, $\underset{\circ}{y}$	ʔ	ʔ, ʔw, ʔy
vowels	V (mid tone)	V̀ (low tone)	V́ (high tone)	voiceless vowels $\underset{\circ}{\textrm{a}}$	breathy vowels $\underset{\cdot\cdot}{\textrm{a}}$			creaky voice vowels $\underset{\sim}{\textrm{a}}$	glot-talized vowels $\textrm{a}^{ʔ}$
spread glottis	−	−	−	+	+	+	−	−	−
constricted glottis	−	−	−	−	−	−	+	+	+
stiff vocal folds	−	−	+	−	−	+	−	−	+
slack vocal folds	−	+	−	−	+	−	−	+	−

lateral affricates, which are [−continuant], as opposed to lateral fricatives [+continuant] (*SPE,* 317; Li 1946), as in (19), where the columns are voiceless, voiced, and voiceless glottalized representatives of the categories listed to the right.

(20)   voiceless   voiced   voiceless
                                          glottalized

t	d	t'	alveolar stops
š	ž		postalveolar fricatives
č	ǰ	č'	postalveolar affricates
$\underset{\circ}{l}$	l		sonorant laterals
t͡ɬ	d͡ɮ	t͡ɬ'	lateral affricates

The nonlateral affricates [č, ǰ, t͡s, d͡z] can then also be considered [−continuant], being differentiated from the corresponding stops with [strident]: the stops are [−strident] while the affricates are [+strident]. Sounds which are [+strident] are acoustically noisy and are produced by directing the airstream in a complex path rather than a direct path, which characterizes [−strident] sounds. We will also use [strident] to distinguish between certain points of articulation in section 3.5.3, where we will see that we need to distinguish between [+strident] and [–strident] affricates in Chipewyan, so that [strident] cannot be the only feature distinguishing between stops and affricates. We will therefore require a feature [delayed release] to differentiate between stops [–delayed release] and affricates [+delayed release]. The lateral affricates are [+strident] (cf. Ladefoged 1971, 106).

Other features for consonant manner of articulation are [nasal] and [lateral]. A sound is [+nasal] if the velum is lowered to allow airflow through the nose, otherwise it is [–nasal]. A sound is [+lateral] if the sides of the tongue are lowered to allow airflow along the molar teeth, otherwise it is [–lateral]. The sounds [ɾ] and [l] are minimally distinguished by the feature [lateral]. The feature [nasal] distinguishes vowels too. French distinguishes the nasal vowel [ɛ̃] in *vin* 'wine' from the oral vowel [ɛ] in *vais* '(I) go.'

3.5.3 Place of articulation

The 1986 revision of the IPA allows for eleven points of articulation, or twelve, if the prepalatals (alveolo-palatals) are reintroduced from earlier versions. But it is by no means necessary or desirable to consider this simply as a continuum, as suggested by Ladefoged (1971, 43). The points of articulation fall into clear groups determined by the articulators involved. For example, both bilabial and labiodental articulations involve the lower lip while the dental, alveolar, postalveolar, retroflex, and prepalatal articulations all involve the blade of the tongue. There are clear acoustic discontinuities as well. In passing from the alveolar [s] to the postalveolar [š], no matter how gradually, there is a clear point at which the sound appears to have a lower pitch, the result of adding acoustic energy in the region of the third formant, which is present in [š] but absent in [s], as discussed in section 1.2 of chapter 1. All this suggests that we should pursue the use of binary features in differentiating places of articulation. The acoustic differentiation between [s] and [š] is the basis of the feature [anterior]. A sound is [+anterior] if its articulation is forward of the dividing line between [s] and [š] (i.e, the bilabials, labiodentals, dentals, and alveolars), otherwise it is [–anterior]. A second binary division that cross classifies with [anterior] is suggested by the articulators involved. The feature [+coronal] distinguishes sounds produced by raising the blade of the tongue; all other sounds are [–coronal]. As expected, these two binary features divide the points of articulation into four regions, as in (21).

Not a class

(21)   Bilabial   dental   Postalveolar   Palatal and beyond
              labiodental   alveolar   retroflex
                                          prepalatal
                                          (Polish)

anterior   +   +   −   −
coronal   −   +   +   −
lab   +   +   +
hi   −   +   +

These four distinctions are adequate for a description of the English stops and affricates, as shown in (22).

(22)   [p]   [t]   [č]   [k]
anterior   +   +   −   −
coronal   −   +   +   −
lab   +   −   −   −
hi   −   −   +   +

We do not need to make a systematic distinction between bilabials and labio-dentals in English. There are bilabial stops [p] and [b] but no labiodental stops (and in fact there are no recognized phonetic symbols for the latter). In English there are labiodental fricatives [f] and [v] but no bilabial fricatives [ɸ] and [β]. Here there are symbols available for the distinction, and indeed this distinction is made in Ewe, as in (23) (Ladefoged 1971, 38).

(23)   èβè   'Ewe language'   èvè   'two'
       éɸá   'he polished'   éfá   'he was cold'
       èβló   'mushroom'   évló   'he is evil'
       éɸlè   'he bought'   éflé   'he split off'

We use [strident] to distinguish these classes of fricatives, the feature we used for certain affricates. The acoustic noise which characterizes [+strident] sounds is produced by directing the airstream in a complex path. In a labio-dental fricative, for example, the airstream is obstructed by the incisor teeth, and is forced to angle downward before it can exit the mouth via the lips, thus executing a complex path and producing considerable noise. A bilabial frica-tive, on the other hand, allows a simple, straight path through the lips. Similarly, [strident] distinguishes interdental from dental and alveolar frica-tives, for example, in English (24).

(24)   thin   [θɪn]   sin   [sɪn]

observ : what fhs
descr : act classes
expl : ? (expl)

Since the airstream is direct in [θ], this sound is [−strident]. In [s], the tongue directs the airstream against the alveolar ridge. From there it must angle downward before exiting through the incisor teeth. Similarly, [+strident] characterizes the postalveolar [š] and the uvular [χ] while the palatal fricative [ç] and the velar [x] are [−strident], though other features differ in these cases. Stridency also distinguishes some liquids: Czech has a strident r-sound, orthographically ř, phonetically [ṛ],[13] as in řada 'row' vs rada 'council.' The contrast of a strident and nonstrident lateral occurs in Bura and Margi, two languages of Africa (Ladefoged 1964). Oral stops and all sonorants are [−strident]. Most affricates are [+strident]; however, Chipewyan has a contrast between a nonstrident interdental affricate in t̄θɛ 'stone' vs t̄sá 'beaver' (SPE, p. 329). This implies that we need an additional feature to distinguish affricates from stops. SPE suggests [delayed release]: affricates are [+delayed release], all other segments are [−delayed release].

In order to make further distinctions in the [−anterior, −coronal] region, we appeal to the features we first established for vowels [high], [low], and [back]. We noted in chapter 1 that the prepalatal, palatal, and velar sounds are produced by an elevation of the body of the tongue, and in fact that these consonant articulations have some similarity to the high vowels [i] and [u]. We therefore regard these articulations as [+high]. In addition, the prepalatals and palatals are [−back], while the velars are [+back]. Some support for this analysis comes from assimilations. In many languages, velars become palatals in the environment of front vowels, as in the examples of exercise 2.15 of chapter 2 from Lumasaaba (Brown 1972). Uvulars and pharyngeals are also [+back] but differ from velars in being [−high]. In exercise 2.6 of chapter 2 we saw examples from Greenlandic Eskimo in which high vowels have mid allophones adjacent to uvular consonants, which can be seen as an assimilation in the feature [−high]. Pharyngeals are [+low], differing in this feature from uvulars. The complete feature specifications for points of articulation are given in (25). The shaded cells are not specified for basic points of articulation, but are reserved for secondary articulations, discussed in section 3.6. Where + appears under [strident] in this chart, it applies to fricatives and affricates only. Stops, nasals, trills, flaps, and approximants are [−strident] at all points of articulation. Note also that there are two dental rows. The first is for interdentals and includes the [−strident] [θ]; the second is for regular dentals and

---

[13] This symbol has been eliminated from the current IPA chart. The sound is that of a trilled [r] with simultaneous [ž].

includes the [+strident] [s̩]. Except for these sounds (and their voiced counterparts), interdentals and dentals are not distinguished.[14]

(25)		ant	cor	stri	dist	high	low	back	round
Bilabial	φ	+	−	−	+				
Labiodental	f	+	−	+	−				
(nonstrident) (inter-)dental	θ	+	+	−	+				
(strident) Dental	s̩	+	+	+	+				
Alveolar	s	+	+	+	−				
Postalveolar	š	−	+	+	−	+	−	−	
Retroflex	ṣ	−	+	+	−	−	−	−	
Prepalatal	ś	−	+	+	+	+	−	−	
Palatal	ç	−	−	−	+	+	−	−	
Velar	x	−	−	−	−	+	−	+	
Uvular	χ	−	−	+	−	−	−	+	
Pharyngeal	ħ	−	−	−	−	−	+	+	
Glottal	h	−	−	−	−	−	−	−	

Distinctive features for points of articulation

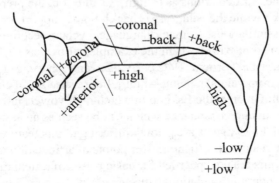

-coronal
−back +back
+coronal
+high
-coronal
+anterior
+high
−low
+low

---

[14] The column labelled [dist] refers to the feature [distributed], defined as follows in *SPE*: "Distributed sounds are produced with a constriction that extends for a considerable distance along the direction of the air flow; nondistributed sounds are produced with a constriction that extends only for a short distance in this direction" (Chomsky & Halle 1968, 312). While we include it here for completeness, this feature is only responsible for the distinctions between the dental and alveolar points of articulation, and for the distinction between the postalveolar and prepalatal and points of articulation, will not be used elsewhere in this book.

In section 3.3 we mentioned German rhymes as a source of external evidence for our feature analysis. Another form of external evidence is speech errors. While many speech errors involve transposition of entire segments, others involve subsegmental elements, i.e., features. The sample in (26) is illustrative. The intended utterance is given to the left of the arrow, the erroneous utterance is given to the right of the arrow, and the right column indicates the nature of the change in terms of features.

(26) *s*pell *m*other → smell ['bəðɾ]   reversal of [nasal]
      *b*ang the *n*ail → mang…mail   anticipation of [nasal],
                                               persistence of labial (noncoronal)
      *c*lear *b*lue sky → glear plue   reversal of [voice]
      *b*ig and *f*at → pig…vat   reversal of [voice]
      *s*catter*b*rain → spattergrain   reversal of [anterior],
                                               maintenance of [voice]
      spa*g*he*tt*i → skabetti   reversal of [anterior]
      *p*e*d*estrian → tebestrian   reversal of [coronal]
      *c*all the *g*irl → gall the curl   reversal of [voice]
      documen*t*ation → documendation   voicing assimilation

3.6   Secondary articulation of consonants

Because the various articulators we have been considering are relatively independent of each other, there are segments in which more than one articulator play a role in their production. This is evident in vowels such as [u] and [ü], where the lips and the tongue body both participate in the production of the sound. When one or more vowel features are superimposed on a consonant articulation, we speak of a *secondary articulation* of the consonant. Common types of secondary articulation are palatalization, velarization, labialization, and pharyngealization. The table in (27) gives the symbols and feature specifications for these, illustrated with the alveolar [t].

(27)		high	low	back	round
palatalized	t^y	+	−	−	−
velarized	$t^ɣ$	+	−	+	−
labialized	t^w	+	−	+	(+)
pharyngealized	$t^ʕ$	−	+	+	−

The superimposed tilde [~] is used to represent a velarized or pharyngealized articulation, where these are not distinguished, as in [ɫ].

3.7   Features for suprasegmentals

As we pointed out in section 1.1.3 of chapter 1, *suprasegmentals* refer to phonetic features outside the linear sequence of segments. For this reason, these properties of utterances are difficult to represent as part of feature matrices of individual segments. Nevertheless, it is common to codify things like stress, length, and tone as segmental properties. Stress can be considered a feature [±stress] on vowels, although it is more properly considered a property of a syllable in relation to neighbouring syllables. This will be explored when we develop syllable structure in section 7.2.1 of chapter 7 and metrical structure in section 7.2.2 of chapter 7. Tone has a certain tendency to act rather independently of the segments that make up an utterance. For example, a tone may remain when the segment it is associated with is deleted, being subsequently linked up to some other segment, or a tone may spread to join up to a number of segments or syllables in an utterance. We will explore this when we discuss autosegmental phonology in section 7.1 of chapter 7. Meanwhile, the glottal features in (19) may be used on vowels to indicate tone, e.g., [+slack (vocal folds)] for high tone and [+stiff (vocal folds)] for low tone. For length we will use the feature [±long] until we explore the concept of mora in section 7.2.1 of chapter 7.

3.8   Redundancy and implications

As we mentioned in section 3.2, in connection with Turkish vowels, not all feature specifications are contrastive in a given language. In Turkish, the feature [low] does not serve to contrast any pair of vowels, although the vowel [ɑ] in Turkish is phonetically [+low] while the other Turkish vowels are [−low]. In this section we consider some ways of determining the redundant feature specifications for some classes of segments in different languages, anticipating more extensive discussion of this question in section 7.3 of chapter 7. For reasons that will become clear as we proceed, we will start with a simpler vowel system, that of Spanish, and return to the Turkish example at the end of this section.

We give a fully specified matrix for the Spanish vowels in (28).

	i	e	a	o	u
(28)					
high	+	−	−	−	+
low	−	−	+	−	−
back	−	−	+	+	+
round	−	−	−	+	+
ATR	+	+	−	+	+

Schane & Bendixen (1978) suggest the following procedure for extracting the redundancies from such a matrix. Starting with the top row of feature specifications, determine if any value of that feature is always associated with the same value for some feature in the second row. That value in the other row is then redundant, which is indicated by circling that value. Continue by checking to see if some value in the first row is consistently associated with the same value in the third row, and so on, until all the predictions from the first row to later rows are discovered. For (28), we observe that [+high] in the first row is always associated with [−low] in the second row, so that we can circle the value [−low] for the vowels *i* and *u*. This is an expected result, since we have observed that the the redundancy relation in (29) is universally observed, due to the nature of these features. We give the required redundancy rule in (29). We prefix *R:* to a redundancy rule to indicate its status and as a reminder that redundancy rules can fill in blank feature specifications but cannot change previously specified features.

(29)   R: [+high] → [−low]

In addition, we see that [+high] vowels in (28) are always [+ATR]. This allows us to state the further redundancy rule (30a), which can be combined with (29) to give (30b).

(30)   a.   R: [+high] → [+ATR]

   b.   R: [+high] → $\begin{bmatrix} -\text{low} \\ +\text{ATR} \end{bmatrix}$

The feature values that are circled by this procedure are redundant, and can be omitted. The interpretation of (30b) is that such redundant values can be recovered by applying the rule. That is, if all the circled feature values in (34) were omitted, they could be replaced by applying the redundancy rules (30b), (31), (32), (33) and (34).

We cannot make any other redundancies on the basis of the first row of features in (28). The feature [+high] is associated with both [+back] and [–back] and with both [+round] and [–round]. Likewise, [–high] is associated with both [+low] and [–low], with both [+back] and [–back], and with both [+round] and [–round].

We then proceed to the second row to see if any features on the lower rows can be predicted from the values found there. Indeed, we find that the value [+low] is associated with [+back, –round, –ATR] (since there is only one low vowel in the system), but that [–low] is associated with both values of [back] and [round]. This allows the implication in (31).

(31)   R: [+low] → $\begin{bmatrix} +\text{back} \\ -\text{round} \\ -\text{ATR} \end{bmatrix}$

We can then look for implications from [back] to [round] and [ATR], and we find (32).

(32)   R: [–back] → $\begin{bmatrix} -\text{round} \\ +\text{ATR} \end{bmatrix}$

Finally, we can look for predictions from [round] to [ATR], and we find (33).

(33)   R: [+round] → [+ATR]

At this point we notice that all values of [ATR] have been circled, that is, all values of [ATR] are redundant in this system.

This is all the implications we can find by working from higher rows to lower ones. If we now reverse the procedure and work from lower rows to higher ones, we can extract the further redundancies in (34).[15] In applying this procedure, it is essential not to use feature values that have been declared redundant to predict any other feature values. For example, since all values of [ATR] are redundant, it is not possible to use any value of [ATR] to predict any other feature value.

---

[15] The redundancy rules (34b, c) can be collapsed as in (i), using the curly braces notation introduced in section 4.9.1 of chapter 4.

(i)   R: $\begin{Bmatrix} [-\text{back}] \\ [+\text{round}] \end{Bmatrix} \to [-\text{low}]$

(34)   a.   R: [+round] → [+back]
          b.   R: [−back] → [−low]
          c.   R: [+round] → [−low]
          d.   R: [+low] → [−high]

In fact, the redundancies in (34) can be derived from the redundancies in (29), (31), and (32) by a simple logical procedure, which consists of interchanging the features and their values on each side of the arrow. For example, (29) says that [+high] vowels are [−low]. Reversing the features puts [low] on the left and [high] on the right of the arrow, and reversing their values puts [+low] on the left of (34d) where we had [−low] on the right of (29) and puts [−high] on the right of (34d) where we had [+high] on the left of (29). To see why this works, consider (29) again. It says that a [+high] vowel is necessarily [−low]. Now consider a [+low] vowel: what can we say about its value for [high]? It cannot be [+high], because (28) requires that [+high] vowels be [−low], which is a contradiction. Therefore it can only be [−high]. In this case we are dealing with two *universal* implications, (29) and (34d), but the same logic applies, for instance in relating (32) to (34a), where the implication is not universal. In the case of (31), where a single feature (here [+low]) implies the presence of two features (here [+back, −round]), the reversed rule (31b) allows either reversed value (i.e., [−back] or [+round]) to imply the reversal of [low], that is, [−low]. This can also be seen if (31) is broken into its two components, as in (32). Reversing the first two of these gives (33), which is equivalent to (34b, c). (Recall that we cannot use the reverse of (35c), i.e. [+ATR] → [−low], since [ATR] is redundant everywhere, even though this implication is true of the matrix in (37), for other reasons.)

(35)   a.   R: [+low] → [+back]
          b.   R: [+low] → [−round]
          c.   R: [+low] → [−ATR]
(36)   a.   R: [−back] → [−low]
          b.   R: [+round] → [−low]

We can now give the matrix for the Spanish vowels again, in (37), this time with the redundant feature values circled. Some circled values may be derived from more than one implication, but are circled only once.

(37)

	i	e	a	o	u
high	+	−	⊖	−	+
low	⊖	⊖	+	⊖	⊖
back	−	−	⊕	⊕	⊕
round	⊖	⊖	⊖	+	+
ATR	⊕	⊕	⊖	⊕	⊕

This procedure can be applied to any feature matrix, but it may not always yield the expected results. If we try it on a matrix of the eight vowels of Turkish, specified in terms of [high], [back], and [round], we will discover that there are no redundancies to be extracted. However, if we try it on a matrix of Turkish vowels that also includes [low], we will generate a matrix in which [+low] is distinctive for *a*, but the other features are redundant for that vowel, as shown in (38). Thus the procedure extracts the maximum amount of redundancy, but fails to reveal that [low] can be considered redundant in Turkish.

(38)

	u	ɨ	ü	i	o	a	ö	e
high	+	+	+	+	−	⊖	−	−
low	⊖	⊖	⊖	⊖	⊖	+	⊖	⊖
back	+	+	−	−	+	⊕	−	−
round	+	−	+	−	+	⊖	+	−
ATR	⊕	⊕	⊕	⊕	⊕	⊖	⊕	⊕

In general, it is better to find the *minimum set of features* required to distinguish the segments in a given system. In (38) we can clearly eliminate the ATR row as redundant. The low row also appears nearly redundant, suggesting that it may be possible to eliminate it also. We can observe that the sole uncircled value in this row, the plus value for [a], is not paired minimally with a minus value in the rest of the row; that is, [a] is distinct from every other segment in the system in at least one of the features [high], [back], or [round]. Constructing a matrix in terms of these three features indeed permits us to distinguish all the vowels of Turkish, as in (4). Since there are eight vowels, and they are distributed symmetrically, it is possible to make all the necessary distinctions with three features, since $2^3 = 8$. For any set of m segments, we need at least n features such that $2^n \geq m$. If the distribution is less symmetrical than the Turkish case, we may need more features than the theoretical minimum.

In some cases we can determine such a minimum set of features by using the method described in this section. For example, Yawelmani has the under-lying vowel phonemes in (39), as we will demonstrate in detail in section 5.6 of chapter 5.

(39) i u

  a o

If we set up a distinctive feature matrix for these vowels, we get the arrangement in (40).

(40)

	i	a	o	u
high	+	–	–	+
low	–	+	–	–
back	–	+	+	+
round	–	–	+	+
ATR	+	–	+	+

Applying the method above yields the circled redundancies in (41) along with the redundancy rules in (42).

(41)

	i	a	o	u
high	+	–	–	+
low	–	+	–	–
back	–	+	+	+
round	–	–	+	+
ATR	+	–	+	+

(42) $[+\text{high}] \rightarrow \begin{bmatrix} -\text{low} \\ +\text{ATR} \end{bmatrix}$

  $[-\text{high}] \rightarrow [+\text{back}]$

  $[+\text{low}] \rightarrow \begin{bmatrix} -\text{high} \\ +\text{back} \\ -\text{round} \\ -\text{ATR} \end{bmatrix}$

  $[-\text{low}] \rightarrow [+\text{ATR}]$

$$[-\text{back}] \rightarrow \begin{bmatrix} +\text{high} \\ -\text{low} \\ -\text{round} \\ +\text{ATR} \end{bmatrix}$$

$$[+\text{round}] \rightarrow \begin{bmatrix} +\text{ATR} \\ +\text{back} \\ -\text{low} \end{bmatrix}$$

This shows that [ATR] is completely redundant in Yawelmani, but at least one value is specified for each of the four other features. However, we shouldn't need four features to distinguish four vowels; ideally we should be able to distinguish four vowels with only two features. Inspection of (40) reveals that the features [high] and [round] are all that are needed to distinguish these four vowels, as shown in (43). This is the minimal set of features needed for the underlying vowels of Yawelmani. Note that no other pair of features serves to distinguish all four vowels. Since Yawelmani phonetically has [e] in addition to these four vowels, the feature [low] is needed in addition for the phonetic distinctions of the language.

(43)

	i	a	o	u	e
high	+	−	−	+	
round	−	−	+	+	

In section 7.3 of chapter 7 we will explore another, more revealing way of extracting redundancies that takes the language system into account.

When we come to writing rules in terms of distinctive features in chapter 4, we will need to be able to determine the minimum set of features required to select the class of segments that undergo the rule. We will need to be able to give a matrix that characterizes just this class in terms of the system of the individual language. The redundancy inherent in each phonological system allows us to simplify phonological rules by not specifying features that are redundant in that system.

3.9   Exercises

3.1   Which segment is *not:*

1.	[+coronal]	s	n̩	χ	t'	ǰ
2.	[−back]	i	ɑ	š	ʔ	ö
3.	[+sonorant]	a	ɹ	l	w	z
4.	[+strident]	θ	z	š	č	v
5.	[−round]	ʌ	tʸ	k	u	ɨ
6.	[−anterior]	ç	d	g	ḍ	ʔ
7.	[+low]	ɒ	ʕ	a	tˢ	ɛ
8.	[−high]	ɛ	χ	h	pʸ	a
9.	[+continuant]	ŋ	ɨ	s	l	r
10.	[−ATR]	ə	ü	e	ɪ	ɒ
11.	[+consonantal]	n	y	l	t	ɾ
12.	[−syllabic]	w	g	n	l̩	ɾ

uvulars are [+hi]

3.2   What distinctive feature differentiates the sounds in each of the following pairs? State which member of the pair has the + value. Ignore [distributed].

1.	u	ʊ
2.	b	d
3.	k	c
4.	ǰ	ź
5.	ü	ö
6.	z	ž
7.	ɛ	æ
8.	ʌ	e
9.	k	x
10.	a	ɒ
11.	θ	ð
12.	l	ɾ

(Continued)

13.   N   ŋ

14.   ɩ   y

15.   t͡s   t͡θ

3.3.   For each segment, if you change the value of the feature indicated, what new segment will be derived?

1.   ŋ   [back]

2.   ɨ   [back]

3.   ʌ   [high]

4.   d   [coronal]

5.   ö   [back]

6.   æ   [low]

7.   ü   [round]

8.   ɸ   [strident]

9.   ɣ   [voice]

10.   tʸ   [high]

3.4.   A *natural class* is a class of related segments such that the class as a whole is defined by a smaller number of features than is required to define any single member of the class. Phonological rules typically affect such a class of segments and are triggered by environments defined as such a class.

Consider the following array of consonants and vowels. Assume that these are the only sounds you need to consider.

Vowels

i	ü	ɨ	u
e	ö	ʌ	o
æ	œ	ɑ	ɒ

(Continued)

Consonants

	ɾ			
	l			
m	n	ɲ	ŋ	
b	d	ɟ	g	
p	t	c	k	ʔ
pʰ	tʰ	cʰ	kʰ	
f θ	s	š	x	

Below are listed some classes of sounds from this array. Characterize each class in terms of distinctive features, using the minimal specification necessary for each class. Treat vowels and consonants separately.

1. {i}
2. {i, ü}
3. {i, ü, ɨ, u}
4. {i, ü, e, ö}
5. {ʌ, o, ɑ, ɒ}
6. {ü, ö, u, o}
7. {e, ʌ}
8. {œ, ɒ}
9. {ü, u}
10. {p, t}
11. {p, t, c, k}
12. {p, t, c, k, ʔ}
13. {d}
14. {ɟ, c, cʰ}
15. {k, g, kʰ, x}
16. {tʰ, cʰ}
17. {θ, s}
18. {s, š}
19. {ɲ, ŋ}
20. {n, l, ɾ}
21. {l, ɾ}

3.5.   Consider the first row of the vowel chart from exercise 3.4:

Three different classes of segments have been enclosed in boxes. What is the relationship between the number of features needed to characterize a natural class and the number of segments in that class?

3.6   Determine the redundant features in the following distinctive feature matrices.

a. Hungarian fricatives

	f	v	s	z	š	ž
[ant]	+	+	+	+	−	−
[cor]	−	−	+	+	+	+
[voice]	−	+	−	+	−	+

b. English fricatives

	f	v	θ	ð	s	z	š	ž
[strid]	+	+	−	−	+	+	+	+
[ant]	+	+	+	+	+	+	−	−
[cor]	−	−	+	+	+	+	+	+
[voice]	−	+	−	+	−	+	−	+

c.   German fricatives and affricates

	f	v	s	z	š	ž	x	p͡f	t͡s
[cont]	+	+	+	+	+	+	+	−	−
[delrel]	−	−	−	−	−	−	−	+	+
[ant]	+	+	+	+	−	−	−	+	+
[cor]	−	−	+	+	+	+	−	−	+
[strid]	+	+	+	+	+	+	−	+	+
[voice]	−	+	−	+	−	+	−	−	−

(Continued)

d.   Estonian vowels (Oinas 1968)

	i	ɛ	æ	ü	ö	ə	ɑ	u	ɔ
[high]	+	–	–	+	–	–	–	+	–
[low]	–	–	+	–	–	–	–	+	–
[back]	–	–	–	–	–	+	+	+	+
[round]	–	–	–	+	+	–	–	+	+
[ATR]	+	–	–	+	–	–	–	+	–

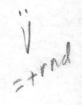

3.7   What is the *minimum* set of feature specifications required for each of the following systems? Draw a feature matrix for each.

a.   Yoruba vowels (Archangeli & Pulleyblank 1989)

        i   u
        e   o
        ɛ   ɔ
                 ɑ

b.   Latvian underlying vowels (Budiņa-Lazdiņa 1966)

        i   u
        æ   ɑ

c.   Samoan consonants (Marsack 1962)

        p   t
        f   s
        v
        m   n   ŋ
                l

d.   Spanish obstruents (European)

        p   t̪   k
        b   d̪   g
        f   θ   s̪   x

Non-overlapping phonemes
= neutralization

wait   dear
wade   tear

$$\acute{V} \; \underline{D} \; V$$
$$* \; t/d$$

4   Alternations

4.1   Alternations as phonology

In chapter 2 we observed how phonological rules can determine the phonetic shape of phonemes. For example, in Farsi, the phoneme /r/ appears as [r], [ɾ], or [ɹ], depending on the phonological environment in which it is found (see 12 of chapter 2). These allophones of Farsi /r/ do not contrast with each other, since no two of them ever appear in the same phonological environment. But phonological rules are more general, in that they can determine the distribution of sounds that in other contexts may contrast. For example, in Latin, long and short vowels ordinarily contrast (see 44 of chapter 2). But in the context before *ns* and *nf,* short vowels do not appear: vowels must be long in this position. This generalization can be expressed as a phonological rule just as the distribution of the Farsi allophones of /r/ can be. In the case of Latin long and short vowels, the rule has an effect on the phonological shape of morphemes. In the case we discussed in chapter 2, the negative prefix *in-* has a long vowel when it is attached to stems beginning with *s* or *f,* as in *iːnsaːnus* and *iːnfeːliks,* while it has a short vowel when attached to other stems, as in *inhuːmaːnus* and *inimiːkus.* Because this rule results in alternations of an otherwise contrastive feature and affects the phonemic shape of morphemes, phonemic theory assigned this study to a separate area of the grammar called *morphophonemics.*

    In generative phonology there is no distinction between these two types of rules. As we saw in section 2.8 of chapter 2, this distinction is somewhat artificial and makes it impossible to capture certain kinds of generalizations. For example, the vowel-length alternation observed in the Latin *in-* prefix is by no means a property of this particular *morpheme:* It arises wherever the appropriate combination of *sounds* appears: it is *phonological,* not *morphological.* For example, the prefix *kon-* shows the same behaviour, and similar alternations appear within morphemes, as shown in (1).

(1)   kondoː   'I found'   koːnsueːwit   'he got used to'
        konkinoː 'I sing in chorus'   koːnfeːkit   'he accomplished'
        fontis   'fountain (genitive)' foːns   'fountain (nominative)'

The purpose of this chapter is to develop the role of phonological rules in accounting for alternations of various types.

4.2 Morphology

Morphology is the study of the internal structure of words. It is concerned with the ways in which morphemes combine to form words, how separate morphemes contribute to the meaning of the word as a whole, and with complex morphological processes like infixation and reduplication. All of these are interesting topics in themselves, but we will for the most part be concerned only with relatively straightforward morpheme combinations.

In some cases morphology provides more than one item with a particular meaning, if the variation is not phonologically predictable. For example, in English, nouns normally form their plurals by the addition of a suffix ordinarily spelled *-(e)s,* with three phonologically predictable pronunciations, [z], [s], and [ɪz]. The plural of *box* is *boxes.* This must be contrasted with the plural of *ox,* which is *oxen.* There is no way to predict the plural of *ox* by purely phonological rules; the morphology must provide a special *allomorph* or *suppletive affix* for this case, with the phonological shape [ɪn], and the noun *ox* must be given a special marker that says it takes this special allomorph rather than the regular allomorph. However, the morphology provides only one phonological shape for the regular plural suffix, namely /z/. The morphology does not have to provide the three pronunciations of this morpheme [z], [s], and [ɪz], because the phonology specifies which of these forms will be used with any regular noun. These phonological variants are known as *alternants.* This is the first principle of phonological alternations, stated in (2).

(2)   Except in cases of suppletion, every morpheme has only one phonological form. Any variation in the phonetic shape of a morpheme results from the operation of regular phonological rules.

In some cases, it may be difficult to determine if the variation in the shape of a morpheme is suppletive or the result of regular phonology. In this chapter, we will deal only with cases of phonological alternation. It may also be difficult to determine the phonological shape of the morpheme as it is supplied by the morphology, known as the *underlying representation*. We will develop a number of principles for determining this underlying shape as we proceed.

4.3   Russian devoicing

In chapter 2, section 2.8.2, we observed that Russian obstruents contrast for voicing. However, we also saw there that the voicing of Russian obstruents is not contrastive in the position before another obstruent: there the voicing assimilates to the voicing of the following obstruent. There is another environment where voicing is nondistinctive. Consider the data in (3).[1]

(3)	nom.sg.	dat.sg.	gloss	voiceless initial		voiced initial	
	'xlep	'xlebu	'bread'	po'ka	'while'	bo'ka	'sides'
	xo'lop	xo'lopu	'bondman'				
	'sat	'sadu	'garden'	'tom	'volume'	'dom	'house'
	͡tsvet	͡tsvetu	'colour'				
	'ras	'razu	'time'	'sloy	'layer'	'zloy	'bad'
	'us	u'su	'whisker'				
	'storoš	'storožu	'guard'	'šar	'sphere'	'žar	'heat'
	'duš	'dušu	'shower'				
	'rok	'rogu	'horn'	'klup	'club'	'glup	'stupid'
	'rok	'roku	'fate'				
	'rak	'raku	'crayfish'				
	po'rok	po'rogu	'threshold'				
	po'rok	po'roku	'vice'				

Morphologically, the nouns in the first column consist of a stem with no affix, while the nouns in the second column consist of the stem plus the suffix *-u,* meaning 'dative singular.' The forms in the right two columns, which are all morphologically simple, are repeated from (52) of chapter 2 (section 2.8.2) to demonstrate phonemic contrasts between voiced and voiceless obstruents. The position of stress is also shown. Although stress is not relevant to this

---

[1] The data in (3) ignore certain vowel alternations, in particular, the reduction of unstressed vowels. See exercise 4.7. Based on Kenstowicz & Kisseberth 1979, 46ff.

problem, it is important in vowel reduction, an aspect of Russian phonology that appears in exercise 4.4.

In some of the cases in (3) we see that there is no change in the shape of the stem between the nominative singular and the dative singular. An example is *xo'lop,* 'bondman,' which has the same form in both columns. In other cases, like *'xlep,* 'bread,' we observe an alternation. The stem has the form *xlep* in the nominative singular and *xleb* in the dative singular (disregarding stress, which is on the stem syllable in both cases). Should we choose one of these two forms as the underlying representation for the morpheme meaning 'bread,' and if so, which one? Either choice requires a rule to generate the other in the appropriate context. Suppose we choose *xlep.* Then we require a rule to turn *p* into *b,* say in the environment between vowels. This is a natural enough rule, a kind of *lenition,* in the terminology introduced in chapter 2, section 2.7.3. Such a rule is contradicted by the data, however, in the sense that there are instances of *p* (and of other voiceless obstruents) between vowels, as in *xo'lopu.* Adopting this solution would require some mechanism for exempting *xo'lopu* from the rule, either marking it as an exception or marking forms like *xlep* so that the rule applies only to them. Once we propose a rule, we have to test it on all the data, that is, on all the forms that it *could* apply to, not just to those forms where it appears actually to have applied. This is the only way to ensure that the rules are perfectly general.

The other possible choice for the underlying representation for 'bread' is *xleb.* This choice of underlying representation requires a rule that converts *b* to *p* in word final position, a *fortition,* as discussed in section 2.7.4 of chapter 2. An examination of all the data reveals that this rule is not contradicted: there are no examples of word-final voiced consonants in these data.[2] There is also pattern congruity, since the rule applies to all obstruents in Russian, not just *b.* Using distinctive features to represent classes of sounds, as we developed in chapter 3, we can express the required rule as in (4).

(4)   *Final Devoicing (Russian)*
        [–sonorant] → [–voice] / ___#

This rule says that any segment that bears the feature [–sonorant] that appears in word-final position acquires the feature [–voice] (overriding an existing

---

2 As discussed in section 2.8.2, word-final voiced obstruents appear in assimilation to an immediately following voiced obstruent. This additional rule does not destroy the generality of word-final devoicing in Russian.

[+voice] specification, if any). Notice that we do not have to specify this change as affecting only [+voice] obstruents. It does no harm to state it in such a way that it applies to all obstruents, and this simplifies the rule by one feature. The application of a rule when it provides a feature already present in its input (for example in *xo'lop*) is termed *vacuous* application.[3] Any form in Russian that includes an obstruent in word-final position is said to *meet the structural description of rule (4)*. We will develop this idea more carefully in section 4.5. We can now state some principles governing the choice of underlying representations and rules required to convert them into phonetic forms. We give these in (5). Some of these will be elaborated on further in chapter 6.

(5)   *Criteria of phonological analysis*

a. Criterion of *predictability:* Underlying phonological representations are chosen in such a way as to maximize predictability of phonetic forms on phonological grounds.

b. Criterion of *naturalness:* Phonological representations are stated in terms of phonetic features. They differ from phonetic representations only to the extent that there is justification for a more abstract representation. Unless some phonological rule intervenes, underlying representations are preserved phonetically. Underlying representations are chosen in such a way that the rules required to produce phonetic forms are maximally natural.

c. Criterion of *simplicity:* Underlying phonological representations and phonological rules are chosen so that the overall grammar is maximally simple.

d. Preference of *phonological* solutions: phonological solutions are preferred to morphological solutions (e.g., arbitrary lexical markings or suppletion), other things being equal.[4]

---

[3] See section 4.7 for another example of vacuous application.

[4] An example of a morphological solution is the plural *oxen* of English *ox*. This noun has to have an arbitrary lexical marker to state that it requires the suppletive plural suffix *-en*, since there is no phonological reason for this choice (compare the regular plural *boxes*).

Our analysis of Russian devoicing meets the criteria in (5). Phonetic forms are predictable by rule (4) if underlying representations are chosen so that alternating morphemes have final voiced obstruents while morphemes with invariant voiceless obstruents have underlying final voiceless obstruents. The analysis is natural, since final devoicing is a natural rule. A rule of intervocalic voicing is also natural, but in this case is contradicted by the data. An analysis incorporating a rule of intervocalic voicing would require a morphological solution, i.e., arbitrary lexical markings of which morphemes undergo the rule, or else suppletive forms, both contrary to principle (5d). The solution is simple in that a simple rule is all that is required, and no arbitrary lexical markings.

To verify that this solution adheres to the criteria of predictability, naturalness, simplicity, and the preference for phonological solutions, we should note that the phenomenon of voice alternation in Russian is by no means confined to the particular morphological categories exemplified in the data of (3). Consider the additional data in (6) (Kenstowicz & Kisseberth 1979, 49).

(6)

nom.sg.	gen.pl.	gloss
'rɨba	'rɨp	'fish'
tro'pa	'trop	'path'
po'beda	po'bet	'victory'
siro'ta	si'rot	'orphan'
gro'za	'gros	'storm'
'liža	'liš	'ski'
du'ša	'duš	'soul'
no'ga	'nok	'leg'
so'baka	so'bak	'dog'

The nouns in (6) are feminine, in contrast to the masculine nouns in (3). Morphologically, the feminine nouns in (6) have a suffix in the nominative singular, namely -a, and no suffix in the genitive plural. Once again, the criterion of predictability obliges us to set up underlying representations with a stem-final voiced consonants for words that show an alternation in voicing, such as 'rɨba. Words whose stem-final consonant is always voiceless, such as tro'pa, are lexically represented with underlying voiceless consonants.

A common error is to try to write phonological rules to change one word into another (for example, the nominative singular into the dative singular of the words in (3) or the genitive plural into the nominative singular of the words in (6). This is incorrect. The function of the phonological rules is to specify the pronunciation (phonetic representation) of words whose morphological form is already specified by rules of morphology. We will consider some refinements of this idea in section 7.4 of chapter 7, where we discuss the interaction of morphology and phonology in terms of lexical phonology.

4.4 More on phonological rules

In section 2.6 of chapter 2 we introduced the standard notation for phonological rules, repeated here as (7).

(7) $A \rightarrow B \, / \, P \_\_\_\_ Q$

In the light of our introduction of distinctive features in chapter 3, we can now be more precise as to the meaning of each part of this rule. A and B must each be a single column of distinctive features. A (the *input* or *focus* of the rule) contains the *minimal* set of features needed to define the set of segments affected by the rule. B (the *structural change*) contains *all* and *only* the features that change by the operation of the rule.[5] P and Q (the *environment*) are also matrices of distinctive features, but these may contain more than one column, and may contain boundary symbols and other abbreviatory conventions. Another way of writing the schema of (7) is shown in (8). It is sometimes easier to see that a form meets the structural description of a rule if written in the format of (8) rather than of (7).

(8)   P   A   Q
            ↓
            B

---

[5] It is sometimes possible to omit features from the structural change if they are redundant concomitant changes of the change indicated. For example, if a rule specifies that a segment changes to become [+sonorant], it should not be necessary to specify that it becomes [+voice] also, since sonorants are normally voiced. It is not always easy to decide which concomitant changes are redundant in a given situation, and a full discussion must await our introduction of underspecification theory in section 7.3 of chapter 7. When in doubt, it is best to indicate all the features that change, even if some are redundant.

Some symbols used in phonological rules are given in (9). A special convention regarding the use of the morpheme boundary (+) should be carefully observed. If a morpheme boundary appears in a form, it need not be matched with a morpheme boundary in a rule in order to say that the form meets the structural description of the rule. On the other hand, a word boundary (#) in a form must be matched with a word boundary in a rule in order for the rule to apply. Either a word boundary or a morpheme boundary may be written into a rule, in which case it must be matched with a corresponding boundary in a form in order to say that the form meets the structural description of the rule.

(9)   *Some conventional symbols used in phonological rules:*

    # = word boundary

    + = morpheme boundary

    $ or . = syllable boundary

    C = [–syll]

    V = [+syll]

    {} enclose alternatives (see §4.9.1)

    () enclose optional elements (see §4.9.2)

    C_0 = zero or more [–syllabic] segments

    C_0^1 = zero or one consonant

    C_a^b = a string of consonants of at least *a* but no more than *b* (rarely used)

P or Q or both may be null. If either is null, this corresponds to the claim that it does not matter what appears in that side of the environment. If both are null, the rule applies regardless of the environment in which A appears. In addition, the expression PAQ is often referred to as the *structural description* of the rule. In addition, A may be null (represented by Ø), in which case the rule is an *insertion*. If B is null, the rule is a *deletion*. Obviously, it is not possible for both A and B to be null in the same rule.

In Russian Final Devoicing (4), the A of our schematic rule (7) is the feature matrix [–sonorant], which minimally defines the set of all obstruents. B corresponds to the feature matrix [–voice] which is the feature changed by the rule. Because P is not expressed in (4), the rule applies regardless of what precedes the obstruent in the form under consideration. Q is expressed as the word boundary, #, which says that the change takes place only if the obstruent occurs in word-final position.

4.5 ATR harmony

In Pulaar (Paradis 1986, Archangeli & Pulleyblank 1994), the feature [±ATR] is not distinctive. The high vowels [i] and [u] are always [+ATR]. The low vowel [ɑ] is always [−ATR]. There are also two mid vowels, which can be [−ATR] [ɛ] and [ɔ], or [+ATR] [e] and [o]. The mid vowels are [+ATR] when they occur to the left of a vowel which is [+ATR], either a high vowel or another mid vowel that is itself followed by a high vowel, as shown in (10).

(10) a. sof+ru   'chick (singular)'
      b. ser+du   'rifle butt (singular)'
      c. m͡beːl+u   'shadow (singular)'
      d. peːc+i   'slit (singular)'
      e. beːl+i   'puddle (singular)'
      f. dog-oː+ru   'runner (singular)'

In other contexts the mid vowel appears as [−ATR], as shown in (11).[6]

(11) a. cɔf-ɔn   'chick (diminutive plural)'
      b. cɛr-kɔn   'rifle butt (diminutive plural)'
      c. m͡beːl-ɔn   'shadow (diminutive plural)'
      d. peːc-ɔn   'slit (diminutive plural)'
      e. m͡beːl-ɔn   'puddle'
      f. ńdɔg-ɔ-w-ɔn   'runner (diminutive plural)'

This demonstrates that there is an alternation in [ATR] in this language, despite the fact that this feature is not distinctive. The morpheme for 'slit' appears in the form *peːc* in the [+ATR] context and as *pɛːc* otherwise.

The low vowel [ɑ] is always [−ATR] regardless of context. It does not assimilate in [+ATR] to a following high vowel, and it does not allow a mid vowel to its left to assimilate to a high vowel following the low vowel, as illustrated in (12).

---

[6] In comparing the forms in (9) and (10) you can ignore other alternations, such as those affecting consonants. In addition, the morphology is not completely transparent in these examples.

(12)   a.   fɑyi   'fat'
        b.   lɑmmi   'salted'
        c.   bɔːt-ɑː-ri   'to dine'
        d.   pɔːf-ɑː-li   'respirations'
        e.   nɔdd-ɑː-li   'call'
        f.   ŋ͡gɔr-ɑː-gu   'courage'

Assuming that all mid vowels are [−ATR] in underlying representation, we can formulate the rule in (13) to account for the [+ATR] form of these vowels in phonetic forms.

(13)   *ATR Harmony (Pulaar)*

$$\begin{bmatrix} +\text{syll} \\ -\text{low} \end{bmatrix} \rightarrow [+\text{ATR}] / \underline{\hspace{1cm}} C_0 \begin{bmatrix} +\text{syll} \\ +\text{ATR} \end{bmatrix}$$

right-to-left iterative

In rule (13) it is not necessary to include [−high] in the input. If a [+high] vowel appears with a following [+high, +ATR] vowel, the assimilation will take place vacuously, i.e., without effecting any change on the input.

Notice that the opposite assumption, that all mid vowels are [+ATR] in underlying representation, is not possible. This would imply that mid [−ATR] vowels would be derived by assimilation, but in the final syllable of a word the [−ATR] quatlity of mid vowels cannot be derived by assimilation to a following vowel, since there is none. Therefore, [−ATR] mid vowels in the final syllable must be underlying. We assume that this is also true in other positions, and derive [+ATR] mid vowels by assimilation to a following vowel.

Rule (13) will not affect the mid vowel in the first syllable of *pɛːc-ɔn* (10d) because the vowel following the mid vowel is [−ATR]. Rule (13) will affect the underlying representation /pɛːc-i/ (from 10). By assumption, the morpheme /pɛːc/ has the same underlying representation in all its occurrences. The interpretation of the rule as applied to /pɛːc-i/ is given in (14).

(14)   / p   ɛː   c   +   i /   underlying representation

            _____   C_0 $\begin{bmatrix} +\text{syll} \\ +\text{ATR} \end{bmatrix}$ structural description of rule (13)

                      ↓
                  [+ATR]   structural change

so [−ATR] is default!

We say that the representation /pɛːc-i/ "meets the structural description" of rule (13). That is, the ɛː matches the input to the rule because it is a nonlow vowel, the c matches the term C_0 in the rule, and the i matches the term $\begin{bmatrix} +\text{syll} \\ +\text{ATR} \end{bmatrix}$. Consequently, the rule applies and supplies the feature [+ATR] to the input vowel, turning it to [eː]. However, a form like bɔːt-aː-ri (12c) does not meet the structural description of (13). Although ɔː fits the description of the input ([+syll, −low]) and i matches the term $\begin{bmatrix} +\text{syll} \\ +\text{ATR} \end{bmatrix}$, the expression intervening between these two, taːr, cannot be matched to the rule's term C_0, since C_0 represents zero or more [−syll] segments and the sequence aː-r includes the [+syll] segment aː. If we try some other ways to match the segments of the form with the terms of the rule, we are still unable to do so. We cannot match the input aː with the rule's $\begin{bmatrix} +\text{syll} \\ +\text{ATR} \end{bmatrix}$, because aː is [−ATR]. Therefore, the rule cannot apply to this form.

In the form dog-oː-ru (10f) we observe two [+ATR] mid vowels. The vowel in the second syllable of this word straightforwardly assimilates to the vowel of the final syllable by (13). The vowel of the first syllable presents a slight problem. We argued on the basis of forms like (12c) that ATR harmony by rule (13) cannot assimilate a vowel across a vowel; that is, the [−ATR] vowel aː blocks propagation of [+ATR]. In order to obtain the right result in (10f), we allow rule (13) to apply *iteratively,* that is, repeatedly, to its own output. This is shown visually in (15).

(15) /#dɔg-ɔː-ru#/   underlying representation
           ɔː   ATR Harmony (first iteration)
           o   ATR Harmony (second iteration)
      [#dog-oː-ru#]   phonetic representation

Iterative rule application is very common in vowel harmony systems. This mode of rule application ensures that all the vowels within the harmonic domain, usually a word, agree in the harmonic feature, here [ATR].

The second ATR harmony system we will examine is that of Yoruba, a Niger-Congo language of Nigeria (Archangeli & Pulleyblank 1989). Like Pulaar, High vowels in Yoruba are always [+ATR] while low vowels are [−ATR], and mid vowels occur in both [+ATR] and [−ATR] variants. Unlike Pulaar, the feature [ATR] is contrastive on mid vowels in Yoruba. This is shown by the near-minimal pairs in (16).[7]

(16)   *mid vowels [+ATR]*   *mid vowels [–ATR]*

ilé	'house'	ilè	'land'
ebi	'hunger'	èbi	'guilt'
ate	'hat'	àǰè	'paddle'
		èpà	'ground nut'
ègè	'dirge'	ègέ	'cassava'
èké	'lie'	εké	'forked stick'
èse	'cat'	εsε	'row'
epo	'oil'	èkɔ	'pap'
olè	'thief'	ɔbὲ	'soup'
owó	'money'	ɔkɔ̀	'vehicle'

When in a bisyllabic word a mid vowel cooccurs with a high vowel on either
side, the mid vowel can be either [+ATR] or [–ATR]. When a mid vowel
occurs to the right of a low vowel, both [+ATR] and [–ATR] vowels also
occur. However when a mid vowel occurs to the left of a low vowel, the mid
vowel can only be [–ATR]. There are no words of the form *eCa*, where C is
any consonant. Finally, if a bisyllabic word has two mid vowels, they must
both be [+ATR] or both [–ATR]; they cannot be one of each. Archangeli &
Pulleyblank (1989) account for this in terms of a rule that assimilates a mid
vowel to a [–ATR] feature to its right, as in (17).[8]

(17)   *ATR Harmony (Yoruba)*

$$\begin{bmatrix} +\text{syll} \\ -\text{high} \\ -\text{low} \end{bmatrix} \rightarrow [-\text{ATR}] \ / \ \underline{\hspace{1cm}} C_0 \begin{bmatrix} +\text{syll} \\ -\text{ATR} \end{bmatrix}$$

Once again we employ the symbol C_0 to allow any number of nonsyllabics to
intervene between the assimilating vowels. The fact that low vowels are con-

---

[7] An acute accent (´) indicates high tone, a grave accent (`) indicates low tone; vowels with
no tone mark have mid tone.

[8] We have reinterpreted their rule in terms of the general format (7) for phonological rules.
Archangeli & Pulleyblank's rule is formulated in terms of autosegmental phonology,
which we discuss in section 7.1 of chapter 7.

sistently [–ATR] explains the occurrence of forms like *èpa* 'ground nut' as well as the nonexistence of words like **eCa*. It also explains words with two [–ATR] mid vowels, if we assume that the rightmost mid vowel is marked [–ATR] in underlying representation. Rule (17) ensures that this feature is assigned to the first mid vowel also. The nonoccurrence of words with two mid vowels, the first of which is [–ATR] and the second of which is [+ATR], is not accounted for by rule (17); Archangeli & Pulleyblank assume an additional constraint that [–ATR] must be assigned to the rightmost mid vowel if more than one mid vowel occurs in the word.[9]

As in Pulaar, ATR harmony in Yoruba results in alternations. Mid vowels are used as nominalizing prefixes. These prefixes are [–ATR] if attached to a stem with a [–ATR] vowel; otherwise they are [+ATR], as in (18).

(18)   Prefix [+ATR]

      èrò   'a thought'   rò   'think'

      òkú   'corpse of person'   kú   'die'

      Prefix [–ATR]

      èrɔ   'machine'   rɔ   'fabricate'

      ɔdɛ   'hunter'   dɛ   'hunt'

These two examples of ATR harmony show that a rule can produce alternations whether or not the feature involved in the rule is contrastive. [ATR] is not contrastive in Pulaar but it is contrastive in Yoruba. In both languages the harmony patterns result in alternations. In the next section we see that a similar situation can arise with other features.

4.6   Spanish lenition; Fortition and nasal assimilation in Lumasaaba

In chapter 2, section 2.4, we observed that the stops [b], [d̪], and [g] contrast with each other in Spanish. We also observed that the approximants [β], [ð̪], and [ɣ] contrast with each other. But the stops do not contrast with the approximants. The sounds [b] and [β] form one phoneme in Spanish, which we can call /b/. Likewise, the sounds [d̪] and [ð̪] form one phoneme, /d̪/, and the

---

[9] Their constraint is stated more compactly in terms of autosegmental phonology and underspecification theory, which we discuss in sections 7.1 and 7.3 of chapter 7, respectively.

sounds [g] and [ɣ] form a phoneme /g/. In chapter 2 we noted that these three phonemes illustrate *pattern congruity*. The three voiced stops of Spanish are all converted into the corresponding approximants in the same environment, namely between vowels or glides. We can make more sense of this pattern congruity by appealing to the theory of distinctive features, developed in chapter 3. Expressing the rule in the format of (7) explicitly captures these ideas, as in (19).

(19)   *Lenition (Spanish)*

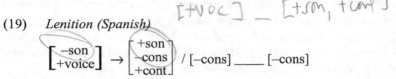

$$\begin{bmatrix} -son \\ +voice \end{bmatrix} \rightarrow \begin{bmatrix} +son \\ -cons \\ +cont \end{bmatrix} / [-cons] \_\_\_\_ [-cons]$$

To make the most sense of this rule, consider the distinctive feature matrix of Spanish consonants, given in (20).

(20)

	p	t̪	k	f	θ	s	x	č	b	d̪	g	β	ð̪	ɣ	r	ɾ	l	m	n	ɲ	w
cons	+	+	+	+	+	+	+	+	+	+	+	−	−	−	+	+	+	+	+	+	−
syll	−	−	−	−	−	−	−	−	−	−	−	−	−	−	−	−	−	−	−	−	−
son	−	−	−	−	−	−	−	−	−	−	−	+	+	+	+	+	+	+	+	+	+
cont	−	−	−	+	+	+	+	−	−	−	−	+	+	+	+	+	−	−	−	−	+
stri	−	−	−	+	−	+	−	+	−	−	−	−	−	−	−	−	−	−	−	−	−
voice	−	−	−	−	−	−	−	−	+	+	+	+	+	+	+	+	+	+	+	+	+
cor	−	+	−	−	+	+	−	+	−	+	−	−	+	−	+	+	+	−	+	−	−
ant	+	+	−	+	+	+	−	−	+	+	−	+	+	−	+	+	+	+	+	−	−
lat	−	−	−	−	−	−	−	−	−	−	−	−	−	−	−	−	+	−	−	−	−
nas	−	−	−	−	−	−	−	−	−	−	−	−	−	−	−	−	−	+	+	+	−
HSP	−	−	−	−	−	−	−	−	−	−	−	−	−	+	−	−	−	−	−	−	−

The feature matrix [−son, +voice] is sufficient to express the class {[b], [d̪], [g]}, since these are the only voiced obstruents in Spanish. The only features that change are [sonorant], [consonantal], and [continuant]. The change consists in making the input segments [+son, −cons, +cont]. The inputs are all [−syll] and this is unchanged; they are all [−strid] and [+voice] and these do not change either, hence these three features are unmentioned in the rule. The context is adequately specified by the matrix [−cons] on each side of the environment bar, indicating that the change takes place if the input segment is both preceded and followed by a vowel or glide. It does not matter that the output segments [β], [ð̪], and [ɣ] are also [−cons], since these segments do not exist in underlying representations; they only exist as a result of this rule.

Consequently they will never be present as conditioning factors in the representations that rule (19) apply to.

Most interestingly, the features [coronal] and [anterior] are also unmentioned in rule (19). The inputs differ in terms of these features for point of articulation, but the point of articulation does not change by the operation of the rule, so these features do not need to be mentioned either, either in the input or in the structural change. In this way the rule correctly expresses the generalization that the voiced stops become the *corresponding* approximants (i.e., at the same point of articulation), which expresses the basic idea behind pattern congruity somewhat more formally.

Like ATR harmony in Pulaar, Lenition in Spanish may result in alternations, even though the segments involved are not contrastive. Consider (21).

(21)	boðeγa	'shop'	la βoðeγa	'the shop'
	daγa	'dagger'	la ðaγa	'the dagger'
	gota	'drop	la γota	'the drop'

Because rule (19) can also apply across word boundaries, at least within close-knit phrases like an article plus noun that are illustrated in (21), the forms in the left column of (21) with initial voiced stops have alternates with initial voiced approximants when the definite article *la* precedes.

Lumasaaba also has alternations involving voiced stops and approximants. Let us consider some forms with labials, as in (22) (Brown 1972).

(22)	cibati	'a knife'	zimbati	'knives'
	kaβua	'a small dog'	zimbua	'dogs'

The forms in (22) are morphologically complex. In the left column, each word consists of a prefix plus a stem. In the right column there are two prefixes preceding the stem. The morpheme for 'knife' appears in a constant phonetic shape, which we can take as its underlying representation: /bati/. In the singular this is preceded by the prefix [ci], whose underlying representation is /ki/ (see exercise 2.16). In the plural, the stem is preceded by two prefixes, phonetically [zi] and [m], whose underlying representations we will return to. The morphological analysis of 'dogs' is like that of knives: two prefixes [zi] and [m] plus the stem. In the singular *kaβua* we have a different prefix from that found in 'a knife': in 'a small dog' it is [ka], which signifies 'small' as well as 'singular.' The morpheme for 'dog' has two phonetic forms: [βua] and [buɑ]. Which of these should we take as its underlying representation? If we choose /buɑ/, we would require a rule like (19) that we proposed for Spanish. But such an analysis does not meet the *criterion of predictability,* because it would predict lenition of /b/ to [β] in *cibati* as well, which would produce the incorrect form **ciβati.* Unlike Spanish, the sounds [b] and [β] contrast in the environment V____V in Lumasaaba. Therefore, let us try the reverse analysis: the underlying representation for 'dog' will be /βuɑ/. This commits us to a rule of the form (23).

(23)   *Postnasal Stopping (Lumasaaba; preliminary)*

$$
\begin{bmatrix} -\text{syll} \\ +\text{son} \\ +\text{cont} \\ +\text{ant} \\ -\text{cor} \end{bmatrix} \rightarrow \begin{bmatrix} +\text{cons} \\ -\text{cont} \\ -\text{son} \end{bmatrix} / \ [+\text{nasal}] \ \underline{\quad}
$$

(i.e., β → b / [+nasal] ____)

This analysis conforms to the criterion of predictability in that it is not contradicted by any of the forms in (22). Now let us consider some additional forms of Lumasaaba in (24).

(24)   ludɑhɑ   'a wing'   zindɑhɑ   'wings'

        luli   'a root'   zindi   'roots'

        luɟeɟele   'a chain'   ziɲɟeɟele   'chains'

        luyoːyo   'a bud'   ziɲɟoːyo   'buds'

        kɑguniyɑ   'a small bag'   ziŋguniyɑ   'bags'

In the plural forms of (24) we see the same prefix [zi] that we had in the plurals of (22). But the prefix that appeared as [m] in (22) appears as [n], [ɲ], and [ŋ] in (24). We can regard these as all being instances of the same underlying prefix, since in each case the point of articulation of this nasal prefix is the same as the following stop: in (22) we have a bilabial nasal [m] before the bilabial stop [b] and in (24) we have the alveolar nasal [n] before the alveolar stop [d], the palatal nasal [ɲ] before the palatal stop [ɟ] and the velar nasal [ŋ] before the velar stop [g]. You probably noticed that the same effect appears in exercise 2.16 of chapter 2, where it appears that [m] and [n] contrast between vowels, and are therefore separate phonemes, but [ɲ] and [ŋ] occur only before homorganic[10] stops. This is clearly a case of assimilation, as discussed in section 2.7.1 of chapter 2. We can write rules for this in features, as in (25), assuming /n/ as the underlying representation of the prefix that appears after /zi/ and before the stem in (22) and (24).

(25)   *Nasal assimilation (Lumasaaba; preliminary)*

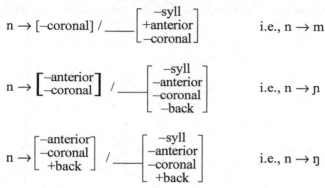

$$n \rightarrow [-\text{coronal}] / \underline{\quad} \begin{bmatrix} -\text{syll} \\ +\text{anterior} \\ -\text{coronal} \end{bmatrix} \qquad \text{i.e., } n \rightarrow m$$

$$n \rightarrow \begin{bmatrix} -\text{anterior} \\ -\text{coronal} \end{bmatrix} / \underline{\quad} \begin{bmatrix} -\text{syll} \\ -\text{anterior} \\ -\text{coronal} \\ -\text{back} \end{bmatrix} \qquad \text{i.e., } n \rightarrow ɲ$$

$$n \rightarrow \begin{bmatrix} -\text{anterior} \\ -\text{coronal} \\ +\text{back} \end{bmatrix} / \underline{\quad} \begin{bmatrix} -\text{syll} \\ -\text{anterior} \\ -\text{coronal} \\ +\text{back} \end{bmatrix} \qquad \text{i.e., } n \rightarrow ŋ$$

In fact, it should be possible to write a single rule for (25), since there is a single generalization involved: a nasal assimilates in point of articulation to a following stop in that it takes on that stop's values for the features [coronal], [anterior], and [back]. The notation for this uses Greek letters α (alpha), β (beta), γ (gamma), δ (delta), ε (epsilon), and so on. Such a Greek letter is interpreted as plus *or* minus, but only one of these in any given application of a rule. That is, if α is plus in one place in a rule on a particular application, it must be interpreted as plus wherever it occurs in that rule on that application. If another Greek letter appears in the same rule, it follows the same conventions, but β is completely independent of α and γ is independent of both. Using this convention, rule (25) is abbreviated as in (26). This notation is further developed in section 4.9.3.

(26)   *Nasal Assimilation (Lumasaaba; revised)*

$$n \rightarrow \begin{bmatrix} α\text{anterior} \\ β\text{coronal} \\ γ\text{back} \end{bmatrix} / \underline{\quad} \begin{bmatrix} -\text{syll} \\ α\text{anterior} \\ β\text{coronal} \\ γ\text{back} \end{bmatrix}$$

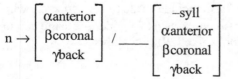

[α place]

---

[10] The term homorganic means having the same point of articulation.

Continuing with the analysis of the Lumasaaba data in (22) and (24), we see in (24) that [d] and [l] contrast between vowels (compare *ludaha* and *luli*), and likewise [ɟ] and [y] (compare *luɟeɟele* and *luyoːyo*).[11] However, these contrasts are neutralized after a nasal, just like the contrast between [β] and [b] observed in (22). This is *pattern congruity* again. We need to generalize rule (23) so that it accounts for (24) as well as (22). To do this, let us construct a feature matrix that shows the contrasts in Lumasaaba consonants, as in (27).

(27)

	p	t	c	k	f	s	z	b	d	ɟ	g	β	l	y	m	n	ɲ	ŋ
cons	+	+	+	+	+	+	+	+	+	+	+	−	+	−	+	+	+	+
syll	−	−	−	−	−	−	−	−	−	−	−	−	−	−	−	−	−	−
son	−	−	−	−	−	−	−	−	−	−	−	+	+	+	+	+	+	+
cont	−	−	−	−	+	+	+	−	−	−	−	+	+	+	−	−	−	−
nas	−	−	−	−	−	−	−	−	−	−	−	−	−	−	+	+	+	+
voice	−	−	−	−	−	−	+	+	+	+	+	+	+	+	+	+	+	+
cor	−	+	−	−	−	+	+	−	+	−	−	−	+	−	−	+	−	−
ant	+	+	−	−	+	+	+	+	+	−	−	+	+	−	+	+	−	−
back	−	−	−	(+)	−	−	−	−	−	−	(+)	−	−	−	−	−	−	+

We can now pick out just the class of segments that our rule will affect: {β, l, y}. These are all and only the segments that are [−syll, +son, +cont] in (27). Therefore, this feature matrix appears on the left of the arrow in (28). The features that change are [consonantal], [continuant], and [sonorant], since the change consists in making these segments into obstruents. The change occurs when these consonants follow a nasal segment. This gives us the rule in (28).

(28)   *Postnasal Stopping (Lumasaaba; revised)*

$$\begin{bmatrix} -\text{syll} \\ +\text{son} \\ +\text{cont} \end{bmatrix} \rightarrow \begin{bmatrix} +\text{cons} \\ -\text{cont} \\ -\text{son} \end{bmatrix} / [+\text{nasal}] \_\_\_\_$$

Notice that (28) is more general than (23), and also simpler, in that the input is expressed in terms of fewer features. In particular, the features for point of articulation (labial) that appeared in (23) have been removed in (28) so that (28) now expresses this process for all points of articulation.

For completeness, we will also include a rule to convert *k* to *c* when it precedes a front vowel (which also converts *g* to *ɟ* under the same conditions, as in exercise 2.15). This rule looks like (29) in features.

---

[11] There does not appear to be a velar continuant that contrasts with [g] in intervocalic position.

(29)   *Velar Fronting (Lumasaaba)*

$$\begin{bmatrix} -son \\ +cont \\ -ant \\ +cor \end{bmatrix} \rightarrow [-back] \; / \; \underline{\hspace{1cm}} \begin{bmatrix} +syll \\ -back \end{bmatrix}$$

$$\left[\begin{array}{c} -son \\ -bk \end{array}\right] = k, g$$

4.7   Steps in phonological analysis

The procedure we followed in analyzing the data of Lumasaaba can be generalized to be applied to developing a phonological analysis of comparable sets of data in any language. We summarize these steps here, bearing in mind that this is not intended as a rigid methodology, but simply as a suggestion as to how to proceed with unfamiliar data.

First step: make a preliminary morphological analysis of the data. Find the common parts of words with similar meaning. You will not always find a morpheme that corresponds to every part of the English gloss. A single morpheme in the language under investigation may correspond to more than one item in the English gloss, or several morphemes may correspond to just one part of the gloss. For example, in Lumasaaba, the prefix *ka-* carries the meanings of 'singular' and 'small,' while the two prefixes *zi-n* are required to express the English meaning of 'plural.' Analyze the language on its own terms. As a further example, consider the forms in (30) from Finnish.

(30)   talo   'house'
        talossa   'in the house'
        taloissa   'in houses'

Here we analyze *talo* as 'house' and *ssa* as 'in.' There is nothing in Finnish that corresponds to the 'the' in the gloss of *talossa*. The suffix *i* means plural in *taloissa*. Notice that this morpheme appears between the morphemes for 'house' and 'in' rather than after both, as in English. In some cases there may be bits that are difficult to assign to a morpheme. Keep the various possibilities in mind until some additional data allows you to decide.

Second step: Determine the morpheme alternants and the phonological relation between them. Construct a phonological feature matrix for the contrasting sounds of the language. Consider some additional Finnish forms in (31).

(31)   isæ   'father'

        isæssæ   'in the father'

From this and the previous data we establish an alternation -*ssa* ~ -*ssæ* 'in.'
These are the same except that the vowel is back in the first and front in the
second. Note that you do not want to try to derive one *word* from another *word*
by means of phonological rules. For example, you are on the wrong track if
your phonological rules derive a plural from a singular (or vice versa). At this
stage, we are assuming that words already contain all their morphemes, in the
correct order, before any phonological rules operate. Phonological rules cannot change the meaning of words, so they don't change singulars to plurals or
vice versa.

Third Step: Set up an underlying representation for each morpheme, and give
the phonological rules necessary to account for the morpheme alternants.
Each morpheme should have just one unique underlying representation. In
Finnish, we might propose the morphemes /talo/ 'house,' /isæ/ 'father,' and
/-ssa/ 'in.' In this case the nonalternating morphemes /talo/ and /isæ/ have
underlying representations identical to their phonetic realizations, while the
morpheme for 'in' has an underlying representation identical to one of its two
phonetic realizations. We then need a phonological rule of Vowel Harmony
that turns the back vowel of -*ssa* to a front vowel [æ] after the front vowel of
a stem such as /isæ/.

   In some cases, the underlying representation of an alternating morpheme
may not correspond to any of its phonetic realizations. In complex cases even
a nonalternating morpheme may have an underlying representation that differs from its phonetic realization. The two main criteria for setting up underlying representations are the predictability criterion and the naturalness of the
rules required.

Fourth Step: Order the rules. So far in our discussion very little ordering has
been required, but this concept will become more important as we proceed. If
in the analysis of a set of data you find two rules A and B, where some of the
forms illustrate the operation of A but not B, while other forms illustrate the
operation of B but not A, there may be some forms which contain potential
inputs to both rules. By trying both orders, A before B and B before A, you
may find that only one order works for all forms; this is therefore the order
required by the data. The rules are *unordered* if there is no form in the data
that requires that the rules have to be tried in some particular order.

Fifth Step: Test the rules. If your underlying representations and rules are all suitable, then you should be able to derive all the correct phonetic forms and no incorrect forms. Any rule you establish must be tested in all contexts in which it is potentially applicable, not just those examples which motivated the rule in the first place. It is always useful to set up a table like the sample derivations in (32, next section) giving the derivation of a representative sample of forms.

4.8   Writing up the analysis

It is convenient to summarize the results of an analysis in a compact form. For the Lumasaaba data just considered in (22) and (24), we could summarize the results as in (32).

(32)   Lumasaaba
        Morphological analysis

singulars consist of one prefix plus stem	plurals consist of two prefixes plus stem
underlying representations of the prefixes: /ki, /kɑ/, /lu/ (only one occurs with any given stem in these data)	underlying representations of the prefixes: /zi+n/ (in these data both always occur, in this order)

Phonological rules

    (29)   *Velar Fronting*

$$\begin{bmatrix} -son \\ -cont \\ -ant \\ -cor \end{bmatrix} \rightarrow [-back] \: / \underline{\hspace{1cm}} \begin{bmatrix} +syll \\ -back \end{bmatrix}$$

    (28)   *Postnasal Stopping*

$$\begin{bmatrix} -syll \\ +son \\ +cont \end{bmatrix} \rightarrow \begin{bmatrix} +cons \\ -cont \\ -son \end{bmatrix} \: / \: [+nasal] \underline{\hspace{1cm}}$$

(26)   *Nasal Assimilation*

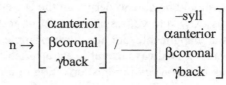

$$n \rightarrow \begin{bmatrix} \alpha anterior \\ \beta coronal \\ \gamma back \end{bmatrix} / \underline{\hspace{1cm}} \begin{bmatrix} -syll \\ \alpha anterior \\ \beta coronal \\ \gamma back \end{bmatrix}$$

Sample derivations

a. /#zi+n+βuɑ#/	b. /#zi+n+li#/	c. /#ki+bɑti#/	Underlying representations
———	———	c	Rule (29)
b	d	———	Rule (28)
m	n	———	Rule (26)
[#zimbuɑ#]	[#zindi#]	[#cibɑti#]	Phonetic representations

The convention followed here for writing up the derivations is to show just the segment (or segments) that changes directly below the input to the rule in the row for each rule. If a given rule does not apply, we have drawn a line ——— in the space under the form for that rule. We show rule (26) as having applied in the derivation of [zindi]; however, it actually does not change the form. This is known as *vacuous* application. In this example the order in which the rules apply does not matter. In chapter 5 we will examine cases where the rules must be ordered. We should emphasize again that the rules developed for this example should be tried for *every* example in the data. That is, given the underlying representation of any word made up of underlying representations of morphemes, taken from the morphological analysis in (32) and combined in a morphologically appropriate way, the application of all the rules developed for the analysis should result in the phonetic form of that word as given in the original data. Of course, not every rule will affect every form. We have given only three sample derivations in the analysis, but you should verify the analysis by trying a few more.

4.9   Further rule writing conventions and abbreviatory devices

In this section we introduce some additional conventions that are used in writing phonological rules.

4.9.1   Curly braces

Curly braces ({}) are used to enclose alternatives that cannot be abbreviated as a natural class using distinctive features. As an example of their use, consider the data in (33) from Polish (Gussmann 1980, Rubach 1984).

(33)

ruf	'ditch'	parta	'party'
vʸatr̥	'wind'	sʸarka	'sulphur'
krfʸi	'bloody'	sʸostra	'sister'
bar	'bar'	gura	'mountain'
kur	'cockerel'	xur	'choir'
kura	'hen'	kr̥tan	'larynx'

The phoneme /r/ has a devoiced allophone [r̥] in two environments: when it is between two voiceless consonants and when it follows a voiceless consonant at the end of a word. This can be expressed by rule (34).

(34)   r-*Devoicing (Polish)*

$$r \rightarrow [-voice] / \begin{bmatrix} -syll \\ -voice \end{bmatrix} \_\_\_ \left\{ \begin{bmatrix} -syll \\ -voice \end{bmatrix} \atop \# \right\}$$

No eff̌x.

4.9.2 Parentheses

Parentheses (()) are used to enclose items that may be present or absent in a rule. Consider the forms in (35) from Karok (Bright 1957).

(35)

Imperative	*1 sg.*	*3 sg.*	*gloss*
pasip	nipasip	ʔupasip	'shoot'
siːtva	nišiːtva	ʔusiːtva	'steal'
ʔikšah	nikšah	ʔuksah	'laugh'

The segment *s* is converted to *š* when the vowel *i* immediately precedes *(nišiːtva)*, or when the vowel *i* precedes with an intervening consonant *(nikšah)*. This is expressed by the rule in (36).

(36)   *Strident Palatalization (Karok)*

$$[+strident] \rightarrow [-anterior] / \begin{bmatrix} +syll \\ -back \end{bmatrix} (C) \_\_\_$$

PIP

The question arises what would happen with a sequence *iss*, that is, where the

intervening consonant is itself *s*. The answer is that both *s* are converted to [š]:
the form /ʔissaha/ is converted to ʔiššaha 'water.' This is known as *conjunctive* application; that is, both parts of the rule apply, here the part with the
parenthesized material (C) and the part without it.

In other cases, rules abbreviated by the parentheses notation apply *dis-
junctively:* only one of the parts of the rule apply in any given derivation. This
occurs most frequently with stress rules. For example, English stress, in the
examples of (37), can be described by the statements in (38), where *ultima*
means 'the last syllable,' *penult* means 'the next-to-last syllable,' and *antepenult* means 'the third syllable from the end.'

(37)   A   B   C   D
       América   balaláika   agénda   capríce
       génesis   muséum   ellípsis   regíme
       alúminum   arthrítis   amálgam   cocaíne
       cínnamon   propósal   galáctin   paróle

(38)   A.   If the ultima has a lax vowel, stess goes on the antepenult if
            the penult has a lax vowel which is followed by no more than
            one consonant
       B.   If the ultima has a lax vowel, stress goes on the penult if the
            penult has a tense vowel
       C.   If the ultima has a lax vowel, stress goes on the penult if the
            penult is followed by two or more consonants
       D.   If the ultima has a tense vowel, it is stressed

This involves much repetition of conditions. It can be made more concise by
otherwise statements, as in (39).

(39)   A′. If the ultima is lax, stress goes on the antepenult if the penult
            is lax and followed by no more than one consonant (=A)
       B′. *Otherwise,* if the ultima is lax, stress goes on the penult
            (combines B, C)
       C′. *Otherwise,* stress goes on the ultima

In formal notation, (39) is expressed as (40), where V̌ abbreviates a lax
([−ATR]) vowel.

(40)   A′   V → [+stress] / _____$C_0(\breve{V}C_0^1)\breve{V}C_0\#$

       B′   V → [+stress] / _____$C_0\breve{V}\ C_0\#$

       C′   V → [+stress] / _____$C_0\#$

The rules of (39) must apply in the order given and must be disjunctive: if any of the rules applies, the others are skipped. Rules A′ and B′ can be combined using the parentheses notation as in (41).

(41)   V → [+stress] / _____ $C_0(\breve{V}C_0^1)\breve{V}C_0\#$

Finally, rule (41) can be combined with C′ to give (42).

(42)   V→ [+stress] / _____ $C_0((\breve{V}C_0^1)\breve{V}C_0)\#$

The simplified rules A′, B′, C′ of (40) (or the combined rule of 42) have an unexpected advantage over the original rules A, B, C, D. Rule (42) automatically accounts for stress on monosyllables like *pig, pen, monk, list, hut,* and two-syllable words like *venom, cabin, syrup, colour, vomit.* With the original rules these would need entirely separate statements.

We have not given any general principles by which we can determine whether rules with parentheses are disjunctive or conjunctive. Stress rules should probably be done in a different way, by building higher level structure (feet) over syllables. We will explore this possibility in section 7.2.2 of chapter 7. With a segmental rule like (36), conjunctive application is expected. It would be most unusual to have a palatalization rule affect only the second *s* in a sequence *iss,* leaving the first *s* unchanged, when an *s* immediately after *i* is affected by the same rule when the segment following is not a possible target of palatalization, giving **?issaha* for 'water' but still *niši:tva* and *nikšah.*

4.9.3   Greek letter variables

In section 4.6 we introduced the use of Greek letter variables in a rule of assimilation in Lumasaaba, rule (26), whereby a nasal takes on the point of articulation of a following obstruent. Let us consider some other examples of the use of this notation. Consider the forms of Pengo in (43) (Burrow 1970; Kenstowicz & Kisseberth 1979, 185, 364).

(43)   *2 sg. imperative*   *3 sg. past*   *gerund*   *gloss*

tuːb-ɑ	tuːp-t-ɑn	tuːb-ǰi	'blow'
tog-ɑ	tok-t-ɑn	tog-ǰi	'step on'
ṛaːk-ɑ	ṛaːk-t-ɑn	ṛaːg-ǰi	'offer worship'
hiːp-ɑ	hiːp-t-ɑn	hiːb-ǰi	'sweep'

Root morphemes may end in voiced or voiceless obstruents, as seen in the 2 sg. imperative forms in the first column of (43). When a suffix beginning with a voiceless consonant is added, as in the 3 sg. past forms of the second column, the root-final consonant appears voiceless. When a suffix beginning with a voiced consonant is added, as in the gerund forms of the third column, the root-final consonant appears voiced. Evidently, assimilation takes place from voiced to voiceless in forms like *tuːp-t-an* and from voiceless to voiced in forms like *hiːb-ǰi*. This can be accounted for by a rule using the Greek letter convention as in (44).

(44)   *Voicing Assimilation (Pengo)*

$$[-son] \rightarrow [\alpha voice] / \underline{\hspace{1cm}} \begin{bmatrix} -son \\ \alpha voice \end{bmatrix}$$

The Greek letter variable notation is also used to express dissimilations. The imperative morpheme *-laʔ* in Huamelultec Chontal (Kenstowicz & Kisseberth 1979, 364; Waterhouse 1949) has an initial voiced *l* after voiceless segments and a voiceless allophone *l̥* after voiced ones. There is also a palatalization process after high vowels, which does not concern us here.

(45) | | | | |
|---|---|---|---|
| koḷɑʔ | 'say it!' | kanḷɑʔ | 'leave it' |
| miiḻʸɑʔ | 'tell him!' | pɑnxlɑʔ | 'sit down!' |
| puḷʸɑʔ | 'dig it!' | fušlʸɑʔ | 'blow it!' |

This can be expressed by the rule in (46).

(46)   *Lateral Dissimilation (Huamelultec Chontal)*
        $l \rightarrow [-\alpha voice] / [\alpha voice] \underline{\hspace{1cm}}$

The minus sign before α reverses its value. Thus $-\alpha$ is interpreted as $-$ when α is $+$ and $-\alpha$ is interpreted as $+$ when α is $-$. Therefore (46) has the desired dissimilatory effect.

The Greek letter does not need to be associated with the same feature in all of its occurrences in the rule. In Chamorro (see exercise 5.4 in chapter 5), [round] is redundant in vowels. This language has the underlying vowel system in (47).

(47)   i   u
       e   o
       æ   ɑ

The feature [round] does not have to be specified in underlying representations in Chamorro. Its value can be predicted by the redundancy rules in (48).

(48)   a. $\begin{bmatrix} +syll \\ +low \end{bmatrix}$ → [–round]

       b. $\begin{bmatrix} +syll \\ -low \\ \alpha back \end{bmatrix}$ → [αround]

That is, by (48a), all [+low] vowels are [–round] and by (48b) nonlow vowels have the same value for [round] as they have for [back]. The back vowels *u* and *o* are [+round] while the front vowels *i* and *e* are [–round].

4.9.4 Angled bracket notation

The angled bracket notation is a variation on parentheses. Two or more sets of angled brackets are used in a rule, with the interpretation that the presence of one of the sets of angled brackets implies the presence of the others, while the absence of one implies the absence of the others. It is used to express a rule like Old High German umlaut (Braune 1975), which has the effect on stem vowels shown in the plural column of (49).

(49)   *sg.*   *pl.*   *gloss*
       wurm   würmi   'worm'
       taːt   tæːti   'deed'
       not   nöti   'need'
       slɑg   slɛgi   'stroke'
       gɑst   gɛsti   'guest'

When followed by *i* over one or more consonants, the stem vowel is fronted. The stem vowel is also raised from low to mid in this environment when it is short, low, and back. This additional condition is expressed in rule (50) by the use of angled brackets.

(50)　*Umlaut (Old High German)*

$$\begin{bmatrix} \left\langle \begin{matrix} +\text{syl} \\ +\text{low} \\ +\text{back} \\ -\text{long} \end{matrix} \right\rangle \end{bmatrix} \rightarrow \begin{bmatrix} -\text{back} \\ \langle -\text{low} \rangle \end{bmatrix} / \underline{\hspace{1cm}} C_1 i$$

English has a rule known as Velar Softening that converts *k* to *s* and *g* to *ǰ* when followed by a nonlow front vowel or glide, in a substantial portion of the vocabulary derived from Latin. This rule is responsible for the alternations observed in (51).

(51)　[k], [g]　　　　　　　[s], [ǰ]

　　　critic, critical　　　criticism, criticize

　　　opaque　　　　　　opacity

　　　analogue　　　　　analogize

　　　regal　　　　　　　regicide

Both velar stops are converted to coronal strident sounds by this rule, but the voiceless one is also converted to an anterior continuant, while the voiced one remains nonanterior and noncontinuant. This is expressed by rule (52), using angled brackets.

(52)　*Velar Softening (English)*

$$\begin{bmatrix} -\text{cor} \\ -\text{ant} \\ -\text{cont} \\ \langle -\text{voiced} \rangle \end{bmatrix} \rightarrow \begin{bmatrix} +\text{coronal} \\ +\text{strident} \\ \left\langle \begin{matrix} +\text{anterior} \\ +\text{continuant} \end{matrix} \right\rangle \end{bmatrix} / \underline{\hspace{1cm}} \begin{bmatrix} -\text{cons} \\ -\text{low} \\ -\text{back} \end{bmatrix}$$

The class of velar stops {k, g} in English is captured by the features [−coronal, −anterior, −continuant]. Both become coronal and strident with no change in voicing. The angle bracket condition is not fulfilled by the voiced stop [g]; converting this to a coronal strident results in the affricate [ǰ]. If it is [−voice], it fulfills the angle bracket condition on the input and the angle bracket requirement on the structural change must also be put into effect, making the output [+anterior, +continuant], i.e., the alveolar fricative [s].

The angled bracket notation can be combined with the Greek letter notation. In section 3.2 of chapter 3 we discussed Turkish Vowel Harmony, with the data in (53), repeated here.

(53)

		nom sg.	*gen.sg.*	*nom.pl.*	*gen.pl.*
1.	'rope'	ip	ipin	ipler	iplerin
2.	'girl'	kɨz	kɨzɨn	kɨzlɑr	kɨzlɑrɨn
3.	'face'	yüz	yüzün	yüzler	yüzlerin
4.	'stamp'	pul	pulun	pullɑr	pullɑrɨn
5.	'hand'	el	elin	eller	ellerin
6.	'stalk'	sɑp	sɑpɨn	sɑplɑr	sɑplɑrɨn
7.	'village'	köy	köyün	köyler	köylerin
8.	'end'	son	sonun	sonlɑr	sonlɑrɨn

The rule of Vowel Harmony in Turkish can be formalized as in (54). As we mentioned in section 4.5 in connection with Vowel Harmony in Pulaar, vowel harmony rules are often iterative, and that is the case in Turkish also. Rule (54) converts any vowel to the same value of [back] as the immediately preceding vowel, expressed by the Greek letter notation as [αback] in both the structural analysis and the structural change of the rule. In addition, the rule affects high vowels further, making them agree in [round] as well as [back] with the immediately preceding vowel. This agreement is expressed by the two occurrences of [βround], and its restriction to [+high] vowels is expressed by placing [+high] in angled brackets in the input to the rule and [βround] in angled brackets in the structural change.

(54)   *Vowel Harmony (Turkish)*

$$\begin{bmatrix} +\text{syll} \\ \langle +\text{high} \rangle \end{bmatrix} \rightarrow \begin{bmatrix} \alpha\text{back} \\ \langle \beta\text{round} \rangle \end{bmatrix} / \begin{bmatrix} +\text{syll} \\ \alpha\text{back} \\ \langle \beta\text{round} \rangle \end{bmatrix} C_0 \underline{\quad} \text{(left to right iterative)}$$

4.9.5 Mirror image rules

We sometimes find that a rule operates in both directions. Such is the case of vowel harmony in Akan, of which we had brief examples in section 3.3 of chapter 3. Consider the forms in (55).

(55)   o-fiti-i   'he pierced it'   ɔ-čɪrɛ-ɪ   'he showed it'
        e-bu-o   'nest'   ɛ-bʊ-ɔ   'stone'

Each form consists of a prefix, a root, and a suffix. ATR harmony affects both prefix and suffix. With our present rule writing conventions we can express this as (56).

(56) $\left[\begin{array}{c}+\text{syll}\\-\text{low}\end{array}\right] \rightarrow [\alpha\text{ATR}] \ / \left\{ \begin{array}{c} \underline{\quad} C_0 \left[\begin{array}{c}+\text{syll}\\\alpha\text{ATR}\end{array}\right] \\ \left[\begin{array}{c}+\text{syll}\\\alpha\text{ATR}\end{array}\right] C_0 \underline{\quad} \end{array}\right\}$

This is unsatisfactory since the environment has to be repeated for suffixes in a mirror image string with respect to the prefix rule. The notation of mirror image rules has been proposed to account for rules of this type, in which the percent sign (%) is substituted for the usual slash (/), which shows that the rule is interpreted as applying to the string as written and also to the mirror image of that string.

(57) *Vowel Harmony (Akan)*

$\left[\begin{array}{c}+\text{syll}\\-\text{low}\end{array}\right] \rightarrow [\alpha\text{ATR}] \ \% \underline{\quad\quad} C_0 \left[\begin{array}{c}+\text{syll}\\\alpha\text{ATR}\end{array}\right]$

4.9.6 Transformational rules

In section 4.4 we restricted the input item in phonological rules to a single feature column. Sometimes it is necessary to write a phonological rule that affects more than one segment simultaneously. This requires a different format, the *transformational* format. It is used to express rules such as metathesis and coalescence. A *metathesis* is a reversal of the linear order of two segments. Lithuanian has a rule that interchanges a fricative followed by a velar stop when a third consonant follows. It shows this effect in certain forms of the verb 'to bind' given in (58) (Kenstowicz 1972, 22).[12]

(58)

	'tear'	*'bind'*	*'toss'*	*suffix*
underlying root	/dreːsk/	/mɛːzg/	/blɔːšk/	
past, 3 singular	dreːskeː	mɛːzgeː	blɔːškeː	/-eː/
imperative plural	dreːkskite	mɛːgskite	blɔːkškite	/-kite/
infinitive	dreːksti	mɛːgsti	blɔːkšti	/-ti/

The rule for this process is given in transformational format in (59).

(59)   *Metathesis (Lithuanian)*

$$\begin{bmatrix} -\text{son} \\ +\text{cont} \\ +\text{cor} \end{bmatrix} \quad \begin{bmatrix} -\text{son} \\ -\text{cont} \\ +\text{back} \end{bmatrix} \quad [-\text{syll}]$$

	1	2	3
$\Rightarrow$	2	1	3

In a transformational rule, each term is given a number in the structural description. The structural change expresses the fate of each term by reference to its number. Conventionally, the double-shafted arrow ($\Rightarrow$) is used instead of a single-shafted arrow ($\rightarrow$) in such rules. In rule (59), the structural change consists of interchanging terms 1 and 2. As an example, the underlying representation /dresk + kite/ is matched to rule (59) as in (60), with the change shown in the line below.

(60)

/...dre	s	k	+	k	ite.../
	1	2		3	

$\Rightarrow$ [dre   k   s   kite]

In a *coalescence,* two (or possibly more) terms are converted to a single

---

[12] The forms for 'bind' also show voicing assimilation in those forms where the suffix begins with a voiceless consonant.

Kenstowicz also notes that the Russian city name [mɑskˈvɑ] 'Moscow' has been borrowed into Lithuanian as [mɑksˈvɑ], evidently having undergone (59), at least historically.

term. For example, a language may have a rule that converts a sequence of two identical vowels into a single long vowel of the same quality. This can be expressed by the transformational rule in (61).

(61)

$$
\begin{matrix}
[+\text{syll}] & & [+\text{syll}] \\
1 & \alpha & 2
\end{matrix} \; \alpha
$$

$$
\Rightarrow \quad \begin{bmatrix} 1 \\ +\text{long} \end{bmatrix} \quad \emptyset \qquad \text{where } 1 = 2
$$

Which √ is ∅!?

This rule operates on a sequence of vowels. Term 1 is replaced by a long version of itself and term 2 is deleted, under the condition that the two vowels are identical in feature composition. This condition is expressed by the statement 1 = 2. (Of course, this condition is not to be interpreted arithmetically!)

The notations discussed in this section will be useful in writing rules in the solution to various problems in this and subsequent chapters.

4.10   Exercises

For each exercise, find the underlying representations for all morphemes and write phonological rules to account for all the alternations you observe. Be sure that your underlying representations conform the the criterion of predictability. Several exercises require more than one rule. Except for exercise 4.7, the rules do not need to be ordered.

1. Morphological analysis
2. Allomorphs
3. Predictability
4. Rules
5. Order rules

4.1 Lac Simon (Kaye 1981)

teːšɨbɨwaːgɨn	'chair'	nɨdeːšɨbɨwaːgɨn	'my chair'
čiːmaːn	'canoe'	oǰiːmaːn	'his canoe'
piːgoška:	'it breaks'	kiːbɨgoška:	'it broke'
šoːškose:	'it slides'	nižoːškose:	'I slide'
kɨn	'bone'	nɨkɨn	'my bone'
šogona:	'nose'	kɨšogona:	'your nose'
towɨk	'ear'	nɨtowɨk	'my ear'
kon	'liver'	okon	'his liver'
kaːt	'leg'	nɨkaːt	'my leg'

Notes: ni- and *nɨ-* are prefixes meaning 'first person singular.' Do not try to account for the difference in the vowel of these two prefixes. The forms glossed with 'it' have no morpheme corresponding to 'it.'

4.2 Maori (Hale 1973, Sanders 1990)
The alternation in the first eight rows is accounted for by a very simple rule if the correct underlying representations are chosen. The last two rows require an additional rule.

Active	Passive	Gerundive	Gloss
awhi	awhitia	awhitaŋa	'embrace'
hopu	hopukia	hopukaŋa	'catch'
mau	mauria	mauraŋa	'carry'
inu	inumia	inumaŋa	'drink'
aru	arumia	arumaŋa	'follow'
tohu	tohuŋia	tohuŋaŋa	'point out'
kimi	kimihia	kimihaŋa	'seek'
wero	werohia	werohaŋa	'stab'
patu	patua	patuŋa	'strike, kill'
kite	kitea	kiteŋa	'see, find'

4.3   German

One rule is required to account for all alternations if the correct underlying representations are chosen.

	nominative	*genitive*	*gloss*
1.	liːt	liːdəs	'song'
2.	kriːk	kriːgəs	'war'
3.	šrɛk	šrɛkəs	'fright'
4.	bɛrk	bɛrgəs	'mountain'
5.	kalk	kalkəs	'lime'
6.	muːs	muːzəs	'jam'
7.	špiːs	špiːsəs	'spear'
8.	alt	altəs	'alto'
9.	muːt	muːtəs	'courage'
10.	man	manəs	'man'
11.	haːr	haːrəs	'hair'
12.	dɔrn	dɔrnəs	'thorn'
13.	talk	talkəs	'talcum'
14.	talk	talgəs	'tallow'

4.4   Russian (Pulkina & Zakhava-Nekrasova 1988)
Note: stress is on the final syllable in the plural of these examples, and on the penultimate (or only) syllable in the singular. You need not write a rule for stress; consider that it is already present for the purpose of this problem. One rule is required to account for the alternation in consonants. Both vowel alternations can be described by a single rule with appropriate use of notational conventions.

[handwritten: -sm → [-vcd] / _#]

[handwritten: o → ʌ]

[handwritten: e → i]

	singular	*plural*	*gloss*
1.	'bok	ba'ka	'side'
2.	'snʸek	snʸi'ga	'snow'
3.	'lʸes	lʸi'sa	'forest'
4.	'glɑs	glɑ'za	'eye'
5.	'gorɑt	gɑrɑ'da	'town'
6.	'ostrɑf	ɑstrɑ'va	'island'
7.	'pogrʸip	pɑgrʸi'ba	'cellar'
8.	'luk	lu'ga	'meadow'
9.	u'čitʸilʸ	učitʸi'lʸɑ	'teacher'

4.5   Palauan (South Pacific; Josephs 1975, Hagège 1986)
Note: stress is on the final syllable of words with suffixes, otherwise it is penultimate. You need not write a rule for stress; consider that it is already present for the purpose of this problem and problem 4.8. One rule accounts for all the vowel alternations with the correct choice of underlying representations.

	Passive verb prefix mə-	*Anticipating State verb (two forms)* *Suffix -all*	*Suffix -l*	*gloss*
1.	mə'silək	sələ'kall	sə'lokl	'wash'
2.	mə'sesəb	səsə'ball	sə'sobl	'burn'
3.	mə'ðaŋəb	ðəŋə'ball	ðə'ŋobl	'cover'
4.	mə'teʔəb	təʔə'ball	tə'ʔibl	'pull out'
5.	mə'ŋatəʔ	ŋətə'ʔall	ŋə'taʔl	'clean'
6.	mə'leʔət	ləʔə'tall	lə'ʔotəl	'tie'

[handwritten: V → ə / unstr.]

4.6   Tibetan numerals (Kjellin 1975)

ǰu	'ten'
ǰig	'one'
ǰugǰig	'eleven'
ši	'four'
ǰubši	'fourteen'
šibǰu	'forty'
gu	'nine'
ǰurgu	'nineteen'
gubǰu	'ninety'
ŋa	'five'
ǰuŋa	'fifteen'
ŋabǰu	'fifty'

[handwritten annotations: bǰu, gǰig, bši, rgu, ŋa]

1. What is the order of morphemes in the Tibetan numeral?
   a. teens (11–19)
   b. tens (40, 50, 90)
2. Give the underlying representation for each of the morphemes. Note that the UR need not be identical to any actually appearing word.
3. Give the phonological rule required to derive all the phonetic forms from the underlying representations of each numeral. Note that only one very simple and natural rule is required. If your rule is complex or if you have more than one rule, you have made an error in your choice of underlying representations.

[handwritten: C → ∅ / # _ C]

*[handwritten: *#CC]*

4.7   Yawelmani (California; Kenstowicz & Kisseberth 1979; Kuroda 1967)

a.   Determine the phonological rule involved in the alternations in vowel length.

	Dubitative	Aorist	gloss
1.	xatal – al	xathin – hin	'eat'
2.	giy'al	giy'hin	'touch'
3.	meːk'al	mek'hin	'swallow'
4.	ṣaːpal	ṣaphin	'burn'

V → [-long] /
_ CC
_ C ·

b.   Determine the phonological rule involved in the alternations in the presence or absence of the vowel.

5.	pa?ṭal	pa?iṭhin	'fight'
6.	?ilkal	?ilikhin	'sing'
7.	lihmal	lihimhin	'run'
8.	?ayyal	?ayiyhin	'pole a boat'

Ø → i / a_CC

c.   Determine the interaction of the two rules developed in parts a and b (the rules must be ordered, as explained in chapter 5).

9.	?amlal	?aːmilhin	'help'
10.	ṣalk'al	ṣaːlik'hin	'wake up'
11.	senṭ'al	seːniṭ'hin	'smell'

Epen. bleeds shortening

4.8   Palauan (South Pacific; Josephs 1975, Hagège 1986)
Note: Recall the remarks on stress in exercise 4.5. You will need the rule developed there for this problem and one additional rule.

	basic noun	'his/her/ its...'	'our...'	gloss
1.	'ʔuɾ	ʔə'ɾal	ʔəɾə'mam	'tongue'
2.	'ðuʔ	ðə'al	ðəʔə'mam	'ability'
3.	'keɾ	kə'ɾil	kəɾə'mam	'question'

(Continued)

V → φ | _V

4.	ʔur	ʔəril	ʔərəˈmam	'laughter'
5.	ˈbuʔ	bəˈʔil	bəʔəˈmam	'spouse'
6.	ˈar	ʔəˈral	ʔərəˈmam	'price'
7.	ˈjar	kəˈul	kərəˈmam	'medicine'
8.	ʔur	ʔəˈrul	ʔərəˈmam	'rib of coconut frond'

4.9   Hungarian (Vago 1980)

One rule is required to account for the consonant alternations in the stems and another for the vowel alternations in the suffixes.

C → [+vcd] / _ [−son, +vcd]

V → [αbk] / [v, αbk] C₀ _

	'in'	'from'	gloss
kɒlɒp	kɒlɒbbɒn̪	kɒlɒpto:l	'hat'
ku:t̪	ku:d̪bɒn̪	ku:tto:l	'well'
ža:k	ža:gbɒn̪	ža:kto:l	'sack'
re:s	re:zben̪	re:stö:l	'part'
lɒka:š	lɒka:žbɒn̪	lɒka:što:l	'apartment'
ke͡tre͡ts	ke͡tred̪zben̪	ke͡tre͡ts͡tö:l	'cage'
vɒra:ž	vɒra:žbɒn̪	vɒra:što:l	'magic'
rɒb	rɒbbɒn̪	rɒpto:l	'prisoner'
ka:d̪	ka:d̪bɒn̪	ka:tto:l	'tub'
mɛlɛg	mɛlɛgben̪	mɛlɛktö:l	'warm'
vi:z	vi:zben̪	vi:stö:l	'water'
a:ɟ	a:ɟbɒn̪	a:cto:l	'bed'

4.10   Spanish

Determine a unique underlying representation for each stem and for each personal form. With the correct underlying representations, two simple rules account for all the alternations.

suffix vowel is suppletive

	'speak'	'eat'	'live'	
1st singular	ablo	komo	biβo	−o
2nd singular	ablas	komes	biβes	−as
3rd singluar	abla	kome	biβe	−e
1st plural	ablamos	komemos	biβimos	< −(e)mos
3rd plural	ablan	komen	biβen	−en

⟨e⟩ i → φ | _ -o, -e

o, e → φ | a − _

abla-
kom- ⟨~ kome -⟩
bibi-

4.11 Old Norse (Gordon 1957, 290)

Five rules are required to account for all the alternations. It may be possible to collapse two of them. No ordering is required.

	'long'	'old'	'middle'	'clear'
singular				
nominative	langr	gamall	miðr	glöggr
genitive	langs	gamals	miðs	glöggs
dative	longum	gomlum	miðyum	glöggum
accusative	langan	gamlan	miðyan	glöggwan
plural				
nominative	langir	gamlir	miðir	glöggwir
genitive	langra	gamalla	miðra	glöggra
dative	longum	gomlum	miðyum	glöggum
accusative	langa	gamla	miðya	glöggwa

[handwritten notes:]

lang
gamal
miðy
glöggw

sg. nom. -r
" gn. -s
" dat. -um
" acc. -an
pl. nom. -ir
" gen. -ra
" dat. -um
" acc. -a

$w, y \rightarrow \emptyset / \_ c$
$y, w \rightarrow \emptyset / \_ i, u$ resp.
$r \rightarrow l / l \_$
$\vartheta \rightarrow a / \_ c, a$
$a \rightarrow \emptyset \ VC\_CV$

[son, +cnt, +cor, +str, (+vcd)]
* [-son, αvcd] [-son, -αvcd] #
∅ → I / [sib] _ [sib] #

        i.e., [sib] [sib] # DNO

5

Rule order

In the last chapter we discussed alternations, with examples from several languages where more than one process could be observed. Although the cases we discussed there did not involve interactions among the various processes, it is very common for processes to interact with each other. This chapter investigates such rule interaction, and in particular the hypothesis that all such rule interaction is explained as sequential rule ordering.

5.1 Russian

In section 4.3 of chapter 4 we established a phonological rule of Russian which we called Final Devoicing, which is responsible for alternations like *xlep~xlebu,* the nominative and dative singular respectively of the word for 'bread.' The underlying representation for the noun stem is /xleb/, and Final Devoicing converts the final voiced obstruent to its voiceless counterpart in word-final position. We will now consider the interaction of this rule with two other rules of Russian. Let us consider the verb forms in (1) and make a morphological analysis.[1]

(1)		*Masculine*	*Feminine*	*Neuter*	*Plural*	
	Infinitive	*past*	*past*	*past*	*past*	*gloss*
	pisat^y	pisal	pisala	pisalo	pisali	'write'
	viset^y	visel	visela	viselo	viseli	'hang'
	govorit^y	govoril	govorila	govorilo	govorili	'speak'
	čitat^y	čital	čitala	čitalo	čitali	'read'
	smotret^y	smotrel	smotrela	smotrelo	smotreli	'look'

---

[1] In the discussion of Russian in this section we ignore certain vowel changes that depend on stress, for the sake of simplicity. Exercise 4.4 in chapter 4 included some of these changes. Based on Kenstowicz & Kisseberth 1979, 55ff.

These verb forms consist of a stem plus one or two suffixes. In the forms of
'write' the constant part is *pisa,* which is the stem. The infinitive consists of
the stem plus the suffix *t*ʸ. The past tense forms all have *l* following the stem,
so we take this to be the past tense suffix. This suffices in the masculine past.
The remaining past tense forms have a second suffix, -*a* for feminine, -*o* for
neuter, and -*i* for plural. Thus the morphological analysis of these verb forms
in Russian is as in (2); note that we do not have any alternations in the data of
(1), so no phonological rules are involved as yet.

(2)   *Masculine* *Feminine*   *Neuter*   *Plural*
          Infinitive *past*   *past*   *past*   *past*
          STEM+tʸ   STEM+l   STEM+l+a   STEM+l+o   STEM+l+i

The stems of the verbs in (1) all end in a vowel. We find alternations when we
examine verbs whose stems end in a consonant, as in (3).

(3)   *1 singular* *Masculine* *Feminine*   *Neuter*   *Plural*
        present   *past*   *past*   *past*   *past*   *gloss*
        peku   pek   pekla   peklo   pekli   'bake'
        seku   sek   sekla   seklo   sekli   'thrash'
        nesu   nes   nesla   neslo   nesli   'carry'
        pasu   pas   pasla   paslo   pasli   'herd'

In (3) we have given the first person singular of the present tense, the suffix
for which is transparently -*u*. Otherwise, we have given the same past-tense
forms as in (1). On the basis of the principle formulated in chapter 4 that a
morpheme has a single underlying representation, we can assume that the
morphological analysis of (2) applies to the forms in (3) equally as to the
forms in (1). The underlying representation of the feminine past of 'bake' is
therefore /pek+l+a/, to which no phonological rules apply. The underlying
representation for the masculine past of 'bake' must be /pek+l/. However, the
past morpheme /l/ is not present phonetically in this form, or in the masculine
past of 'thrash,' 'carry,' or 'herd.' We can assume that this alternation is the
result of a rule of *l*-Deletion, which we formalize in (4).

(4)   l-*Deletion (Russian)*
        l → Ø / C ____ #

Rule (4) deletes *l* when it appears in word-final position after a consonant. It correctly deletes *l* in the masculine past forms of (3) but leaves the other past forms of (3) intact, because in them the *l* is followed by a vowel. It also has no effect on the masculine past forms of (1), because there the *l* is preceded by a vowel in the masculine past, since the verb stems end in a vowel. We can show the operation of rule (4) by giving some sample derivations in (5).

(5)　/#pisɑ+l#/　/#pek+l#/　/#pek+l+ɑ#/　underlying representation

　　　———————　　　Ø　　　　———————　　　*l*-Deletion (4)

　　　[#pisɑl#]　　[#pek#]　　　[#peklɑ#]　　phonetic representation

In *pek*, *l*-Deletion applies since its structural description is met. In *pisal*, *l*-Deletion does not apply, since *l* is preceded by a vowel. In *pekla*, *l* is not followed by a word boundary, so *l*-Deletion fails here also.

　　　Having considered two rules of Russian, Final Devoicing in chapter 4, and *l*-Deletion (4), in contexts where there is no interaction, we now investigate what happens when the rules have a chance to interact. Consider the examples in (6).

(6)

1 singular present	Masculine past	Feminine past	Neuter past	Plural past	gloss
grebu	grep	grebla	greblo	grebli	'row'
skrebu	skrep	skrebla	skreblo	skrebli	'scrape'
lezu	les	lezla	lezlo	lezli	'crawl'
mogu	mok	mogla	moglo	mogli	'be able'
beregu	berek	beregla	bereglo	beregli	'guard'

Where an alternation between a voiced and voiceless obstruent is observed, as in *greb~grep* 'row,' we assume that the underlying representation of the stem contains a voiced obstruent, as we did with alternations like *xlep~xlebu* in chapter 4. The underlying representation of the feminine past of 'row' is then /greb+l+ɑ/, to which no phonological rules apply. The voiced obstruents in this word are not in word-final position, and so are not affected by Final Devoicing. The underlying representation for the masculine past of 'row' must be /greb+l/, by reasoning similar to what we used in taking /pek+l/ as the underlying representation for the masculine past of 'bake.' With this underlying representation it is apparent that *l*-Deletion has applied, since no *l* appears in the phonetic representation *grep*. It would also appear that Final Devoicing has applied, since we have assumed that the stem has the underlying representation /greb/. But Final Devoicing is not applicable to the underlying representation /greb+l/, since *b* is not word final here. It becomes word final only by the application of *l*-Deletion. In other words, *l*-Deletion must precede Final Devoicing. Let us set this out in derivation (7).[2]

(7) /#greb+l#/   underlying representation
        greb   *l*-Deletion
        grep   Final Devoicing
     [#grep#]   phonetic representation

In order for the derivation to work, the rules must apply in this order, with each rule applying to the results of the previous rule. If they were to apply in the reverse order (or simultaneously) an incorrect form would result, as shown in (8).

(8) /#greb+l#/   underlying representation
     ———   Final Devoicing
        greb   *l*-Deletion
     *[#greb#]   phonetic representation

In (8), Final Devoicing cannot apply, because there is no word-final obstruent. When *l*-Deletion applies, it produces such a word-final obstruent, but by then it is too late. With ordered rules we cannot return to an earlier rule once later rules have applied. The derivation ends with an incorrect phonetic representation. We conclude that the order of these two rules must be as in (7). The rule order in (7), in which one rule creates a structure to which a later rule could apply, and where the later rule could not have applied had it not been for the application of the first rule, is known as a *feeding* order. The first rule *feeds* the second rule by creating its structural description, which did not appear in that form before.

The data in (9) introduce an additional alternation in Russian, which requires another rule.

---

[2] In derivations (7) and (8) we set out the entire representation after the application of each rule, for the sake of clarity. Subsequently we will use the usual convention of writing just the items that change by the application of a rule, aligned with the forms above.

(9)

	1 singular present	Masculine past	Feminine past	Neuter past	Plural past	gloss
	meţu	mel	mela	melo	meli	'sweep'
	pleţu	plel	plela	plelo	pleli	'plait'
	breḍu	brel	brela	brelo	breli	'lounge'
	klaḍu	klal	klala	klalo	klali	'place'
	rosţu	ros	rosla	roslo	rosli	'grow'

dental?

The first person singular present forms in (9) show that the verb stems here end in dental stops, *t* or *d*. This stop does not appear in the past tense forms, but the past tense suffix *l* does appear, except in the masculine past of 'grow.' By our previous reasoning, the masculine past of 'sweep' must be /meţ+l/ in underlying representation. The nonappearance of *t* in the phonetic form [mel] must be due to a rule that deletes dental stops before *l*. We formulate this rule in (10).

(10) *Dental Stop Deletion (Russian)*

$$\begin{bmatrix} -son \\ -cont \\ +ant \\ +cor \end{bmatrix} \rightarrow \emptyset \ / \ \underline{\quad} \ l$$

PIP

What is the ordering relation between Dental Stop Deletion (10) and the two rules we developed earlier? If we examine the underlying representation /meţ+l/, we notice that *both l*-Deletion and Dental Stop Deletion *could* apply to it, but in fact only Dental Stop Deletion *does* apply in this case. We can ensure this by ordering Dental Stop Deletion before *l*-Deletion. We illustrate these rules and their ordering in (11).

(11)

/#meţ+l#/	/#meţ+l+a#/	/#rosţ+u#/	/#rosţ+l#/	/rosţ+l+a/	
					underlying representation
Ø	Ø	——	Ø	Ø	Dental Stop Deletion
——	——	——	Ø	——	*l*-Deletion
——	——	——	——	——	Final Devoicing
[#mel#]	[#mela#]	[#rosţu#]	[#ros#]	[#rosla#]	phonetic representation

In the derivations of (7) and (8) we demonstrated that *l*-Deletion must precede Final Devoicing. We have now shown that Dental Stop Deletion must precede *l*-Deletion. Therefore the ordering of the three rules must be that shown in (11). Since Dental Stop Deletion is ordered before *l*-Deletion and *l*-Deletion is ordered before Final Devoicing, Dental Stop Deletion must be ordered before Final Devoicing. This is known as *transitivity* of rule order.

The interaction of Dental Stop Deletion and *l*-Deletion in the derivation of [mel] is such that Dental Stop Deletion makes it impossible for *l*-Deletion to apply. Just by inspecting the underlying representation, we might have expected *l*-Deletion to apply, since the *l* is after a consonant and in word-final position, which are the conditions under which (4) applies. But, because of Dental Stop Deletion, *l* no longer follows a consonant at the time that *l*-Deletion becomes available. This situation, where one rule destroys a configuration that a later rule could otherwise have applied to, is known as a *bleeding* order of rules. Dental Stop Deletion *bleeds* *l*-Deletion in the derivation of [mel]. However, Dental Stop Deletion does not bleed *l*-Deletion in the derivation of [ros], because the form /ros+l/, after Dental Stop Deletion, still has a consonant before *l*, so that both Dental Stop Deletion and *l*-Deletion apply in this derivation. However, the order is the same in both cases. If the order were reversed in the case of [ros], Dental Stop Deletion would not be able to apply, because *l*-Deletion would have eliminated the *l* that is part of the condition for Dental Stop Deletion. This is one of the most striking observations about ordered rules. The order remains the same for all derivations in the language, but the relations of the rules may be different in various derivations. We will see several examples of this observation in this chapter.

5.2   Methodology: discovering rule order

In chapter 4, section 4.7, we discussed the steps to follow in phonological analysis. Step 4 was to order the rules. We can now make this step more explicit. The first thing to do is find examples of alternations that involve only one rule, and use those alternations to formulate that rule, adhering as closely as possible to the criteria of predictability and naturalness. For example, in Russian, we first formulate the Final Devoicing rule on the basis of alternations that involve only this rule, such as *xlep~xlebu*. Do the same with other rules. In Russian, *l*-Deletion is the only rule involved in *pek*. Then investigate representations where more than one rule is potentially applicable. The derivation of *grep* is one such case in Russian, since *l*-Deletion causes the preceding consonant to be word final. We tried both possible orders, and only one order gives correct outputs. In the case of Dental Stop Deletion, it could only be investigated in conjunction with its effect on other rules, since Dental Stop Deletion and *l*-Deletion are both potentially applicable to the same forms. In such cases, the one that is found to apply is ordered first. Continue until a single order of rules is discovered that is correct for all derivations. It may happen that some pairs of rules need not be ordered, as with some of the examples we discussed in chapter 4.

5.3 Formulation of the ordered rule hypothesis

According to Chomsky & Halle, "[t]he hypothesis that rules are ordered…seems to us to be one of the best-supported assumptions of linguistic theory" (1968, 342). This hypothesis can be made explicit by the statements in (12). *SPE* attributes (12a, b) to Bloomfield (1939).

(12) a. It is always possible to order the rules in a sequence and to adhere strictly to this ordering in constructing derivations without any loss of generality as compared to an unordered set of rules or a set ordered on a different principle (*SPE*, 18).

b. Such linear ordering makes it possible to formulate grammatical processes that would otherwise not be expressible with comparable generality (*SPE*, 18).

c. Rules are applied in a linear order, each rule operating on the string as modified by all earlier applicable rules (*SPE*, 341).[3]

The only major modification we will make to (12) is the proposal that some rules apply cyclically (this idea will be discussed in section 7.4 of chapter 7). In this proposal, rules still apply in a linear order, but that order is repeated after the addition of some morphological information. Since this requires discussion of the overall organization of a grammar and the relationship between phonology and morphology and the lexicon, we defer this refinement until then. For now we assume that all morphology precedes the phonology, and that phonological rules apply in a strict linear order, according to (12).

---

[3] A string is defined as any sequence of segments and boundaries that is considered for a derivation.

The proposal that rules are ordered has considerable empirical support, but has not been uncontroversial. Linguists have experimented with a fair number of alternative hypotheses. For example, phonemic theory assumed that all rules apply simultaneously. As we argued in section 2.8 of chapter 2, such a theory is not capable of capturing appropriate generalizations about the language. Consider how our analysis of Russian in section 5.1 would fare under such an assumption. An underlying representation such as /met+l/, as we said, meets the structural description of both Dental Stop Deletion and *l*-Deletion; under simultaneous application, both rules would apply, giving the incorrect output *[me]. To prevent this outcome, we would have to add a condition to *l*-Deletion, such as (13).

(13)   l-*Deletion (Russian; simultaneous version)*
        l → Ø / C _____ #
        unless C is a dental stop

The added condition "unless C is a dental stop" will block *l*-Deletion in /met+l/. But this condition repeats part of the statement of Dental Stop Deletion, since this rule precisely affects dental stops. Not only that, but this move obscures the phonetic motivation for *l*-Deletion. It would seem that *l*-Deletion has the effect of reducing the complexity of clusters, and there is no reason why such reduction should not operate in the context of dental stops.

Similarly, Final Devoicing would have to be reformulated under the hypothesis of simultaneous application of rules. Given the underlying representation /greb+l/, Final Devoicing is inapplicable, since this form has no word-final obstruent. Simultaneous application will thus produce the same incorrect result, *[greb], as the derivation (8) with *l*-Deletion and Final Devoicing in the wrong order. In order for simultaneous order to work, Final Devoicing would have to be revised as in (14).

(14)   *Final Devoicing (Russian; simultaneous version)*
        [−sonorant] → [−voice] / _____ (l) #

That is, in (14) Final Devoicing is complicated by adding an optional *l* between the obstruent that undergoes devoicing and the word boundary. Once again part of another rule has been added to Final Devoicing, in this case *l*-Deletion, just to make simultaneous application possible. Also, this move obscures the motivation of Final Devoicing. Devoicing of obstruents in word-final position is common and appears in many languages, but devoicing before a word-final sonorant would be a rather unusual rule.

In general, as the depth of ordering in an ordered-rule analysis increases, the complications in the statement of the rules required for simultaneous application increases geometrically, requiring endless repetition of conditions of some rules into other rules (cf. *SPE*, 344ff. for an extended discussion of a similar but more complex example). This repetition of conditions not only complicates the rules but obscures their very motivation. Under the hypothesis that the rules apply in a linear order, the rules can be stated much more generally and their motivation appears clearly.

5.4   Iterative rules

As we observed in chapter 4, section 4.5, some phonological rules apply *iteratively*, that is, they apply repeatedly to their own output in a particular direction within a given domain. This mode of application is particularly common with rules of vowel harmony and stress. In section 4.5 of chapter 4 we discussed two examples of vowel harmony involving the feature [ATR], one of which, Pulaar, involved an iterative vowel assimilation rule. We will discuss another, similar example in section 5.6, where we will investigate the interaction of an iterative vowel harmony rule with a number of other rules in Yawelmani. In this section we will mention a few general properties of rules of this type. First of all, an iterative rule must be specifically designated as having this property. A rule will not apply iteratively just because it happens to create possible inputs to itself. For example, in exercise 4.2 of chapter 4 a vowel deletion rule is required to account for alternations in the passive and gerundive suffixes in Maori, as in (15).

(15) | Active | Passive | Gerundive | Gloss |
|--------|---------|-----------|-------|
| awhi | awhitia | awhitaŋa | 'embrace' |
| hopu | hopukia | hopukaŋa | 'catch' |
| patu | patua | patuŋa | 'strike, kill' |
| kite | kitea | kiteŋa | 'see, find' |

The first two examples show that the passive suffix is *-ia* and the gerundive suffix is *-aŋa*. These suffixes appear in these forms when the stem ends in a consonant. This consonant is deleted in the active form, which has no suffix, because no word of Maori ends in a consonant. However, in the last two examples, the passive and gerundive suffixes show loss of their initial vowel after a stem that ends in a vowel. The rule in (16) accounts for this alternation.

(16)   *Vowel Deletion (Maori)*
        $V \rightarrow \emptyset \ / \ V + \underline{\quad\quad}$

[handwritten: Exceptions will appear.]

[handwritten margin: Nature]

A morpheme boundary is required in the rule, because Maori does not simplify vowel clusters within a morpheme, as shown by the passive suffix *-ia* after a consonant. Now consider the derivation of the passive form *kitea* 'see, find' in (17).

(17)   /#kite + ia#/   underlying representation
            $\emptyset$ Rule (16)
     [#kite + a#]   phonetic representation

[handwritten margin: –(V)X]

[handwritten: (V) → ∅ / V—]

The first vowel of the passive suffix is deleted by rule (16). The result of this operation is another form that has a vowel sequence across a morpheme boundary, but this representation is not further simplified, and in fact is the phonetic representation of this word. Because rule (16) is not designated as iterative, it does not reapply to its own output.[4]

If a rule is designated as iterative, the direction of iteration must also be specified. For ATR harmony in Pulaar, we proposed the rule in (18) in chapter 4.

(18) $\begin{bmatrix} +\text{syll} \\ -\text{low} \end{bmatrix} \rightarrow [+\text{ATR}] \ / \ \underline{\quad\quad} \ C_0 \begin{bmatrix} +\text{syll} \\ +\text{ATR} \end{bmatrix}$
      right-to-left iterative

The derivation in (19), repeated from chapter 4, illustrates the iterative application of this rule.

---

[4] Designating rule (16) as right-to-left iterative would also ensure that it applies only once in derivations like (17). With this designation, the rule would first check *a,* which is not in the context for deletion, then check *i,* which is in the context for deletion and so would get deleted. By the convention of iterativity the rule cannot go back and check *a* again, so it would not get deleted.

(19) /#dɔg-ɔː-ru#/ underlying representation

         oː   ATR Harmony (first iteration)

       o   ATR Harmony (second iteration)

    [#dog-oː-ru#] phonetic representation

We can state the principle of iterative rule application in (20).

(20) *Iterative rule application*

To apply a rule designated as right-to-left iterative to a string, S_0, in a domain, determine the rightmost substring of S_0 that meets the structural description of the rule. If no such substring is found, the rule does not apply. If a substring is found, the rule applies to obtain the derived string S_1. Then find the next rightmost substring that meets the structural description, if any, and reapply the rule. Continue in this manner until the left edge of the string is reached and no further substrings can be found that meet the structural description of the rule. To apply a rule designated as left-to-right iterative, apply the procedure starting at the left and moving rightward, until the right edge of the string is reached.

In the case of a vowel harmony rule such as (18), it may seem most natural to apply the rule in the direction that maximizes the possibilities for applying the rule. That is, applying (18) from left to right would allow only a single application, giving the output **dɔg-oː-ru*. In the terminology of section 5.1, the right-to-left directionality of rule (18) is *feeding* or *self-feeding,* since the first iteration of vowel harmony in the derivation (19) sets up a situation for an additional application of the rule that did not exist before the first iteration.

    We can demonstrate that direction of iteration can be the only difference between two instances of the same rule. In Slovak (Kenstowicz & Kisseberth 1979, 319–320) we find that suffix vowels exhibit alternations of length, as in (21).

(21)

1sg.	*3sg.*	*1pl.*	*gloss*
vol-ɑː-m	vol-ɑː	vol-ɑː-me	'call'
čiːt-ɑ-m	čiːt-ɑ	čiːt-ɑ-me	'read'
čes-ɑːv-ɑ-m	čes-ɑːv-ɑ	čes-ɑːv-ɑ-me	'comb'
vol-ɑːv-ɑ-m	vol-ɑːv-ɑ	vol-ɑːv-ɑ-me	'call'

$$V \rightarrow [\text{-long}] \ / \ {}'\bar{V} \ C_1 -$$

čiːt-av-a-m	čiːt-av-a	čiːt-av-a-me	'read'
piːs-av-a-m	piːs-av-a	piːs-av-a-me	'write'

The verb forms in (21) are formed of a verb root plus one to three suffixes. The final suffix indicates the person and number: -m for first person singular, -me for first person plural, and no suffix in the third person singular. Before the suffix for person and number is the vowel, /-aː/ in underlying representation, that indicates the conjugation (other verb classes, not illustrated here, use other vowels in this position). In the third to sixth lines of (21) there is a frequentative suffix, /-aːv/ in underlying representation, between the verb stem and the conjugation vowel. The verb stem /vol/ 'call' has an underlying short vowel, and the conjugation vowel appears long after it, as in the first line of (21). The verb stem /čiːt/ 'read' has an underlying long vowel, and the conjugation vowel is shortened following this stem. The conjugation vowel is systematically short after the frequentative suffix, as in lines three and four of (21); if the verb stem has a long vowel, as in the last two lines of (21), *both* the vowel of the frequentative suffix and the conjugation vowel appear shortened. This allows us to propose the rhythmic rule in (22) for Slovak.

(22)   *Rhythmic Rule (Slovak)*

$$V \rightarrow [\text{-long}] \ / \ \begin{bmatrix} +\text{syll} \\ +\text{long} \end{bmatrix} C_0 \underline{\hspace{1cm}}$$

Iterative: right to left

The Australian language Gidabal (Geytenbeek 1971; Kenstowicz & Kisseberth 1979, 320–321) has a pattern very similar to the Slovak rhythmic rule, in that many suffixes with an underlying long vowel appear with a short vowel when the preceding syllable has a long vowel. Compare the subjunctive suffix, with the underlying representation /-yaː/, which alternates between a long and a short vowel, with the potential suffix /-ye/, which always has a short vowel, in the forms in (23).

(23)

badi-yaː	'should hit'	badi-ye	'may hit'
yagaː-ya	'should fix'	yagaː-ye	'may fix'
gaːda-yaː	'should chase'	gaːda-ye	'may chase'

By the criterion of predictability the rule must be one of shortening; it would be difficult to motivate a lengthening rule that would lengthen vowels in just the right environment and would not affect the suffix /-ye/. As we will see, vowels other than *a* participate in the length alternation.

Other suffixes that alternate in terms of vowel length include intensifiers /-daːŋ/, and /-beː/, and the locational /-yaː/. The initial *y* of locational /-yaː/ becomes a voiced stop homorganic with a preceding nasal. These are illustrated in (24).

(24) a. ɲule-daːŋ   'he (emphatic)'
         nuːn-daŋ   'too hot'
         yuː-daŋ   'much later'

      b. gadi-beː   'right here'
         bugal-beː   'very good'
         buruːr-be   'only two'

      c. baːm-ba   'is halfway'
         gilaː-ya   'that'
         ɟubuɲ-ɟaː   'is night'

      d. babar-aː-daŋ   'straight above'
         /babar-yaː-daːŋ/
         ɟalum-baː-daŋ-beː   'is certainly right on the fish'
         /ɟalum-baː-daːŋ-beː/
         gunuːm-ba-daːŋ-be   'is certainly right on the stump'
         /gunuːm-baː-daːŋ-beː/

In (24a, b, c) we find that these suffixes shorten their vowels when the vowel of the preceding syllable is long; otherwise they appear long. In (24d) we see what happens with two or more of these suffixes in a sequence. With two long-vowelled suffixes after a shortvowel, as in *babar-aː-daŋ*, The second long vowel shortens but not the first. When three long-vowelled syllables appear in succession in underlying representation, as in *ɟalum-baː-daŋ-beː*, only the middle long vowel shortens. With four long-vowelled syllables in a row, as in *gunuːm-ba-daːŋ-be*, we see shortening in the second and fourth, but not in the other two. These facts can be predicted by assuming that Gidabal has a vowel shortening rule much like that of Slovak, but that iterates in the opposite direction, as in (25).

(25)   *Vowel Shortening (Gidabal; GVS)*

$$V \rightarrow [-\text{long}] / \begin{bmatrix} +\text{syll} \\ +\text{long} \end{bmatrix} C_0 \underline{\qquad}$$

Iterative: left to right

The derivation in (26) illustrates the operation of Gidabal Vowel Shortening with an input containing a sequence of long-vowelled syllables.

(26)   /#gunuːm-baː-daːŋ-beː#/   underlying representation

                    ɑ   GVS first iteration

        —————   GVS second iteration

                            e   GVS third iteration

        [#gunuːm-bɑ-dɑːŋ-be#]   phonetic representation

On its first iteration GVS shortens the vowel of the first suffix. The second iteration is blocked, or, more accurately, the vowel of the second suffix is not in a position to be shortened after the first iteration since the preceding syllable does not contain a long vowel. (There is a long vowel before it, to be sure, the *uː* of the second syllable of the stem, but the structural description of GVS in (25) does not allow an intervening vowel, so the rule fails to apply to the vowel of the suffix -*daːŋ.* On the final iteration, the structural description is met once again, and the vowel of the final suffix is shortened at this stage. Gidabal Vowel Shortening thus applies in a *bleeding,* or *self-bleeding* fashion. The first iteration of GVS bleeds the potential application to the long vowel of the second suffix.

The right-to-left application of the Slovak rhythmic law is not bleeding, since no application destroys the possibility of a following iteration. Nor is it feeding in Slovak. Successive applications do not create the possibility of further iterations (as they do in vowel harmony rules, such as 18 in Pulaar). The relationship in Slovak is *counterbleeding:* a relationship that is potentially bleeding (and actually bleeding in Gidabal) but, because of the directionality, not actually bleeding. We will find examples of counterbleeding relations between rules as well, and a fourth relation known as *counterfeeding,* where one rule potentially feeds another but in fact does not because the potentially feeding rule is ordered after the rule it would feed. These concepts are developed further in section 5.7.

5.5   Spanish *r*-sounds

In section 2.3 of chapter 2 we observed that trilled [r] and flapped [ɾ] in Spanish are contrastive within words between vowels, and concluded that they are therefore separate phonemes. However, we also observed that the distribution is somewhat complex, and that no contrast is possible in other positions. This is therefore a case of *overlapping distribution.* The situation in which sounds contrast in some environments but not in others is often indicative of a rule, and frequently figures in alternations, as we observed in chapter 4. We may now observe that a rule may be involved even in the absence of alternations. With respect to Spanish *r*-sounds, we stated that the trilled [r] occurs to the exclusion of the flap [ɾ] in initial position in the word. We therefore do not need to assume that lexical representations distinguish these two sounds in that position. If we assume that only one *r*-sound (or an *r*-sound unspecified for [HSP][5]) appears lexically in this position, we can have the rule in (27) produce the trill in word-initial position.

(27)   *Word-initial Trill (Spanish)*

$$\begin{bmatrix} -syll \\ +cons \\ +son \\ +cont \\ -lat \end{bmatrix} \rightarrow [+HSP] \; / \; \# \underline{\hspace{2em}}$$

Harris (1983, 64) observes that this rule may be involved in alternations, although it is difficult to find convincing examples. The words of (28) are the best he could find, although the synchronic relations of the two columns may be open to question.

---

[5] See section 3.5.2 of chapter 3 for this feature as providing the relevant distinction between the trill and the flap.

(28) [r]   [ɾ]

    rec+titud [rɛkti'tud] 'uprightness e+rec+ción [ɛɾɛk'syon] 'erection'

    rup+tura [rup'tura] 'rupture' e+rup+ción [ɛɾup'syon] 'eruption'

    rub+or [ru'βoɾ] 'blush' e+rub+escente [ɛɾuβesɛnte] 'blushing'

    ro+er [ro'ɛɾ] 'to eat away' e+ro+sión [ɛɾo'syon] 'erosion'

    rud+o ['ruðo] 'stupid' e+rud+ición [ɛɾuði'syon] 'erudition'

A second environment where we find trilled [r] to the exclusion of flap [ɾ] is at the beginning of a syllable inside a word after a consonant. Spanish syllables can begin with any single consonant or with two consonants, but only if the first is an obstruent other than [s] and the second is a liquid. The words in (29) have a trill, not a flap (data from Harris 1983, 63).

(29) hon[r]a   ['onra]   'honour'

    al[r]ededor   [alreðe'ðoɾ]   'about'

    En[r]ique   [ɛn'rike]   (name)

    Is[r]ael   [isra'ɛl]   'Israel'

This can also be attributed to a rule, which we give as (30).[6]

(30) *Syllable-initial Trill (Spanish)*

$$\begin{bmatrix} -\text{syll} \\ +\text{cons} \\ +\text{son} \\ +\text{cont} \\ -\text{lat} \end{bmatrix} \rightarrow [+\text{HSP}] \ / \ [+\text{cons}] \ \$ \ \underline{\hspace{1cm}}$$

Within the same syllable after a consonant, the flap occurs to the exclusion of the trill, as in the examples of (31).

---

[6] We use the symbol $ informally to indicate syllable boundary. See section 7.2.1 of chapter 7 for a more careful discussion of syllable theory. Note that rules (27) and (30) could be collapsed using the brace notation, as in (i); we have left them separate here for ease of exposition.

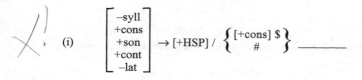

(i) $$\begin{bmatrix} -\text{syll} \\ +\text{cons} \\ +\text{son} \\ +\text{cont} \\ -\text{lat} \end{bmatrix} \rightarrow [+\text{HSP}] \ / \ \begin{Bmatrix} [+\text{cons}] \ \$ \\ \# \end{Bmatrix} \ \underline{\hspace{1cm}}$$

(31) p[ɾ]ado   ['pɾaðo]   'meadow'
      f[ɾ]asco   ['fɾasko]   'flask'
      t[ɾ]apo   ['tɾapo]   'rag'
      d[ɾ]ama   ['dɾama]   'drama'
      c[ɾ]áter   ['kɾatɛɾ]   'crater'
      g[ɾ]ato   ['gɾato]   'pleasing'

The next point to note is that, within a phrase, the sequence [rr] is not distinct from the single segment [r]. Harris (1983, 63) notes the lack of contrast in such phrases as those in (32).

(32) salí rápido   [sa'li'rapiðo]   'I left rapidly'
      salir rápido   [sa'li'rapiðo]   'to leave rapidly'

      gamba rara   ['gamba'raɾa]   'strange shrimp'
      ámbar rara   ['amba'raɾa]   'strange amber'

Harris accounts for this by means of the rule in (33).

(33) *Flap Deletion (Spanish)*
      ɾ → Ø / ____ (#) r

Note that we have been assuming that trill [r] is a single segment. An alternative analysis might be to assume that the trill is actually a geminate [rr] at some level of analysis. It would not be possible to make this assumption of the phonetic level. The trills that appear in word-initial position and at the beginning of a syllable within words, as in (34), would violate well motivated syllable structure constraints in Spanish.

(34) ropa   ['ropa]   *['rropa]   'clothing'
      Enrique   [ɛn'rike]   *[ɛn'rrike]   (name)

This is because [rr] is not a possible syllable onset in Spanish, nor is [nr] a possible syllable-final cluster. Indeed we have proposed that the words in (34) contain a single /r/ in underlying representation, the trill being produced by rules (27) and (30). But what about the contrast between the trill and the flap in word-internal position between vowels? Harris gives a number of examples

of this contrast (already illustrated in section 2.3 of chapter 2), that we repro-
duce in (35).

(35)   torero   [toˈreɾo]   'bullfighter'

        torrero   [toˈreɾo]   'lighthouse keeper'

        caro   [ˈkaɾo]   'expensive'

        carro   [ˈkaro]   'car'

        cero   [ˈθeɾo]   'zero'

        cerro   [ˈθeɾo]   'hill'

Harris proposes that indeed the trill in this position should be analyzed as a
sequence /rr/ in underlying representation. This means that trilled [r] does not
have to figure in underlying representations as distinct from flap [ɾ]. Trilled
[r] is always derived, by rules (27) and (30), contrary to the conclusion in
chapter 2 that this distinction is "phonemic." For example, a word like 'light-
house keeper' is derived as in (36) (compare 'honour').

(36)   /#torrero#/   /#onra#/   underlying representation

        tor$rero   on$ra   rules of syllabification

        torrero   onra   rule (30)

        torero   ———   rule (33)

        [#torero#]   [#onra#]   phonetic representation

Harris points out that there is no reason not to expect underlying representations like (36), which would actually be an unexplained gap if the phonetic
trill [r] had to be analyzed as an underlying trill /r/ distinct from the underlying flap /ɾ/. The flap regularly occurs in syllable-final position before various
consonants in words like (37).

(37)   arpa   [ˈaɾpa]   'harp'

        árbol   [ˈaɾbol]   'tree'

        arte   [ˈaɾte]   'art'

        sarna   [ˈsaɾna]   'scabies'

        Carlos   [ˈkaɾlos]   (name)

| marcha | ['marča] | 'departure' |
| arco | ['arko] | 'bow' |

Furthermore, the flap regularly occurs in syllable-initial position, as in the examples of (35) *torero, caro, cero,* and, according to our analysis, in the examples of (29) and (34), where a rule converts it to a trill. It would be surprising if no underlying forms existed with consecutive flaps, one that can be syllable final and one that can be syllable initial, according to principles of syllabification. The analysis in (36) fills this gap.

Harris notes some other advantages of this analysis. The first concerns the placement of stress. The main stress in Spanish (clitics aside) is on one of the last three syllables of the word. However, stress can appear on the antepenultimate (third from last) syllable only if the penultimate (second from last) syllable ends in a simple vowel (i.e., not a diphthong). Thus, the words in (38a) have antepenultimate stress, but the hypothetical words in (38b), where the penultimate syllable ends in a consonant, cannot be stressed on the antepenult. The examples in (38c) show that antepenultimate stress is possible in words whose penultimate syllable is open before a flap, while (38d) shows that such stress is impossible if a trill appears in this position.

(38) a. teléfono   [tɛ'lɛfono]   'telephone'
          número   ['numɛro]   'number'

      b. *teléfosno [tɛ'lɛfosno]
          *númelro   ['numɛlro]

      c. cámara   ['kamara]   'chamber'
          víbora   ['biβora]   'viper'

      d. *cámarra   ['kamara]
          *víborra   ['biβora]

The distribution in (38c, d) is explained in a way that is exactly parallel to (38a, b) if, at the point where stress is assigned, the trill in intervocalic position is represented as a sequence of two flaps. For, at that point in the derivation, the words in (38d) have the penultimate syllable closed by a flap, preventing antepenultimate stress, exactly as in (38b), where the penultimate syllable is closed by some other consonant.

A second result of this analysis appears in the irregular future tense of the verb *querer* 'to want.' The future tense of regular verbs is formed by adding person-number endings to the infinitive, as in (39a). Certain irregular verbs, such as *poder* 'to be able,' lose the vowel of the infinitive suffix in this construction, as in (39b). That is, the future stem of 'be able' has the suppletive underlying form and /podɾ/ which is not identical to the infinitive /podɛɾ/. (Recall that the approximant [ð] in [po'ðɛɾ] is not underlying but derived by rule 19 of chapter 4.) The same analysis applies to the verb *querer* if we assume the analysis of the intervocalic trill in (36). That is, the future stem of 'want' has the suppletive underlying forms /kɛrr/ which is not the same as the infinitive /kɛrɛɾ/, but which is parallel to 'be able.' Otherwise, we would need to assume that the verb *querer* has an otherwise unattested suppletive form /kɛr/ in the future tense, which is not parallel to 'be able.'[7]

(39)   a.   comer   [ko'mɛɾ]   'to eat'

             como   ['komo]   'I eat'

             comeré   [komɛ're]   'I will eat'

      b.   poder   [po'ðɛɾ]   'to be able'

             puedo   ['pweðo]   'I can'

             podré   [po'dre]   'I will be able'

      c.   querer   [kɛ'rɛɾ]   'to want'

             quiero   ['kyɛɾo]   'I want'

             querré   [kɛ're]   'I will want'

This analysis is clearly possible only if rules can be ordered. In (40) we summarize the underlying representations and ordered rules involved in the analysis of the Spanish *r*-sounds. The syllable structure rules are ordered before the stress rules, though these rules are not given here, as they are quite complex and require appeal to metrical structure developed in section 7.2 of chapter 7. Stress assignment in turn is ordered before rule (v). Rules (iii) and (iv) are also ordered before (v).

---

[7] The diphthongization of the stressed vowel in *puedo* and *quiero* is the result of another rule that is not immediately relevant to the question at hand.

(40)   a.   Underlying segment inventory: one *r*-sound: /ɾ/

    b.   Rules (in order)

        (i)   Syllable structure rules

        (ii)   Stress assignment

        (iii) $\begin{bmatrix} -\text{syll} \\ +\text{cons} \\ +\text{son} \\ +\text{cont} \\ -\text{lat} \end{bmatrix} \rightarrow [+\text{HSP}] \, / \, [+\text{cons}] \, \$ \text{\_\_\_\_}$ (rule 30)

        (iv) $\begin{bmatrix} -\text{syll} \\ +\text{cons} \\ +\text{son} \\ +\text{cont} \\ -\text{lat} \end{bmatrix} \rightarrow [+\text{HSP}] \, / \, \# \text{\_\_\_\_}$ (rule 27)

        (v) $ɾ \rightarrow \emptyset \, / \, \text{\_\_\_\_} \, ɾ$ (rule 33)

In the next section we turn to an example that requires more extensive use of rule ordering.

5.6   Yawelmani

The Yawelmani dialect of Yokuts, an Amerindian language of California (Newman 1944; Kuroda 1967; Kenstowicz & Kisseberth 1979), is of considerable interest in illustrating the principles of analyzing phonological alternations and rule ordering. We therefore offer an extended discussion of the language here, with a miniature grammar of nine rules with many (eleven) crucial ordering relationships. This discussion will serve as a background to some of the discussion of abstractness in phonology in chapter 6.

5.6.1   Vowel Shortening and Epenthesis

In exercise 4.7 of chapter 4 we encountered the data in (41).[8]

---

[8] The feature [ATR] is redundant in Yawelmani vowels, as we showed in section 3.8 of chapter 3. All vowels except *a* are [+ATR]. We will therefore ignore it in this discussion, assuming that it can be specified only after all phonological rules have applied. See section 7.3 of chapter 7 for further discussion.

(41)   *Dubitative*   *Aorist*   *gloss*

   a. 1.   xatɑl   xathin   'eat'

        2.   giy'ɑl   giy'hin   'touch'

        3.   meːk'ɑl   mek'hin   'swallow'

        4.   ṣaːpɑl   ṣaphin   'burn'

   b. 5.   paʔtɑl   paʔiṭhin   'fight'

        6.   ʔilkɑl   ʔilikhin   'sings'

        7.   lihmɑl   lihimhin   'run'

        8.   ʔayyɑl   ʔayiyhin   'pole a boat'

   c. 9.   ʔamlɑl   ʔaːmilhin   'help'

     10.   ṣalk'ɑl   ṣaːlik'hin   'wake up'

     11.   ṣenṭ'ɑl   ṣeːniṭ'hin   'smell'

From the first two lines it is possible to identify the verb stems *xat* 'eat' and *giy'* 'touch.' We also can isolate two suffixes: -*al* 'dubitative' and -*hin* 'aorist.' In the next two lines we see stems whose vowels alternate in length. It is reasonable to propose underlying representations for these verb stems with a long vowel, /meːk'/[9] and /ṣaːp/, along with a rule that shortens a vowel when it is followed by a sequence of two (or more) consonants. We give a slightly more general form of the rule in (42) that also shortens a vowel followed by a single consonant at the end of a word, although this context will not be seen until we discuss echo verbs (54) in section 5.6.2. The general context for this shortening is actually a closed syllable,[10] although we have not formally introduced syllable structure into our model of phonology yet (see section 7.2.1 of chapter 7). These underlying representations and rule (42) conform to the criterion of predictability.

(42)   *Vowel Shortening (Yawelmani)*

$$V \rightarrow [-\text{long}] / \_\_\_ C \begin{Bmatrix} \# \\ C \end{Bmatrix}$$

A conceivable alternative would be to propose underlying short vowels in the alternating cases and a rule to lengthen a vowel in the context ___CV. Such

---

[9] The underlying representation of 'swallow' is actually /miːk'/. See the discussion of echo verbs later in this section.

[10] A closed syllable is one that ends in a consonant. See section 7.2.1 of chapter 7 for fuller development of syllable structure.

an alternative does not conform to the criterion of predictability: it would incorrectly produce lengthening in the dubitative of 'eat' and 'touch,' where there is no long vowel, in addition to lengthening the vowel in this tense of 'swallow' and 'burn.' In other words, length is not predictable in general in the context ____CV, but, since vowels are invariably short in the context of (42), a shortening analysis conforms to the criterion of predictablility.

In lines 5 to 8 of (41) we find verb roots that alternate schematically in the two shapes of (43).

(43)   a.   CVCC   (before -*al*)
         b.   CVC*i*C   (before -*hin*)

If we take (43a) as the basic shape af a root like 'fight,' that is, *pa?t*, we will require an epenthesis rule (44). As with Vowel Shortening, we anticipate slightly by including the environment C____C# for epenthesis, even though this will not be exemplified until we discuss verbal nouns in section 5.6.3; see (66). Epenthesis is also concerned with syllable structure, but cannot be stated in a syllablic environment. In effect, Epenthesis makes syllabification possible, since Yawelmani does not allow more than one consonant in syllable onsets or codas; i.e., no more than two consonants can appear between vowels internal to a word and no more than one consonant can appear at the beginning or at the end of a word.

(44)   *Epenthesis (Yawelmani)*

$$\emptyset \rightarrow i \: / \: C\_\_\_\_C \: \begin{Bmatrix} \# \\ C \end{Bmatrix}$$

The alternative would be to assume (43b) as the underlying shape of roots like 'fight' and to assume a rule of vowel deletion. There are two reasons to reject this alternative. The first is that, when a root shows the alternation of (43), the second vowel is always the same, namely *i*.[11] If deletion were involved, we would expect that any vowel of Yawelmani could appear in this position. In addition, when we discuss echo verbs (55) in section 5.6.2, we will see that verb roots of two syllables have the same vowel quality in both syllables (before the operation of certain phonological processes). If verb roots could

---

[11] The epenthetic vowel sometimes appears as *u*, due to the effects of Vowel Harmony, to be discussed in section 5.6.2. The point still holds, because these roots never exhibit a nonhigh vowel in this position.

have the underlying shape (43b) they would be an exception to this generalization.

The verbs in lines 9–11 of (41) show both alternations. The root for 'help'
has the two forms ʔaml and ʔaːmil. How do we select the underlying representation for this root? As we have seen, e.g., in Russian and Palauan, we cannot always select one of the phonetic forms of a morpheme as the underlying
representation of that morpheme. We apply the reasoning that we used in the
case of each alternation individually. When the vowel of a morpheme alternates in length, we take the long vowel as belonging to the underlying representation, since the appearance of the short version is predictable by Vowel
Shortening (42). When a morpheme alternates between the shapes in (43), we
take the form without the second vowel as underlying, since the appearance
of the second vowel is predictable by Epenthesis (44). Taken together, this
implies that the underlying representation for 'help' is /aːml/, with a long
vowel and without the *i* in the second syllable. The phonetic shapes of this
morpheme are predicted by the two rules already at hand, as long as
Epenthesis (44) is ordered before Vowel Shortening (42). This is shown by the
derivations in (45).

(45)   /#ʔaːml+al#/   /#ʔaːml+hin#/   underlying representation
        ───────   i   Epenthesis (44)
           a   ───────   Vowel Shortening (42)
        [#ʔamlal#]   [#ʔaːmilhin#]   phonetic representation

If Vowel Shortening were ordered before Epenthesis, or if the two rules could
apply simultaneously, the vowel of such roots would always appear short. We
thus establish the order in (45); note that this ordering does not affect the
forms discussed previously, in which only one of these two rules is ever applicable.

5.6.2   Vowel Harmony

We encountered vowel harmony in Turkish and Akan in chapter 3 and in
Pulaar and Yoruba in chapter 4. In general, this is a process that requires
agreement of vowels in a particular feature, generally within the domain of a
word, but the exact conditions vary from one language to another. The data in
(46) illustrate this process in Yawelmani.

(46)

Aorist	Consequential gerundial	Dubitative	Precative	gloss
xathin	xatmi	xatal	xatxa	'eat'
maxhin		maxal		'procure'
bok'hin	bok'mi	bok'ol	bok'xo	'find'
k'oʔhin		k'oʔol		'throw'
xilhin	xilmi	xilal		'tangle'
giy'hin	giy'mi	giy'al	giy'xa	'touch'
dubhun	dubmu	dubal	dubxa	'lead by the hand'
hudhun		hudal		'recognize'

The suffix -*hin* has the alternant -*hun* when the preceding vowel is both high and round, as in *dubhun*. The suffix remains -*hin* following vowels that are nonround, as in *xathin, xilhin,* or nonhigh (even if round), as in *bok'hin.* Other suffixes with this vowel behave similarly. The suffix -*al* has the alternate -*ol* when the preceding vowel is both nonhigh and round, as in *bok'ol.* It remains -*al* if the preceding vowel is nonround, as in *xatal, xilal,* or high (even if round), as in *hudal.* In other words, the harmony is agreement in the feature [round] between vowels that agree in the feature [high]. Like vowel harmony in Turkish and Pulaar, vowel harmony in Yawelmani is iterative, as can be seen from the forms in (47a) with more than one suffix, such as -*sit* 'to, into, for' followed by -*hin* or with disyllabic suffixes, as the reflexive-reciprocal suffix -*iwis* (underlying /-iws/) and the gerundial suffix /-ʔin'ay/ in (47b).

(47)   a.   k'oʔsithin   'throws to'
              maxsithin   'procures for'
              xip'wiysithin   'makes a rubbing motion for'
              t'ulsuthun   'burns for'
       b.   ʔoyowxiwis   'one who feels sorry for himself'
              t'uyuwus   'act of shooting at one another'
              dos-ʔin'ay   'reporting'
              dub-ʔunay   'leading by the hand'

We can state the Vowel Harmony rule for Yawelmani in (48), in formal notation.

(48)   *Vowel Harmony (Yawelmani)*

$$\begin{bmatrix} +syl \\ \alpha high \end{bmatrix} \rightarrow \begin{bmatrix} +round \\ +back \\ -low \end{bmatrix} / \begin{bmatrix} +syl \\ +round \\ \alpha high \end{bmatrix} C_0 \underline{\hspace{2em}}$$

(left-to-right iterative)

Since the epenthetic vowel is *i,* we might expect it to undergo Vowel Harmony when it appears in the environment of a preceding high round vowel. Indeed, as the data in (49) demonstrate, this is the case.

(49)   *aorist*   *dubitative*   *precative*   *gloss*

logiwhin   logwol   logiwxɑ   'pulverize'

t'oyixhin   t'oyxol   'give medicine'

soːnilhin   sonlol   'pack on the back'

hoːtinhin   hotnol   'take the scent'

moːyinhin   moynol   'become tired'

ʔugunhun   ʔugnɑl   'drink'

luk'ulhun   luk'lɑl   'bury'

This implies that Epenthesis (44) is ordered before Vowel Harmony (48). The effects of this ordering can be seen in the derivations of (50).

(50)   a. /#ʔugn+hin#/   b. /#logw+xɑ#/   underlying representation

        i   i   Epenthesis (44)

        u   u   ———   Vowel Harmony (48)

    [#ʔugunhun#]   [#logiwxɑ#]   phonetic representation

The effect of this ordering is that both the epenthetic vowel and the suffix vowel undergo vowel harmony in (50a) while neither undergoes harmony in (50b). The reverse ordering (or simultaneous application) would produce the incorrect forms **ʔuginhun* and **logiwxo.*

The data in (51) at first appear problematic for our analysis of vowel harmony.

(51)

aorist	dubitative	gloss
doshin	doːsol	'report'
ts'omhun	ts'oːmal	'destroy'
wonhin	woːnol	'hide'
ṣoghun	ṣoːgal	'pull out the cork'
soːnilhin	sonlol	'pack on the back'
woːʔuyhun	woʔyal	'fall asleep'
hoːtinhin	hotnol	'take the scent'
doːlulhun	dollal	'climb'

The forms for 'report' are quite normal, assuming an underlying representation /doːs/ for the root. That is, shortening applies as expected in *doshin,* but harmony is not observed because the vowels differ in [high]. On the other hand there is harmony but no shortening in *doːsol,* again exactly as expected. But in the forms for 'destroy,' while shortening applies as expected, harmony is the reverse of what we expect. Why should the suffix have a round vowel in *ts'omhun,* where the vowels differ in [high], while there is no rounding of the suffix in *ts'oːmal,* where the vowels are both [–high]? We cannot simply say that 'destroy' is an exception to vowel harmony. While it unexpectedly fails to condition harmony of a following nonhigh vowel, it equally unexpectedly does condition harmony of a following high vowel. To answer this question, let us review the roots that display alternation in vowel length, given in (52).

(52)

meːk'al	mek'hin	'swallow'
ṣaːpal	ṣaphin	'burn'
doːsol	doshin	'report'

We have observed vowel-length alternation only with the three nonhigh vowels [e, a, o] and not with the high vowels [i, u]. In fact, in the data so far, we have not encountered a single instance of a phonetically long high vowel [iː, uː]. Furthermore, the irregular harmony that we have seen in 'destroy' appears only with roots that show vowel-length alternation. That is, there are no roots with invariant short *o* that take round alternants of high-vowel suffixes *(-hun)* and nonround variants of nonhigh-vowel suffixes *(-al).* As we noted in the discussion of the underlying representation for 'help,' /aːml/, we are not obliged to select one of the phonetic alternants of a morpheme as its underlying representation. The root for 'destroy' in fact behaves as if it had a high vowel at the time vowel harmony is applicable. If we assume that its underlying form has a high vowel, that is /ts'um/, its harmonic properties follow. We can then account for the phonetic nonhigh vowel in this root, and generally for the lack of long high vowels, with a rule of Vowel Lowering (53), ordered after Vowel Harmony.

Absolute neutralization

(53)   *Vowel Lowering (Yawelmani)*

$$\begin{bmatrix} +\text{syl} \\ +\text{long} \end{bmatrix} \rightarrow [-\text{high}]$$

It is also necessary to assume that Vowel Lowering is ordered before Vowel Shortening, since underlying long high vowels are realized as mid phonetically whether they are long or short. The derivations in (54) illustrate the interaction of these rules in some of the forms of (51).

(54)

/#ts'um+hin#/	/#ts'um+al#/	/#wu?y+hin#/	/#wu?y+al#/	underlying
			re	
———	———	i	———	Epenthesis
u	———	u u	———	Vowel Harmony
oː	oː	oː	oː	Vowel Lowering
o	———	———	o	Vowel Shortening
[#ts'omhun#]	[#ts'oːmal#]	[#woː?uyhun#]	[#wo?yal#]	phonetic representations

Although the derivations in (54) illustrate Vowel Lowering only with /uː/, we formulated the rule generally enough to affect /iː/ as well. While we have been tacitly assuming that forms like *meːk'al* 'swallow (dubitative)' have underlying /eː/, the rules so far allow them to be analyzed with underlying /iː/; indeed all phonetic [e] and [eː] can be analyzed as coming from underlying /iː/. Note too that there are no roots with an invariantly short [e]. Some evidence for this position comes from a group of verbs known as 'echo verbs,' some examples of which appear in (55).

i(ː)   u(ː)

a(ː)   o(ː)

(55)

aorist	dubitative	gloss
p'axat'hin	p'axaːt'al	'mourn'
hiwethin	hiweːtal	'walk'
ʔopothin	ʔopoːtol	'arise from bed'
ṣudok'hun	ṣudoːk'al	'remove'
yawalhin	yawaːlal	'follow'
hibeyhin	hibeːyal	'bring water'
yolowhin	yoloːwol	'might assemble'
t'unoyhun	t'unoːyal	'scorch'

of forms

The verbs in (55) are the first we've seen with more than a single syllable. The vowels of the two syllables cannot be selected independently: all verb stems of this form have one of the vowel patterns in (56).

(56) a. CaCaːC
      b. CiCeːC
      c. CoCoːC
      d. CuCoːC

The echo verbs of the form (56d) in fact have the harmonic properties of roots with high round vowels, and can be analyzed as having such a vowel in both syllables in underlying representation, so that 'remove' has the underlying representation /ṣuduːk'/. Likewise, echo verbs of the form (56b) can be analyzed as having the vowel /i/ in both syllables, so that 'walk' is underlyingly /hiwiːt/. This means that echo verbs have identical vowel qualities in their two syllables, with the first short and the second long, in underlying representation. That is, the echo verbs have the forms of (57).

(57) a. CaCaːC
      b. CiCiːC
      c. CoCoːC
      d. CuCuːC

No e?

The sample derivations in (58) should make this clear.

(58)

/#ṣuduːk'+hin#/	/#ṣuduːk'+al#/	/#hiwiːt+hin#/	/#hiwiːt+al#/	underlying representations
———	———	———	———	Epenthesis
u	———	———	———	Vowel Harmony
oː	oː	eː	eː	Vowel Lowering
o	———	e	———	Vowel Shortening
[#ṣudok'hun#]	[#ṣudoːk'al#]	[#hiwethin#]	[#hiweːtal#]	phonetic representations

A second group of echo verbs have the same vowel pattern as those in (55), namely the vowel patterns of (56), underlyingly (57), but differ in not having a final consonant. We give a sample of such forms in (59).

(59)

aorist	dubitative	gloss
panaːhin	panal	'arrive'
ʔileːhin	ʔilel	'fan'
hoyoːhin	hoyol	'name'
t͡sʼuyoːhun	t͡sʼuyol	'urinate'
taxaːhin	taxal	'bring'
nineːhin	ninel	'get quiet'

In (59) the dubitative suffix appears as -l, rather than as -al, as in previous examples. Since the verb roots in (59) are vowel final, we can account for this with a truncation rule, (60).

(60)   *Truncation (Yawelmani)*
        $V \rightarrow \emptyset\ /\ V$____

Truncation must be ordered before Vowel Shortening. Vowel Shortening (42) was formulated to shorten vowels in the context ____C# as well as in the context ____CC. In the derivations of (61), Vowel Shortening occurs in the context ____C#. The derivations in (61) should clarify the situation of the vowel-final echo verbs.

(61)

/#ʔiliː+hin#/	/#ʔiliː+al#/	/#t͡sʼuyuː+hin#/	/#t͡sʼuyuː+al#/	
				underlying representations
———	———	———	———	Epenthesis
———	———	u	———	Vowel Harmony
eː	eː	oː	oː	Vowel Lowering
———	Ø	———	Ø	Truncation
———	e	———	o	Vowel Shortening
[#ʔileːhin#]	[#ʔilel#]	[#t͡sʼuyoːhun#]	[#t͡sʼuyol#]	phonetic representations

We have now discussed five rules of Yawelmani and established their ordering. We summarize the ordering in (62). A curved line between any pair of
rules indicates that the top rule is crucially ordered before the rule that the line
connects to. For example, the curved line connecting Truncation to Vowel
Shortening indicates that Truncation is ordered before Vowel Shortening, but
the order of Truncation with respect to Epenthesis, Vowel Harmony, and
Vowel Lowering has not been established. No curved lines are drawn in these
cases, as these orders are not crucial.

(62)

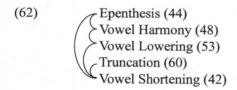

Epenthesis (44)
Vowel Harmony (48)
Vowel Lowering (53)
Truncation (60)
Vowel Shortening (42)

5.6.3   Some additional rules

There are two future suffixes in Yawelmani. Vowel-final echo verbs require
the suffix -ʔ. We give some examples in (63).

(63)   panaʔ   'will arrive'
        ʔiliʔ   'will fan'
        hoyoʔ   'will name'
        t͡sʼuyuʔ   'will urinate'

The final stem vowel is short in the futures of (63), but not, apparently, as a result of Vowel Shortening (42). Since Vowel Shortening is ordered after Vowel Lowering (53), we might expect the second stem vowel of ʔiliʔ and ʦ'uyuʔ to be lowered as well as shortened; however, these vowels remain high. This implies that we need a special rule to shorten vowels before this suffix, ordered before Vowel Lowering. While this rule is of little interest in itself, it does allow the underlying vowel quality of the vowel-final echo verb stem to appear phonetically, thus providing an additional argument for that underlying vowel quality independent of vowel harmony. We can state this rule as in (64).

(64)   *Shortening before word-final ʔ (Yawelmani)*
        $V \rightarrow [-long] / \underline{} ʔ\#$

The second future suffix has alternants *-en, -on,* as shown in the forms in (65). This suffix expresses the future with verbs other than the vowel-final echo verbs.

(65)   bok'en   'will find'
        dubon   'will lead by the hand'
        xɑten   'will eat'
        ɡiy'en   'will touch'
        pɑʔṭen   'will fight'
        lihmen   'will run'
        logwen   'will pulverize'
        ʔugnon   'will drink'
        ṣɑːpen   'will burn'
        doːsen   'will report'
        lɑːnen   'will hear'
        meːk'en   'will swallow'
        woːnen   'will hide (tr.)'
        ʦ'oːmon   'will destroy'

The vowel alternation seen in the future suffix in (65) is unlike any we've encountered to this point. At first sight it would appear to require an additional rule of vowel harmony. However, as we hinted in section 5.6.2, we do not need to assume that the vowel *e,* long or short, appears in underlying representations. The verb 'swallow,' with the alternants *meːk'* and *mek',* can be derived from underlying /miːk'/. For example, the forms *meːk'al* and *mek'hin* are derived as in (66), with the rules developed to this point.

(66)

/#miːk'+al#/	/#miːk'+hin#/	underlying representations
———	———	Shortening before word-final ? (64)
———	———	Epenthesis (44)
———	———	Vowel Harmony (48)
eː	eː	Vowel Lowering (53)
———	———	Truncation (60)
———	e	Vowel Shortening (42)
[#meːk'al#]	[#mek'hin#]	phonetic representations

In the same way, the alternants of the future suffix in (65) can be derived from an underlying representation /-iːn/. This is a rather abstract underlying representation, in that the vowel has two underlying features, [+long, +high], which are not manifest phonetically in any of its alternants. The derivations in (67) show the derivations of the two forms of this suffix.[12] This is the second case in which we see shortening taking place in the context ____C#. (The first was in conjunction with Truncation in 61.)

(67)

/#bok'+iːn#/	/#dub+iːn#/	underlying representations
———	———	Shortening before word-final ? (64)
———	———	Epenthesis (44)
———	uː	Vowel Harmony (48)
eː	oː	Vowel Lowering (53)
———	———	Truncation (60)
e	o	Vowel Shortening (42)
[#bok'en#]	[#dubon#]	phonetic representations

An additional argument for underlying long high vowels comes from certain verbal nouns formed from a verb root with no affix. In this usage the first root

---

[12] For brevity we include only rules relevant to the discussion in this and some subsequent derivations. The reader should verify that applying the complete set of rules (summarized in 76) would give the same result.

vowel is always short, though not by Vowel Shortening. As with the shortened vowels in the future with the suffix -ʔ, these shortened vowels are not also lowered. A sample of such forms is given in (68), along with the underlying representation of each root.

(68)   bok'   'finding'   /bok'/
        ʔuṭ'   'stealing'   /ʔuːṭ'/
        ʔidil   'getting hungry'   /ʔiːdl/
        logiw   'pulverizing'   /logw/
        moyin   'getting tired'   /moːyn/
        ʔutuy   'falling'   /ʔuty/
        wuʔuy   'falling asleep'   /wuːʔy/

Forms like *moyin* and *wuʔuy* undergo Epenthesis; the latter also undergoes Vowel Harmony of the epenthetic vowel. Epenthesis (44) was formulated to apply in the context C____C# as well as in C____CC to allow for this case. Shortening must take place before Epenthesis in (67) and before Lowering. As with the shortening before the future suffix -ʔ, we need a special rule to shorten vowels in verbal nouns, a rule of little interest in itself, except in that it allows the underlying [+high] quality of the vowel of /ʔuːṭ'/ and /ʔiːdl/ to appear phonetically, thereby providing additional justification for this analysis. This special shortening rule, stated in (69), is also ordered before Vowel Lowering.

(69)   *Shortening of vowels in verbal nouns (Yawelmani)*
        V → [–long] / ____C# *in verbal nouns*

Another rule of Yawelmani deletes the final vowel of suffixes of the form -CV when they appear after a vowel-final echo verb root (which happen to be the only vowel-final roots of the language). The examples in (70) are representative, with suffixes -*k'a* 'imperative' and -*mi* 'consequential gerundial.'

(70) ʔilek'   'fan!'   *cf.* giy'k'a   'touch!'

      t͡s'uyok'   'urinate!'   *cf.* dubk'a   'lead by the hand!'

      taxak'   'bring!'   *cf.* xatk'a   'eat!'

      ʔilem   'having fanned' *cf.* giy'mi   'having touched'

      t͡s'uyom   'having urinated' *cf.* dubmu   'having led by the hand'

      taxam   'having brought' *cf.* xatmi   'having eaten'

The required rule is one of Vowel Drop, given in (71).

(71) *Vowel Drop (Yawelmani)*
      V → Ø / V+C____#

Vowel Drop is formulated with a morpheme boundary, indicating that it
applies only when the consonant preceding the vowel to be dropped is morpheme initial. This is shown by the failure of the final vowel of the gerundial
suffix -eːni (underlying /-iːni/) to drop in words like *xateːni* 'in order to eat'
or *ʔaːxeːni* 'in order to stay overnight,' or *ṣalk'eːni* 'waking up.' Vowel Drop
must be ordered before Vowel Shortening in order that Vowel Shortening can
apply in derivations like (72). This is the third instance where Vowel
Shortening takes place in the context ____C#.

(72)	/#taxaː + k'a#/	/#ʔiliː + ka#/	underlying representations
	———	———	Shortening of vowels in verbal nouns
	———	———	Shortening before word-final ʔ
	———	———	Epenthesis
	———	———	Vowel Harmony
		eː	Vowel Lowering
	———	———	Truncation
	Ø	Ø	Vowel Drop (67)
	a	e	Vowel Shortening (41)
	[#taxak'#]	[#ʔilek'#]	phonetic representations

According to the rules for Yawelmani developed to this point we predict that
phonetic long high vowels can never appear. When such vowels occur in
underlying representations they are either lowered or shortened or both. It
turns out, however, that there are phonetic long high vowels from another

source. The reflexive-reciprocal suffix *-iwis* (underlying /-iws/, already met in 47b) is added to a verb root to form a verbal noun, which in the nominative case has no further affix but can take a further suffix *-a* to form the objective case, as seen in (73).

(73)   *nominative*   *objective* (suffix *-a*)
         waǧtṣ-iwis   waǧtṣiːsa   'act of dividing'
         huwṭuwus   huwṭuːsa   'a shell game'

In the nominative we see the effects of Epenthesis and, where appropriate, Vowel Harmony. This is the second instance where Epenthesis takes place in the context C____C#. In the objective Epenthesis is inapplicable, but the sequence of a high vowel followed by *w* and a consonant is collapsed into a long high vowel by a rule of Contraction, formulated in (74) in terms of the transformational format of section 4.9.6 of chapter 4.[13]

(74)   *Contraction (Yawelmani)*

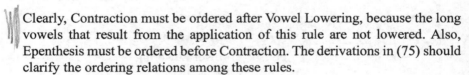

$$\begin{bmatrix} +\text{syl} \\ +\text{high} \end{bmatrix} \quad w \quad C$$

$$\begin{array}{ccc} 1 & 2 & 3 \\ \Rightarrow \quad 1 & \emptyset & 3 \\ [+\text{long}] \end{array}$$

Clearly, Contraction must be ordered after Vowel Lowering, because the long vowels that result from the application of this rule are not lowered. Also, Epenthesis must be ordered before Contraction. The derivations in (75) should clarify the ordering relations among these rules.

---

[13] Kenstowicz & Kisseberth point out that Contraction "must be restricted to the reflexive/reciprocal suffix, since the sequences *-iw-* and *-uw-* occur elsewhere in preconsonantal position" (1979, 99). For example, it must not be allowed to affect the root *huwṭ-*. We allow for the possibility that certain phonological rules are restricted to certain morphemes or certain classes of morphemes.

(75)   /#huwṭ + iws#/   /#huwṭ + iws + a#/   underlying representations

   ———   ———   Shortening of vowels
                                                       in verbal nouns (69)

   ———   ———   Shortening
                                                       before word-final ʔ (64)

         i   ———   Epenthesis (44)

     u u   u   Vowel Harmony (48)

   ———   ———   Vowel Lowering (53)

   ———   ———   Truncation (60)

   ———   ———   Vowel Drop (71)

   ———   ———   Vowel Shortening (42)

   ———   uː   Contraction (74)

[#huwṭuwus#]   [#huwṭuːsa#]   phonetic representations

The final order of all the rules of Yawelmani is given in (76). As in (62), a curved line connects pairs of crucially ordered rules, where the rule at the top end of the line is crucially ordered before the one at the bottom of the same line. For example, the curved line joining Truncation to Vowel Shortening indicates that Truncation is crucially ordered before Vowel Shortening. But not all orderings are crucial. For example, Truncation is not crucially ordered with respect to any rule other than Vowel Shortening. As long as it comes before Vowel Shortening, its position in the list in (76) is essentially arbitrary.

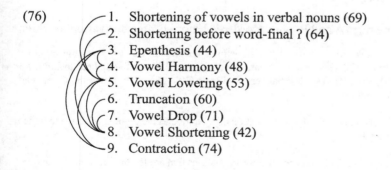

(76)
1. Shortening of vowels in verbal nouns (69)
2. Shortening before word-final ʔ (64)
3. Epenthesis (44)
4. Vowel Harmony (48)
5. Vowel Lowering (53)
6. Truncation (60)
7. Vowel Drop (71)
8. Vowel Shortening (42)
9. Contraction (74)

5.7   Rule ordering relationships

We have already introduced the term *feeding* in reference to certain ordering relations among rules and within certain iterative rules. The purpose of this section is to systematize some of this terminology and to give further examples.

5.7.1   Feeding order

Assume that the grammar of a particular language has two rules, A and B, with A ordered before B. If, in a given derivation, the application of rule A creates a representation to which rule B can apply that was not present before the application of rule A, then rules A and B are in a *feeding* relation, or, equivalently, rule A is said to *feed* rule B.[14] In the derivation (7) from Russian, we said that *l*-Deletion, applying prior to Final Devoicing, is a feeding order, since the output of *l*-Deletion contains a word-final voiced consonant, which can then be devoiced by Final Devoicing. See the illustration of feeding order on page 191.

A number of examples of feeding order occur in our Yawelmani example. In derivations like *ʔugunhun* (50a), Epenthesis feeds Vowel Harmony, since the latter affects the epenthetic vowel. In derivation (72), Vowel Drop feeds Vowel Shortening.

We have also encountered the feeding relation within a single iterative rule in the vowel harmony rules of Turkish and Yawelmani. When a word contains enough vowels of the appropriate type, an iterative harmony rule creates potential structural descriptions for itself with each iteration.

5.7.2   Bleeding order

Again assume rules A and B, with A ordered before B. In a derivation in which

---

[14] An incorrect definition of feeding is sometimes encountered that ignores the relations within individual derivations and treats the concept in a kind of statistical fashion, for example (i), from Koutsoudas, Sanders, and Noll (1974, 2), who define the other relations in this section analogously.

(i)   A FEEDS B if and only if the application of A INCREASES the number of forms to which B can apply.

This definition is unable to account for rule relations that are feeding in some derivations and bleeding in others. It would, apparently, have to count the relevant derivations and declare the relationship to be feeding if there were more derivations in which it was feeding than those in which it was bleeding, an impractical and pointless exercise. This error is repeated in the recent textbook treatment of the subject (Gussenhoven & Jacobs 1998, 98ff).

Cart before the horse illustrates *feeding order*.

Horse before the cart illustrates *counterfeeding order*.

rule A destroys a representation to which B could have applied, we say that A
and B are in a *bleeding* order. In the derivation of *mel* in (11), in Russian,
Dental Stop Deletion bleeds *l*-Deletion. In Yawelmani, the special shortening
rule of shortening before final -ʔ bleeds Vowel Lowering in derivations like
t͡s'uyuʔ 'will urinate,' and the special rule of shortening in verbal nouns bleeds
Vowel Lowering in derivations like ʔuṭ' 'stealing.' See the illustration of
bleeding order on page 193.

It is important to note that terms like feeding and bleeding refer not just to
a pair of rules but to a pair of rules *in a particular derivation* (see footnote 14).
Thus, the order Epenthesis before Vowel Harmony in Yawelmani is feeding in
derivation ʔugunhun (50a), but the same order is bleeding in derivation
logiwxa (50b). The underlying representation /logw+xa/ would be expected to
undergo Vowel Harmony, with the /a/ turning to [o], but, once Epenthesis has
applied, the structural description of Vowel Harmony is no longer met and so
it does not apply. The important thing is that Epenthesis is ordered before
Vowel Harmony as part of the grammar of Yawelmani, but this order might
have different effects in different derivations.

We also encountered bleeding within a single iterative rule in Gidabal
Vowel Shortening. As shown in the derivation in (26), the application of this
rule on any given iteration destroys the possibility of applying it to the next
vowel to the right of the shortened vowel.

5.7.3   Counterfeeding order

We again assume a pair of rules A and B, with A ordered before B. If B cre-
ates a representation to which A could have applied, B is said to *counterfeed*
A and the order is *counterfeeding*. In Yawelmani, the ordering of Vowel
Lowering (53) before Contraction (74) is counterfeeding, since Contraction
creates long high vowels which are the target of Vowel Lowering, but Vowel
Lowering cannot apply because it comes earlier in the ordering. It has missed
its chance, so to speak. Another example in Yawelmani comes from Vowel
Harmony and Vowel Lowering. In the derivation of t͡s'oːmal in (54), Vowel
Lowering produces a sequence of vowels *o...a* with only consonants intervening, to which Vowel Harmony could apply, as it does in *doːsol,* (51), for
example. But Vowel Harmony does not apply because it is earlier in the ordering than Vowel Lowering, and its description is not met at the time it becomes
applicable. See the illustration on page 191.

Locking the barn door while the horse is still inside illustrates *bleeding order*.

Locking the barn door after the horse has run off illustrates *counterbleeding order*.

5.7.4   Counterbleeding order

The final rule ordering relation is known as counterbleeding order. A pair of rules A and B, with A ordered before B, is in a *counterbleeding* relation if B destroys a representation that A applies to, and in fact has already applied. B, ordered after A, has missed its chance to bleed A. For example, in Russian, the derivation of *ros* in (11) shows that Dental Stop Deletion and *l*-Deletion are in a counterbleeding relationship. *L*-Deletion destroys the context for Dental Stop Deletion, but to no avail, as Dental Stop Deletion has already applied, since it is ordered earlier. In Yawelmani, we find that Vowel Harmony and Vowel Lowering are in a counterbleeding relation in the derivation of *ts'omhun* in (54), for example. The root vowel is underlyingly high, so Vowel Harmony can apply to the suffix vowel, which is also high. Once Vowel Lowering has applied the two vowels no longer agree in [high], so Vowel Harmony would be inapplicable, but at the point in the ordering where Vowel Harmony became applicable, its conditions were indeed met and so it applied. Once again we see that these notions are relative to specific derivations, not statistically derived from all derivations in the language. The order Vowel Harmony before Vowel Lowering in Yawelmani is counterfeeding in *ts'oːmal* but counterbleeding in *ts'omhun*. See the illustration on page 193.

5.7.5   Mutually bleeding order

A pair of rules may exhibit a bleeding and a counterbleeding relation in the same derivation. We stated in section 5.7.4 that Dental Stop Deletion and *l*-Deletion in Russian are in a counterbleeding relation in derivations like *ros* in (11). Both these rules actually apply in this derivation. But consider the derivation of *mel* in (11) involving the same two rules. Here Dental Stop Deletion applies, but *l*-Deletion is blocked; in this derivation Dental Stop Deletion bleeds *l*-Deletion by removing the consonant before the *l,* leaving the *l* in a context where it does not get deleted. But, for the same reason as in the derivation of *ros,* the same two rules are in a counterbleeding relation. If *l*-Deletion could apply first, it would bleed Dental Stop Deletion by removing the *l* that forms the context for Dental Stop Deletion. Here is a pair of rules of which, in certain derivations, only one can apply, namely, whichever one is ordered first. This is called a *mutually bleeding* relation. As we saw in the derivations of (11), the applicational order of these rules is the same in each derivation, but the relationships among the rules may be different in different derivations. So we say that Dental Stop Deletion and *l*-Deletion are mutually bleeding (i.e., bleeding and counterbleeding) in the derivation of *mel,* but only counterbleeding (not bleeding) in the derivation of *ros.*

5.7.6 Opacity

Another way of viewing rule ordering relationships is in terms of *opacity.* Kiparsky (1973) defines opacity as in (77).

(77)   …a process P of the form A → B /C____D is *opaque* to the extent that there are phonetic forms in the language having either (i) or (ii).

    (i)   A in the environment C____D

    (iia)   B derived by the process P in the environment other than C____D

    (iib)   B not derived by the process P (i.e., either underlying or derived by another process) in the environment C____D

Another way of stating (77i) is to say that process P is *not surface true.*[15] For example, Vowel Lowering in Yawelmani is not surface true, since there are phonetic occurrences of long high vowels, derived by Contraction, which is ordered after Vowel Lowering. In counterfeeding relations, the counterfed rule is frequently opaque by (77i). In a similar way, Vowel Harmony in Yawelmani is not surface true given phonetic representations such as *ʦ'oːmal.*

Another way of stating (77iia) is to say that the process P is *not surface apparent.* In Russian, Dental Stop Deletion is not surface apparent, given forms like *ros,* where this rule has applied, but where the conditioning element, the *l,* has itself been deleted by a later rule, *l*-Deletion. Counterbleeding relations often result in opacity of this type.

Opacity of type (77iib) is simply any case of *neutralization.* For example, since Russian has underlying /p/, at the end of words like *xoʾlop* 'bondman' as well as [p] derived from /b/ in words like *xlep* 'bread,' also in word-final position, (77iib) regards this as opacity. Neutralization of this type is not normal-

---

[15] *Surface* is another term for phonetic representation.

ly considered to be opaque; however, we include it here for the sake of completeness. Neutralization of another type, known as *absolute neutralization,* in which all instances of some sound are neutralized with some other sound, is opaque, however, but is usually accompanied by opacity of type (77i) or (77iia). An example of absolute neutralization is Yawelmani Vowel Lowering, by which all underlying /uː/ merge with underlying /oː/, regardless of context. We will consider additional cases of absolute neutralization in chapter 6.

5.8   Exercises

5.1   Indonesian (Kwee 1976)

Determine the underlying representation of the prefix and all the stems. Two rules are required to describe the alternations of the prefix and some of the stems. These rules must be ordered.

1.	aǰak	məŋaǰak	'invite'
2.	əmbus	məŋəmbus	'blow'
3.	iris	məŋiris	'slice'
4.	omel	məŋomel	'grumble'
5.	uǰi	məŋuǰi	'examine'
6.	lipat	məlipat	'fold'
7.	rombak	mərombak	'break up'
8.	wakil	məwakil	'represent'
9.	muat	məmuat	'contain'
10.	hapus	məŋhapus	'erase'
11.	bantu	məmbantu	'help'
12.	didik	məndidik	'educate'
13.	goda	məŋgoda	'tease'
14.	pəriksa	məməriksa	'investigate'
15.	tələn	mənələn	'swallow'
16.	karaŋ	məŋaraŋ	'compose'
17.	čoba	məňčoba	'try'
18.	ǰahit	məňǰahit	'sew'

5.2 Polish (Corbridge-Patkaniowska 1964. Thanks to Magdalena Golędzi-
nowska and Anna Boroń for discussion of these data).

Three phonological rules are required to account for these data. The
two that are most important account for the alternation in voicing and
the alternation between *o* and *u*. These two rules must be ordered. A
third rule accounts for the alternation of the plural suffix. (You may
write two rules for this alternation first, then collapse them using the
conventions of section 4.9 of chapter 4.) In accordance with the criterion of predictability, determine the underlying representations of all
the stems and the affix and formulate the required rules.

	singular	plural	gloss
1.	trup	trupɨ	'corpse'
2.	šum	šumɨ	'noise'
3.	žur	žurɨ	'soup'
4.	snop	snopɨ	'sheaf'
5.	kot	kotɨ	'cat'
6.	nos	nosɨ	'nose'
7.	dom	domɨ	'house'
8.	d͡zvon	d͡zvonɨ	'bell'
9.	klup	klubɨ	'club'
10.	trut	trudɨ	'labour'
11.	grus	gruzɨ	'rubble'
12.	bur	borɨ	'forest'
13.	vuw	vowɨ	'ox'
14.	stuw	stowɨ	'table'
15.	žwup	žwobɨ	'crib'
16.	lut	lodɨ	'ice'
17.	vus	vozɨ	'cart'
18.	wuk	wuki	'bow'
19.	sok	soki	'juice'
20.	wuk	wugi	'lye'

(Continued)

[handwritten margin notes:]

(1) $[-son] \rightarrow [-vcd] /$ __ • (with "-nas" written above)

(2) $o \rightarrow u /$ __ $[C, +vcd]\#$

(3) $i \rightarrow i /$ velars __
$e /$ palatals __

(2)–(1) counterbleeding

[vowel diagram: i ɨ u / e o]

21.	ruk	rogi	'horn'
22.	koš	koše	'basket'
23.	nuš	nože	'knife'
24.	sul^y	sol^{y}e	'salt'
25.	buy	boye	'fight'

5.3   Hanunoo (Philippines; Gleason 1955, 30)

Begin by isolating the suffix for 'make it' and proposing a rule to account for the alternation exhibited by this suffix. (Note: two solutions are possible.) Then isolate a prefix for 'times' and formulate a rule to account for the stem alternations in 'one,' 'two,' 'three,' 'four,' and 'six.' (Note: two solutions are possible here also.) Then formulate a rule to account for the additional stem alternation in 'one,' 'four,' and 'six,' using the transformational format (see section 4.9.6 of chapter 4). Finally, order the rules.

1.	?usa	'one'	kas?a	'once'	?usahi	'make it one!'
2.	duwa	'two'	kadwa	'twice'	duwahi	'make it two!'
3.	tulu	'three'	katlu	'three times'	tuluhi	'make it three!'
4.	?upat	'four'	kap?at	'four times'	?upati	'make it four!'
5.	lima	'five'	kalima	'five times'	limahi	'make it five!'
6.	?unum	'six'	kan?um	'six times'	?unumi	'make it six!'
7.	pitu	'seven'	kapitu	'seven times'	pituhi	'make it seven!'

5.4   Chamorro (Guam: Topping 1968).

a. On the basis of these forms, formulate a rule of Vowel Fronting that affects the first vowel of a root. The superior tick marks main stress; particles and affixes carry a secondary stress, marked with the lower tick. Hint: see section 3.3 in chapter 3.

'gwihən	'fish'	ˌi 'gwihən	'the fish'
'gumə?	'house'	ˌi 'gimə?	'the house'
'tuŋu?	'to know'	ˌen 'tiŋu?	'you (pl.) know'

(Continued)

'hulʊʔ	'up'	ˌsæn 'hilʊʔ	'in the direction up'
'petsʊ	'chest'	ˌi 'petsʊ	'the chest'
'tomʊ	'knee'	ˌi 'temʊ	'the knee'
'otdʊt	'ant'	ˌmi 'etdʊt	'lots of ants'
'oksʊʔ	'hill'	ˌgi 'eksʊʔ	'at the hill'
'lahɪ	'male'	ˌi 'læhɪ	'the male'
'lagʊ	'north'	ˌsæn 'lægʊ	'toward north'

b. The next set of data allow for the formulation of a rule of main stress and a rule of vowel reduction. Determine the underlying representation of each root. To formulate vowel reduction using features you may want to give two rules, one affecting [+low] vowels and one affecting [–low] vowels. It is possible to provide a single rule by means of the abbreviatory devices explained in chapter 4. You need not write a rule for secondary stress, which appears on all affixes and particles. Morphologically, the forms in the right column contain the definite particle *i* plus the possessive suffix -*hu* 'my.' The nominals derived from the verbs 'lie' and 'tie' also contain an infix -*in*- that appears immediately after the first consonant of the root.

'dægɪ	'to lie'	ˌi ˌdinə'giˌhu	'my lie'
'godɪ	'to tie'	ˌi ˌginɪ'deˌhu	'my thing tied'
'dagʊ	'yam'	ˌi də'guˌhu	'my yam'
'petsʊ	'chest'	ˌi pɪ'tsoˌhu	'my chest'
'gwihən	'fish'	ˌi gwɪ'hænˌhu	'my fish'
'pigwəʔ	'betel nut'	ˌi pɪ'gwaʔˌhu	'my betel nut'

5.5 Tonkawa (Texas; extinct. Hoijer 1933; 1946; 1949)

Determine the underlying representations of the suffixes associated with the subjects 'I' and 'he' and the progressive and the prefixes associated with the objects 'me' and 'them' and the causative. The third person singular objects 'him' and 'it' have no overt expression; nominal forms (21, 25, and 29) are bare stems without affixes. Determine the underlying representation of all stems and state three phonological rules that determine the alternations of the stems. One of these is an iterative rule.

1.	yakpo?s	'I strike him'
2.	keykapo?	'he strikes me'
3.	weykapo?	'he strikes them'
4.	yakpono?s	'I am striking him'
5.	keykapono?	'he is striking me'
6.	weykapono?	'he is striking them'
7.	yamxo?s	'I paint his face'
8.	keymaxo?	'he paints my face'
9.	weymaxo?	'he paints their faces'
10.	nesyamxo?s	'I cause him to paint his face'
11.	kenesyamxo?	'he causes me to paint my face'
12.	netlo?s	'I lick him'
13.	kentalo?	'he licks me'
14.	wentalo?	'he licks them'
15.	netleno?s	'I am licking him'
16.	kentaleno?	'he is licking me'
17.	wentaleno?	'he is licking them'
18.	notxo?s	'I hoe it'
19.	wentoxo?	'he hoes them'
20.	notxono?	'he is hoeing it'
21.	notox	'a hoe'
22.	pitsno?	'he cuts it'
23.	pitsnano?	'he is cutting it'
24.	weptseno?	'he cuts them'
25.	pitsen	'steer, castrated one'
26.	yawyo?	'he plants it'
27.	yawyeno?	'he is planting it'
28.	weyweyo?	'he plants them'
29.	yawey	'field'

5.6 Lamba (Doke 1938)

Analyze the words into morphemes and determine the underlying representation of each morpheme. The final -*a* of all words is a verbal suffix. Three rules are required to account for the phonetic forms, two of which are crucially ordered. Prove your analysis by giving derivations for *fišika, koseka* and *menena*. Hint: see section 3.3 in chapter 3.

	stem	*passive*	*neuter*	*applied*	*reciprocal*	*gloss*
1.	cita	citwa	citika	citila	citana	'do'
2.	fula	fulwa	fulika	fulila	fulana	'undress'
3.	pata	patwa	patika	patila	patana	'scold'
4.	ceta	cetwa	ceteka	cetela	cetana	'spy'
5.	soŋka	soŋkwa	soŋkeka	soŋkela	soŋkana	'pay tax'
6.	fisa	fiswa	fišika	fišila	fisana	'hide'
7.	lasa	laswa	lašika	lašila	lasana	'wound'
8.	masa	maswa	mašika	mašila	masana	'plaster'
9.	cesa	ceswa	ceseka	cesela	cesana	'cut'
10.	kosa	koswa	koseka	kosela	kosana	'be strong'
11.	šiːka	šiːkwa	šiːčika	šičila	šiːkana	'bury'
12.	βuːka	βuːkwa	βuːčika	βuːčila	βuːkana	'make up'
13.	kaka	kakwa	kačika	kačila	kakana	'tie'
14.	seka	sekwa	sekeka	sekela	sekana	'laugh at'
15.	poka	pokwa	pokeka	pokela	pokana	'take'
16.	ima	imwa	imika	imina	imana	'rise'
17.	tiːna	tiːnwa	tiːnika	tiːnina	tiːnana	'fear'
18.	kaɲa	kaɲwa	kaɲika	kaɲina	kaɲana	'throw down'
19.	ŋaɲa	ŋaɲwa	ŋaɲika	ŋaɲina	ŋaɲana	'snigger'
20.	kuma	kumwa	kumika	kumina	kumana	'touch'
21.	funa	funwa	funika	funina	funana	'draw bow'
22.	foma	fomwa	fomeka	fomena	fomana	'froth'
23.	pema	pemwa	pemeka	pemena	pemana	'breathe'

(Continued)

24.	βona	βonwa	βoneka	βonena	βonana	'see'
25.	mena	menwa	meneka	menena	menana	'grow'
26.	fweɲa	fweɲwa	fweɲeka	fweɲena	fweɲana	'scratch'

5.7 Serbo-Croatian (Ivanić 1926)

The underlying representation of the Active Participle suffix is /l/. In
the masculine, this is converted to [o] by a rule. In the feminine, it is
followed by an additional suffix /a/. Formulate and order the required
rules. Stress and length have been omitted.

	1st person singular present tense	Active participle Masculine	Feminine	gloss
1.	grebem	grebao	grebla	'scratch'
2.	nesem	nesao	nesla	'carry'
3.	pečem	pekao	pekla	'bake'
4.	pletem	pleo	plela	'braid'
5.	kradem	krao	krala	'steal'
6.	pasem	pasao	pasla	'graze'
7.	pišem	pisao	pisala	'write'
8.	rastem	rastao	rasla	'grow'

5.8 Karok (Bright 1957)

Some of these data were introduced in section 4.9.2 to illustrate the
parentheses convention. Formulate two additional rules to account for
the ʔ~Ø alternation and the V~Ø alternations and order all three rules.

Imperative	1 singular	3 singular	gloss	
pasip	nipasip	ʔupasip	'shoot'	
siːtva	nišiːtva	ʔusiːtva	'steal'	
kifnuk	nikifnuk	ʔukifnuk	'stoop'	
suprih	nišuprih	ʔusuprih	'measure'	
ʔifik	niʔifik	ʔuʔifik	'pick up'	
ʔaktuv	niʔaktuv	ʔuʔaktuv	'pluck at'	*(Continued)*

ʔaxyɑr	nixyɑr	ʔuxyɑr	'fill'
ʔimniš	nimniš	ʔumniš	'cook'
ʔiškɑk	niškɑk	ʔuskɑk	'jump'
ʔikšɑh	nikšɑh	ʔuksɑh	'laugh'
ʔišriv	nišriv	ʔusriv	'shoot at a target'
ʔuksup	nikšup	ʔuksup	'point'

5.9   Basque (Biscay; de Rijk 1970; Hualde 1991)

Five rules are required to account for all alternations illustrated. Four of these must be crucially ordered.

	one	*the*	*gloss*
1.	sagɑr bat	sagɑrɑ	'apple'
2.	alaba bat	alabea	'daughter'
3.	neska	neskea	'girl'
4.	gisom bat	gisona	'man'
5.	mutil bet	mutile	'boy'
6.	egum bet	egune	'day'
7.	seme bat	semia	'son'
8.	eče bat	ečia	'house'
9.	asto bat	astua	'donkey'
10.	eri bet	eriye	'village'
11.	mendi bat	mendiye	'mountain'
12.	buru bet	buruwe	'head'
13.	esku bet	eskuwe	'hand'

Some speakers have the following alternative definite forms:

alabie	'the daughter'
semie	'the son'
astue	'the donkey'

How can you account for these alternative forms without any additional rules?

5.10   Japanese (Vance 1987, Lange 1971)

Give the underlying representations of all stems and suffixes. Detetrmine the rules required to derive the phonetic representations (eleven rules in all) and establish the order of the rules. Characterize the orderings as feeding, bleeding, counterfeeding, or counterbleeding.

	present	*past*	*negative*	*desiderative*	*gloss*
1.	miɾu	mita	minai	mitai	'look at'
2.	kiɾu	kita	kinai	kitai	'wear'
3.	taberu	tabeta	tabenai	tabetai	'eat'
4.	kaeɾu	kaeta	kaenai	kaetai	'change'
5.	kau	katta	kawanai	kaitai	'buy'
6.	iu	itta	iwanai	iitai	'say, tell'
7.	kaku	kaita	kakanai	kakitai	'write'
8.	hiku	hiita	hikanai	hikitai	'pull'
9.	kagu	kaida	kaganai	kagitai	'sniff'
10.	isogu	isoida	isoganai	isogitai	'hurry'
11.	kasu	kašita	kasanai	kašitai	'lend'
12.	hanasu	hanašita	hanasanai	hanašitai	'speak'
13.	kat͡su	katta	katanai	kačitai	'win'
14.	ut͡su	utta	utanai	učitai	'hit'
15.	šinu	šinda	šinanai	šinitai	'die'
16.	yobu	yonda	yobanai	yobitai	'call'
17.	tobu	tonda	tobanai	tobitai	'jump'
18.	yomu	yonda	yomanai	yomitai	'read'
19.	sumu	sunda	sumanai	sumitai	'reside'
20.	yoɾu	yotta	yoɾanai	yoɾitai	'approach'
21.	kiɾu	kitta	kiɾanai	kiɾitai	'cut'

5. 11   Latin (Lane 1903)

Determine the underlying representations of the roots and the affixes
for nominative singular and genitive singular. Determine the rules and
their order (ten rules in all). Characterize the orderings as feeding,
bleeding, counterfeeding, or counterbleeding. Provide complete derivations for 'weːr, 'noks, 'merkeːs, 'os, 'ossis, 'ass, 'floːs, 'floːris, 'leoː.

	Nominative sg.	Genitive sg.	Gloss
1.	'paːks	'paːkis	'peace'
2.	'duks	'dukis	'leader'
3.	'seːps	'seːpis	'snake'
4.	'daps	'dapis	'feast'
5.	'marmor	'marmoris	'marble'
6.	'weːr	'weːris	'spring'
7.	'wigil	'wigilis	'watchman'
8.	'saːl	'saːlis	'salt'
9.	'reːks	'reːgis	'king'
10.	'striːks	'striːgis	'screech-owl'
11.	'urps	'urbis	'city'
12.	'pleːps	'pleːbis	'people'
13.	'traps	'trabis	'beam'
14.	'aytaːs	ay'taːtis	'age'
15.	'laws	'lawdis	'praise'
16.	'froːns	'frontis	'brow'
17.	'deːns	'dentis	'tooth'
18.	'ars	'artis	'art'
19.	'noks	'noktis	'night'
20.	'froːns	'frondis	'leaf'
21.	'nepoːs	ne'poːtis	'grandson'
22.	'iŋkuːs	iŋ'kuːdis	'anvil'
23.	'kaliks	'kalikis	'cup'

(Continued)

24.	'radiːks	ra'diːkis	'root'
25.	'merkeːs	mer'keːdis	'reward'
26.	'forkeps	'forkipis	'pincers'
27.	'polleks	'pollikis	'thumb'
28.	'ekwes	'ekwitis	'horseman'
29.	'lapis	'lapidis	'stone'
30.	'opses	'opsidis	'hostage'
31.	'noːmen	'noːminis	'name'
32.	'mel	'mellis	'honey'
33.	'os	'ossis	'bone'
34.	'as	'assis	'whole'
35.	'floːs	'floːris	'flower'
36.	'yuːs	'yuːris	'right'
37.	'leoː	le'oːnis	'lion'
38.	'praydoː	pray'doːnis	'robber'
39.	o'piːnioː	opiːni'oːnis	'notion'

6   Abstractness

6.1   Phonetic representations

As we pointed out in chapter 1, a phonetic representation is a somewhat abstract record of a speech event. A phonetic transcription cannot record every detail of a speech act, but it must record the linguistically significant aspects of that act. As *SPE* (Chomsky & Halle 1968) notes, "even the most skillful transcriber is unable to note certain aspects of the signal, while commonly recording in his transcription items for which there seems to be no direct warrant in the physical record" (1968, 293). They emphasize that phonetic transcription should not be understood "as a direct record of the speech signal, but rather as a representation of what the speaker of a language takes to be the phonetic properties of an utterance..." (p. 294). Any discussion of the abstractness of phonological underlying representations must keep this abstractness of the phonetic representation in mind.

6.2   The null hypothesis

Kenstowicz & Kisseberth (1979, 26ff) use the term *null hypothesis* to refer to the claim that a speaker simply memorizes the phonetic representation of every word he or she encounters and slots that pronunciation into appropriate syntactic slots in producing sentences. They then go on to show that the null hypothesis cannot be correct, and that in fact the aspects of pronunciation that must be memorized by a speaker are more abstract than the phonetic representation. They distinguish between the concepts *list* and *rule,* which we introduced in section 2.9 of chapter 2. The *list* includes all aspects of a lexical item that must be memorized, that is, that are in no way predictable. A *rule* describes the predictable elements of the pronunciation of many lexical items in the different contexts in which they can appear. It is possible to significantly reduce the amount of information that is necessary for a speaker to memorize by expressing predictable information in rules rather than in the list of lexical items.

Any language can be used to produce an infinite number of utterances. These utterances pair a phonetic representation with a meaning. The language produces this infinitude of utterances with finite means, which includes a grammar and a lexicon. The lexicon minimally includes a list of morphemes.[1] Each morpheme in this list must include the minimal amount of information necessary for a speaker to use the morpheme correctly—information about its pronunciation, syntactic properties, and its meaning. For example, the morpheme for 'cat' in English might be represented as in (1).

(1)
$$\begin{bmatrix} \text{/kæt/} \\ [+N, -V, -abstract, +count] \\ \textit{Felis domesticus} \end{bmatrix}$$
Phonological form
Syntactic features
Semantics

Under the heading of phonological form we have given the phonological underlying representation, where the phonetic symbols are understood to represent distinctive feature complexes (chapter 3). The actual phonetic representation might be somewhat different. In (2) we give two sentences using the word *cat* and the phonetic representation that might be associated with each occurrence of this word, in a North American pronunciation. (The symbol [t'] is to be understood as a glottalized [t] rather than as an ejective here.)

(2)   a. I saw the cat.   [kʰæt'], [kʰæʔ]
       b. The cat is on the mat.   [kʰær]

In each case in (2), the initial velar stop is pronounced with aspiration. This aspiration is not an idiosyncratic aspect of the pronunciation of this morpheme, but a predictable part of the pronunciation of voiceless stops in English when they stand at the beginning of a word or at the beginning of a stressed syllable. Therefore this information can be omitted from the lexical representation, since it is predictable by a rule. The morpheme-final stop has (at least) two different pronunciations. In (2a) the stop has a glottalized realization, while in (2b) it is pronounced as a flap (see the discussion in chapter 2, section 2.4). The null hypothesis would require listing both pronunciations

---

[1] In section 7.4 of chapter 7 we will consider a more fully articulated approach to the lexicon.

in (2), as though these were idiosyncratic aspects of this morpheme. What *is* idiosyncratic about the final segment of this morpheme is that it is an alveolar segment, and basically a voiceless stop, but its phonetic realizations as [t], [t'], [tʰ], [ɾ], or [ʔ] are governed by rules, as discussed in chapter 2. We therefore remove these aspects of the pronunciation of this morpheme from its listing in (1), restricting the list to contain only the unpredictable, idiosyncratic aspects of each morpheme.

6.3   Two levels of representation

Typically, a morpheme in any language will have more than one phonetic realization. Besides the example of *cat* in the last section we have seen numerous examples of this phenomenon in previous chapters. The basic claim of generative phonology is that, except for cases of suppletion, only one phonological form of each morpheme needs to be listed in lexical entries. We refer to the phonological aspect of this listing as the *underlying representation* of the morpheme. A particular phonological underlying representation is associated in its lexical representation with syntactic and semantic information, since this association is essentially arbitrary. Except for a very small number of onomatopoetic items there is no natural association between a phonological representation and its meaning. For example, the phonological representation /bɛt/ in English is associated with the meaning 'wager,' in French with the meaning 'animal,' and in German with the meaning 'bed.' Conversely, French associates the meaning 'wager' with the phonological representation /pæri/ and German associates this meaning with the phonological representation /vɛtə/. Hence, for completeness every lexical representation contains an association of phonological, syntactic, and semantic information, as in (1). For brevity, we usually give only the underlying phonological representation, in slant brackets (e.g., /kæt/) along with an indication of its meaning in single quotes (in this case, 'cat'). Morphemes are combined to form words in accordance with the principles of morphology, and words are combined into sentences by the principles of syntax. The first step in phonological analysis, as detailed in section 4.7 of chapter 4, is to make a preliminary morphological analysis of the data. When faced with words made up of several morphemes, we seek the most general way of accounting for the phonetic shape of those morphemes. For example, the regular plural suffix in English has three phonetic shapes, given in (3), along with some examples of words formed with each.

(3)   a. [ɪz]   horses, faces, kisses, crutches, lunches, wishes, skir-
                    mishes, judges, garages, buzzes, boxes

        b. [s]   cats, ducks, tips

        c. [z]   cows, days, pins, chickens, burrs, bells, pigs, cabs, lads

One way of accounting for these facts would be to give rules for the selection
of each morpheme alternant, what Kenstowicz & Kisseberth (1979, 180) call
the *morpheme alternant theory*. These rules might take the form of (4) in
accounting for the English regular plural. In this theory there are no underlying
representations, only a listing of all the phonetic alternants of each morpheme.

(4)   a. Choose [ɪz] if the stem ends in a $\begin{bmatrix} +\text{strident} \\ +\text{coronal} \end{bmatrix}$

        b. Choose [s] if the stem ends in a voiceless segment which is not
            $\begin{bmatrix} +\text{strident} \\ +\text{coronal} \end{bmatrix}$.

        c. Choose [z] if the stem ends in a voiced segment which is
            not $\begin{bmatrix} +\text{strident} \\ +\text{coronal} \end{bmatrix}$.

The morpheme alternant theory is insufficiently general. For example, the
statements in (4) all say to choose a phonetic representation ending in an anterior coronal fricative (the natural class of {s, z}). Furthermore, each of (4a, b,
c) mentions the feature complex $\begin{bmatrix} +\text{strident} \\ +\text{coronal} \end{bmatrix}$. It would be desirable to simplify the description by eliminating these multiple references to each of these
items. A partial simplification is possible within the morpheme alternant theory by the use of "otherwise" statements, as in (5).

(5)   a. Choose [ɪz] if the stem ends in a $\begin{bmatrix} +\text{strident} \\ +\text{coronal} \end{bmatrix}$.

        b. Otherwise, choose [s] if the stem ends in a voiceless segment.

        c. Otherwise, choose [z].

However, a greater degree of simplification is possible by abandoning the
morpheme alternant theory and developing an analysis within generative

phonology. Furthermore, there are cases where the morpheme alternant theory does not work at all, but where generative phonology provides a satisfactory analysis. In the generative analysis there is only one listed form for the regular plural, the underlying representation. The phonetic representations are then the result of applying regular phonological rules. Along the lines of our lexical representation (1) for 'cat' we could have (6) as a lexical representation for 'plural.'

(6)
$$\begin{bmatrix} /z/ \\ [+N, -V] \ _____ \\ \text{'plural'} \end{bmatrix} \quad \begin{array}{l} \text{Phonological form} \\ \text{Syntactic features} \\ \text{Semantics} \end{array}$$

The phonological representation says simply that the regular plural morpheme *is* /z/, its syntactic representation says that it subcategorizes to appear in the position after nouns, and its semantics is that it means 'plural.' We now need to specify the phonological rules, which we give in (7).

(7) a. *Vowel Insertion (English)*

$$\emptyset \rightarrow \iota \ / \begin{bmatrix} +\text{strident} \\ +\text{coronal} \end{bmatrix} \ _____ + z$$

     b. *Devoicing (English)*

$$z \rightarrow [-\text{voice}] \ / \ [-\text{voice}] \ _____$$

With the single underlying representation in (6) and the rules in (7), we can predict all the forms of the regular plural forms in English. Sample derivations are given in (8).

(8)	a. /#kɑw#/	b. /#kæt#/	c. /#hɔrs#/	underived lexical items
	/#kɑw+z#/	/#kæt+z#/	/#hɔrs+z#/	Morphology: Add plural /-z/
				Phonology:
	———	———	hɔrs+ɪz	(7a)
	———	kæt+s	———	(7b)
	[#kɑwz#]	[#kæts#]	[#hɔrsɪz#]	phonetic representations

In order to state these rules in their maximally general form, they must be ordered as given, a bleeding order in the case of *hɔrsɪz*. Otherwise we might derive *[hɔrsɪs] for the plural of 'horse' if (7b) applied before (7a).

In discussing the plurals in (3) we were careful to qualify it by the term 'regular plurals.' While the vast majority of plurals in English are regular and are derived from the underlying representation (6) with the aid of the rules in (7), there are some plural forms that do not conform to these principles, e.g., *oxen, children, foci*. The lexical entries for *ox, child, and focus* have to be provided with some information to this effect. In other words these lexical items are irregular. There is no *phonological* reason why the plural of *ox* should be *oxen* while the plural of *box* is *boxes*. But only irregular items have to be provided with this extra information. In the absence of such specification the regular rules apply.

6.4   The simplicity criterion

You may have thought that the phonological analyses so far in this book have been anything but simple. However, phonological analyses strive for simplicity as defined in (9). This notion was introduced somewhat informally in (5c) of chapter 4.

(9)   *Simplicity criterion*

The optimal grammar of a language is one in which the total number of phonological features required to state all the underlying representations and rules is reduced to the minimum.

The simplicity criterion will normally select a phonological grammar over a morphological solution. For example, it selects the phonological solution to the regular English plural as expressed by the underlying representation in (6) and the rules in (7) over the solution of the morpheme alternate theory, expressed by the statements in (4). This is because the statements in (4) contain a considerable amount of redundancy, which is eliminated by adopting a phonological solution. In fact, as the analysis is extended to cover more data, the phonological grammar is seen to be even more general. For example the rules of (7) also govern the distribution of the possessive morpheme and the reduced form of the auxiliary verbs *have* and *be* in the third person singular, as seen in (10).

(10)   *Possessive* -'s

Liz's book   [ɪz]

Jack's book   [s]

Bob's book   [z]

Auxiliary is

Liz's here   [ɪz]

Jack's here   [s]

Bob's here   [z]

Auxiliary has

Liz's gone   [ɪz]

Jack's gone   [s]

Bob's gone   [z]

*[handwritten margin note: Assuming reduction to /ɪ/ of *is* and *has*. (?)]*

Therefore the phonological analysis makes predictions beyond the data it was originally created to explain. The morpheme alternant theory, by contrast, is forced to make statements like (4) for every morpheme, thus becoming ever more complex.

The inadequacies of the morpheme alternant theory become even clearer when we consider similar examples in other languages where more morphemes are affected by the same process. In section 4.9.3 of chapter 4 we introduced the data in (11) from Pengo in order to illustrate the use of Greek letter variables in rules.

(11)
2 sg. imperative	3 sg. past	gerund	gloss	underlying representation of root
tuːb-a	tuːp-t-an	tuːb-ǰi	'blow'	/tuːb/
tog-a	tok-t-an	tog-ǰi	'step on'	/tog/
ṛaːk-a	ṛaːk-t-an	ṛaːg-ǰi	'offer worship'	/ṛaːk/
hiːp-a	hiːp-t-an	hiːb-ǰi	'sweep'	/hiːp/

In our analysis in chapter 4 we pointed out that the correct phonetic representations are derived by assuming the underlying representations shown in the last column of (11), that is, the form of the root that appears before vowel-initial suffixes. We require the phonological rule in (12).

(12)   *Voicing Assimilation (Pengo)*

$$[-\text{son}] \rightarrow [\alpha\text{voice}] / \underline{\hspace{1cm}} \begin{bmatrix} -\text{son} \\ \alpha\text{voice} \end{bmatrix}$$

The morpheme alternant approach would have to give statements like (13) to account for these forms.

(13)   When a root has alternants whose final segment is a voiced or voiceless obstruent, select the alternant with a final voiced obstruent if the next morpheme begins with a voiced obstruent and select the alternant with a final voiceless obstruent if the next morpheme begins with a voiceless obstruent.

The formulation in (13) is unable to account for the alternant that appears before *vowel*-initial suffixes, since this is voiced in some cases and voiceless in others. The morpheme alternant approach would have to make a special statement about each such root morpheme, since no general statement is possible in the absence of a unique undelrying representation for each root. Clearly the generative approach, with the underlying representations in (11) and the rule in (12) is more general, and simpler.

When the selection of the alternant of one morpheme depends on the selection of the alternant of another (usually adjacent) morpheme, the inadequacies of the morpheme alternant approach become even more apparent. An example is provided by the Russian data we examined in section 5.1 of chapter 5. We recall a selection of those data in (14).

(14)	stem	masc. past	fem. past	neuter past	gloss
	/pisa/	pisa-l	pisa-l-a	pisa-l-o	'write'
	/nes/	nes	nes-l-a	nes-l-o	'carry'
	/met̪/	me-l	me-l-a	me-l-o	'sweep'
	/ved̪/	ve-l	ve-l-a	ve-l-o	'lead'

According to our analysis in chapter 5, we assumed stems as in the left column of (14), a suffix /l/ for 'past' that appears in all past forms (in underlying representations), no suffix for masculine, a suffix /-ɑ/ for feminine, and a suffix /-o/ for neuter. We also assumed two rules that apply in order, given in (15).

(15)   *Dental Stop Deletion (Russian)*

$$\begin{bmatrix} -son \\ -cont \\ +ant \\ +cor \end{bmatrix} \rightarrow \varnothing / \underline{\quad} 1$$

l-Deletion (Russian)
$1 \rightarrow \varnothing / C \underline{\quad} \#$

How would this be analyzed in the morpheme alternant approach? The past tense morpheme has two alternants, [l] and Ø. If we say that the Ø alternant is chosen when it is word final and preceded by a consonant, otherwise the [l] alternant is chosen, this will correctly choose the Ø alternant for [nes] and the [l] alternant for [pisɑl]. However, in the case of [mel] and [vel], that is, stems that alternate between the presence and absence of a final dental stop, the rule presupposes that the choice of [me] (instead of [meţ]) has been made. This choice can be made only on the basis of a statement that chooses the stem alternant without a final dental stop in case it is followed by the [l] alternant, rather than the Ø alternant, of the past tense suffix . This statement in turn presupposes that the choice of the [l] over the Ø alternant of the past tense morpheme has been made. In other words, the choice of the correct alternant of each morpheme depends on the prior choice of the correct alternant of the other, and there is no way to break out of this vicious circle. The alternative generative analysis, however, has no problem producing the correct forms, as we saw in chapter 5.

6.5   The naturalness condition

Implicit in our discussion of underlying representations is the idea that they are composed of the same set of phonetic features as phonetic representations. This may seem obvious, but there have been fairly influential theories that maintained that phonological representations should be completely abstract, and not based on phonetics (e.g., Lamb 1966, Fudge 1967, Householder 1965). The claim that underlying representations are phonetic in nature is part of what Postal (1968) calls the *naturalness condition,* and it follows from the simplicity criterion. For example, if we were to represent the phonological form of the morpheme 'cat' in terms of arbitrary symbols, say /ψ∇ϑ/,[2] instead of as /kæt/, as we did in (1). we would need otherwise unnecessary rules to convert, say, /ψ/ into [k], /∇/ into [æ], and /ϑ/ into [t]. There would be absolutely no justification for such underlying forms or for the rules required. Another aspect of the naturalness condition is that it requires underlying representations to resemble the corresponding phonetic representations. Let us state this more formally in (16).

(16) *Naturalness condition*
The underlying representation of a morpheme is identical to its phonetic representation, unless there is evidence for a more abstract representation.

Evidence to the contrary could include alternations and predictable properties of pronunciation that are rule governed, regardless of whether or not alternations are involved. Alternations have been familiar since chapter 4. Another aspect of the naturalness condition is the requirement that each alternating morpheme have a single underlying representation, from which its alternants are derived by phonological rules that apply to fully formed words composed of the underlying representations of morphemes. Other justifications for more abstract representations come from the consideration of allophones as discussed in chapter 2. The morpheme 'cat' in (1) is an example. Although the initial segment of this morpheme does not alternate, and in fact is always phonetically [kʰ], we are justified in representing it phonologically as /k/, by virtue of the simplicity criterion. We vastly simplify the lexicon by omitting aspiration from the initial stops of words like *cat,* since we can predict that such segments are aspirated by a rule. We can omit the feature [+HSP] from such stop in hundreds of words,[3] while the rule required to aspirate these stops takes only a few features to state.

---

[2] For the sake of argument we assume three arbitrary symbols, the same as the number in the phonological underlying representation. If forms could have arbitrary symbols, there could just as well be more or less than the number of phonological segments, with the ad hoc rules converting these to phonetic segments adjusted accordingly.

[3] It might be objected that we need to specify them as [–HSP], and so we are no further ahead. Actually we will claim that no segments in underlying representation in English have to be specified for any value of [HSP]. The value [+HSP] is specified by the rule alluded to in the text and any segment not specified by this rule gets assigned [–HSP] by default. See section 7.2.2 of chapter 7, where we show that the precise environment for the operation of Aspiration is in foot-initial position. See section 7.3 of chapter 7 for a discussion of underspecification theory that allows this feature to be lexically unspecified.

In fact, there are alternations involving aspiration in English, even though this feature is not contrastive. We pointed out in section 4.6 of chapter 4 that lenition in Spanish, a rule that governs the distribution of voiced stops and their corresponding approximants, can have an alternating effect in expressions like *boḍeya* 'shop' and *la ḅoḍeya* 'the shop.' A similar situation appears in English aspiration and flapping. Consider the words in (17).

(17)   *atom*   ['ærəm]

       atomic   [ə'tʰɒmɪk]

       underlying representation: /ætɒm/

The morpheme 'atom' has varying pronunciation depending on the location of stress, which in turn depends on the morphological makeup of the word in which this morpheme appears. With no affix the stress is on the first syllable, the second vowel is reduced to [ə], and the underlying /t/ is converted to [ɾ]. With the adjectival suffix -*ic,* the stress appears on the syllable before the suffix, putting the /t/ in a position to be aspirated. In this case, the first vowel is reduced to [ə]. This example, like the Spanish expressions just mentioned, shows alternation of a nondistinctive feature. These considerations lead us to set up the underlying representation for the stem in (17) as /ætɒm/. We assume that stress is assigned by rule, that unstressed vowels are reduced, and that the stress-dependent allophones of /t/ appear in appropriate places.

6.6   Degrees of abstractness in underlying representations

6.6.1   Concrete underlying representations

According to the naturalness condition, the underlying representation of a morpheme is identical to its phonetic representation unless there is evidence for a more abstract representation. An underlying representation which is identical to the phonetic representation is referred to as a *concrete* underlying representation. The underlying representation is abstract to the extent that it differs from the phonetic representation. As an example of a maximally concrete representation, consider the English word *bid* [bɪd]. Its underlying representation must contain enough information to distinguish it from other words of English by incorporating the contrastive features of each segment. So the first segment has to be specified as a voiced labial oral stop, to distinguish it from *mid* or *did,* the second segment must be specified as a high front lax vowel to distinguish it from *ban* or *bun,* and the final segment as a voiced alveolar stop to distinguish it from *bill* or *big.* This morpheme does not enter into any alternations, nor does any segment in it have noticeable allophonic features. If there is no reason to represent it more abstractly, we can take its underlying representation to be identical with its phonetic representation: /bɪd/. In fact, it is somewhat difficult to find examples of maximally concrete underlyng representations in English. Many segments exhibit predictable allophonic variation, which should not be present in the underlying representations. For example, *bin* is phonetically [bĩn], but the nasality of the vowel is predictable in the position before a syllable-final nasal consonant, and so is omitted from the underlying representation /bɪn/. Similarly, the final segment of *bill* is a velarized lateral in the phonetic representation [bɪɫ], but this predictable velarization is omitted from the underlying representation /bɪl/.

Underlying representations may differ from phonetic representations when the latter contain predictable, noncontrastive information. In our example of *cat* (1), we gave the underlying representation as /kæt/, even though the initial segment of this morpheme is always realized as an aspirated stop [kʰ]. Since aspiration is never distinctive in English, the feature [+HSP] need not be present in underlying representations, even in those morphemes where it is always present phonetically. Its phonetic appearance is due to a rule. In chapter 2 we contrasted English in this respect with Hindi. In (14) of chapter 2 we provided evidence that aspiration is contrastive in Hindi, repeated here as (18).

(18)   pal   'take care of'   pʰal   'knife blade'
       ṭal   'beat'   ṭʰal   'plate'
       ṭal   'postpone'   ṭal   'wood shop'
       kan   'ear'   kʰan   'mine'

Unlike English, the presence of [+HSP] on stops in Hindi cannot be predicted. In Hindi the underlying representations of the words on the left in (18) must be specified [–HSP] in their initial segment, while those on the right must be specified [+HSP] on this segment.

6.6.2   Underlying representation as one of the phonetic alternants

When a morpheme exhibits alternation, its underlying representation may be one of its phonetic alternants, unless there is a reason to choose a more abstract form. For example, in discussing the Russian voicing alternation in section 4.3 of chapter 4, we observed that the Russian morpheme for 'bread' has the two alternants [xleb] and [xlep]. The underlying representation for this morpheme is /xleb/ with a final voiced stop. The rule we proposed devoices obstruents in word-final position. Other morphemes, like [xolop] 'bondman,' do not alternate in voicing, but always have a morpheme-final voiceless stop. These have an underlying representation identical to the phonetic representation: /xolop/. Since /p/ and /b/ contrast phonetically in positions other than the word-final one, this alternation involves *neutralization*. In cases of neutralization, the underlying form of the alternating segment is always the form that appears *in environments other than* the position of neutralization. These two words have dative singulars ['xlebu] and [xo'lopu], where the alternating segment of /xleb/ is kept away from word-final position (the neutralizing environment) by the suffix -*u*. Therefore the underlying representation is selected on the basis of the dative singular: /xleb/ and /xolop/. Notice that the underlying form of the morpheme, while identical to one of its alternants in the case of /xleb/, is not identical to any actual *word*. The morpheme /xleb/ with no affix can form a word, but in that case the final obstruent is put in word-final position and so undergoes neutralization.

6.6.3   Morphemes with several alternations

When a morpheme exhibits more than one alternation, each alternation should be considered separately in determining the underlying representation. This is because a given word might exhibit neutralization with respect to one alternation but not another. An example is provided by exercise 4.4 of chapter 4, using data from Russian. Some of the forms are repeated here in (19).

(19)		*singular*	*plural*	*gloss*
	1.	'glɑs	glɑ'zɑ	'eye'
	2.	u'čitʸilʸ	učitʸi'lʸɑ	'teacher'
	3.	'lʸes	lʸi'sɑ	'forest'
	4.	'snʸek	snʸi'gɑ	'snow'

The word for 'eye' shows the familiar voicing alternation that we saw in 'bread.' These examples show vowel alternations as well. It is often the case that a language distinguishes more vowels in stressed than in unstressed syllables. To simplify slightly, Russian distinguishes only three vowels in unstressed syllables, here transcribed as [u, i, ɑ]. In (19) the plural suffix -*a* is always stressed and there is only one stress per word. Consequently the stem vowels will be limited to these three in the plural, but the vowels [e, o] may appear in singular forms under stress. The word for 'forest' shows an alternation between [e] and [i] whereas the word for 'teacher' shows phonetic [i] both when stressed and unstressed. There is a neutralization whereby both /e/ and /i/ are realized as [i] when unstressed. For 'forest' we therefore select /lʸes/ as the underlying representation. We assume that stress is assigned by rule and not present in the underlying representation. The underlying /e/ is justified by the criterion of predictability. We can predict when underlying /e/ will appear as [i], namely when it is unstressed, but we cannot predict when an unstressed [i] will appear as [e] when stressed. Now, the word for 'snow' exhibits both alternations. Its underlying representation is /snʸeg/. The stem-final voiced obstruent is justified by our previous argument that a voiced obstruent is underlying in the case of segments that alternate in voicing. The underlying /e/ is justified by the argument that /e/ underlies the alternation [e] (stressed)~[i] (unstressed). We consider each of these alternations separately because neither of the given forms of 'snow' exhibits both underlying segments. The necessity of selecting an underlying representation containing only unneutralized versions of neutralized segments results in an underlying representation that corresponds to neither of the phonetic alternants originally given.[4]

This situation can also arise when the same alternation affects a morpheme in more than one place. Palauan, a language we encountered in exercises 4.5 and 4.8 of chapter 4, exhibits vowel alternations that depend on stress, similar to Russian. Consider the data in (20).

(20)		*Passive verb*	*Anticipating State verb (two forms)*		*gloss*
			Suffix -all	*Suffix -l*	
	1.	mə'ðaŋəb	ðəŋə'ball	ðə'ŋobl	'cover'
	2.	mə'teʔəb	təʔə'ball	tə'ʔibl	'pull out'
	3.	mə'silək	sələ'kall	sə'lokl	'wash'
	4.	mə'sesəb	səsə'ball	sə'sobl	'burn'

---

[4] The palatalization observed in some segments in these examples is probably also predictable and can be omitted from the underlying forms in a more detailed analysis. In fact the alternant ['snʸeg] appears in the dative singular ['snʸegu], although this was not given in the original problem.

As in Russian, there is only one stress per word in Palauan. Stress falls on the
final syllable of words with a suffix, here the two forms of the Anticipating
State verb, formed with the suffixes -*all* and -*l,* otherwise it is penultimate,
here in the Passive verb, which is formed with the prefix *mə-*. The only vowel
that can appear in unstressed syllables is [ə], while stressed syllables can have
any of the vowels [i, e, ɑ, o, u]. We can assume an underlying [ə] for the prefix *mə-*,[5] since we never see any other vowel in this morpheme, as it always
appears unstressed in our data. But we cannot assume any underlying [ə] in
the verb roots, because we could not tell which other vowel it will become
when it happens to be stressed. If we assume that the underlying representation contains those vowels that show up under stress, then we have to construct underlying representations for the verb roots that do not correspond to
any phonetic alternant. For example, the root for 'cover' is /ðaŋob/. By the criterion of predictability, we can predict all the phonetic vowels that appear in
inflected forms of this root with a single rule (21).

(21)   *Vowel Reduction (Palauan)*

$$\begin{bmatrix} +\text{syll} \\ -\text{stress} \end{bmatrix} \rightarrow ə$$

This same rule covers all the cases, with underlying representations /ðaŋob/
'cover,' /teʔib/ 'pull out,' /silok/ 'wash,' and /sesob/ 'burn.' These underlying
representations are somewhat abstract, since the vowels in them do not all
appear together in any one phonetic alternant of the morpheme, but every segment of the underlying representation appears in at least one phonetic alternant of the morpheme.

Russian has an exactly parallel situation as we can see from the forms in
(22).

(22)   'head'

     a.   gɑlɑ'v-ɑ   nominative singular

     b.   'golɑv-u   accusative singular

     c.   gɑ'lof   genitive plural

     d.   /golov/   underlying representation of root

The root contains two instances of the vowel /o/, but, since there can be only

---

[5] Alternatively, we could assume an archiphoneme [+syll] that would be realized as [ə] by
virtue of vowel reduction.

one stress per word, one or both /o/ will be unstressed and consequently merged with [ɑ]. The underlying representation must contain two /o/ on the basis of the criterion of predictability, we can determine its phonetic outcome when unstressed. Given only an unstressed [ɑ], however, we cannot determine if its source is /o/ or /ɑ/.

The situation in Tonkawa, seen in exercise 5.5, is similar, but it involves the deletion of a segment rather than the merger of one segment with another, as is the case in Russian. The underlying representation of the root 'cut' is /piˈtseno/, but at least one of these vowels is deleted in phonetic forms, as seen in (23).

(23)   piˈtsno?   'he cuts it'   piˈtsnɑno?
        weˈptseno?   'he cuts them'   weˈptsenɑno?
        keˈptseno   'he cuts me'   keˈptsenɑno
        piˈtsen   'castrated one, steer'

A comparison with other roots in the language shows that the vowel patterns are not predictable, hence the vowels must appear in the underlying representations of the roots. There are a number of vowel deletion rules in the language, resulting in the pattern of (23), so we can predict the patterns on the basis of these rules on the assumption that the underlying representations have all the possible vowels, even though they do not all appear in any single phonetic alternant of the roots.

6.6.4   More abstract underlying representations

It may happen that an underlying representation contains elements that appear in none of the phonetic alternants of that morpheme, in which case we observe an underlying representation more abstract than those of Russian, Palauan, or Tonkawa discussed in the previous subsection. The analysis of Yawelmani, discussed at length in section 5.6 of chapter 5, is an excellent example. The key lies in the vowel harmony system of the language. Recall that vowel harmony operates from left to right and makes a vowel round (and back) in assimilation to a preceding round vowel that has the same value for [high]. Thus, suffixes with a high vowel appear with the vowel [u] if the preceding vowel is /u/; otherwise they have the vowel [i]. The epenthetic vowel is subject to the same alternation under the same conditions. Suffixes with a non-high vowel appear with the vowel [o] if the preceding vowel is /o/; otherwise they have the vowel [ɑ]. We give some representative data in (24).

(24)		Dubitative	Aorist	gloss
	1.	xatal	xathin	'eat'
	2.	giy'al	giy'hin	'touch'
	3.	meːk'al	mek'hin	'swallow'
	4.	ṣaːpal	ṣaphin	'burn'
	5.	paʔtal	paʔiṭhin	'fight'
	6.	ʔilkal	ʔilikhin	'sings'
	7.	lihmal	lihimhin	'run'
	8.	ʔayyal	ʔayiyhin	'pole a boat'
	9.	ʔamlal	ʔaːmilhin	'help'
	10.	ṣalk'al	ṣaːlik'hin	'wake up'
	11.	ṣenṭ'al	ṣeːniṭ'hin	'smell'
	12.	bok'ol	bok'hin	'find'
	13.	dubal	dubhun	'lead by the hand'
	14.	k'oʔol	k'oʔhin	'throw'
	15.	hudal	hudhun	'recognize'
	16.	logwol	logiwhin	'pulverize'
	17.	sonlol	soːnilhin	'pack on the back'
	18.	ʔugnal	ʔugunhun	'drink'
	19.	doːsol	doshin	'report'
	20.	woːnol	wonhin	'hide'
	21.	hotnol	hoːtinhin	'take the scent'

In order to account for the harmony of these forms, we proposed a vowel harmony rule of the form (25).

(25)   *Vowel Harmony (Yawelmani)*

$$\begin{bmatrix} +\text{syl} \\ \alpha\text{high} \end{bmatrix} \rightarrow \begin{bmatrix} +\text{round} \\ +\text{back} \\ -\text{low} \end{bmatrix} / \begin{bmatrix} +\text{syl} \\ +\text{round} \\ \alpha\text{high} \end{bmatrix} C_0 \underline{\hspace{1cm}}$$

(left-to-right iterative)

We also proposed a rule of Epenthesis that inserts the vowel i in the environ-

ment C____C $\left\{\begin{matrix} \# \\ C \end{matrix}\right\}$, ordered before Vowel Harmony (to account for the fact

that epenthetic vowels harmonize) and a rule of Vowel Shortening to account
for the alternations in vowel length. Vowels are shortened in the context ____

C $\left\{\begin{matrix} \# \\ C \end{matrix}\right\}$. Underlying representations are quite straightforward. They are iden-

tical with the phonetic form in the case of nonalternating roots, like /xɑt/ 'eat,'
the form with a long vowel in the case of roots that alternate in length, like
/ṣɑːp/ 'burn,'[6] and the form lacking the epenthetic vowel in the case of roots
that alternate in the presence or absence of such a vowel, like /ʔilk/ 'sing.' The
roots that alternate both in vowel length and in the epenthetic vowel have an
underlying representation with the long vowel but without the epenthetic
vowel such as /ʔaːml/ 'help,' which does not correspond to one of the phonetic alternants and is therefore slightly abstract.

A number of forms, such as those in (26), are problematic for this analysis of vowel harmony.

(26)   *Dubitative*   *Aorist*   *gloss*
    1.   t͡s'oːmɑl   t͡s'omhun   'destroy'
    2.   ṣoːgɑl   ṣoghun   'pull out the cork'
    3.   woʔyɑl   woːʔuyhun   'fall asleep'
    4.   dollɑl   doːlulhun   'climb'

If we only had the dubitative forms, we might be tempted to say that these
roots are simply exceptions to vowel harmony, since here they fail to condition harmony where they would be expected to condition it. But the aorist
forms show the opposite behaviour: here the roots condition harmony where
they would be expected not to. The other curious aspect of the roots with this
unexpected behaviour is that they all alternate in length. That is, there are no
roots in Yawelmani with invariably short o that take the u form of high-vowel
suffixes and the a form of nonhigh-vowel suffixes. Our approach to this problem was to adopt a relatively abstract underlying representation for such roots
with a long high round vowel, e.g., /t͡s'uːm/ 'destroy' or /wuːʔy/ 'fall asleep.'

---

[6] The underlying form of 'swallow' is /miːk'/ rather than /meːk'/, since we argued for the
lack of vowels of /e/ quality in underlying representations.

The reasoning that led to these underlying representations made use of the lack of phonetic long high vowels[7] and the fact that the roots in (26) behave harmonically as if they had high vowels. In other words, the underlying representation of these roots is determined not only from the alternations that the roots themselves undergo (in this case vowel length and epenthesis), but also from the harmonic effect of these roots on suffixes (and on the epenthetic vowel, where it appears). It should be clear that the choice of /uː/ for the vowel of /ts'uːm/ 'destroy' is entirely determined by these facts, and is not arbitrary in any way. The feature matrix of this vowel is (27).[8]

(27)
$$\begin{bmatrix} +\text{syll} \\ +\text{high} \\ -\text{low} \\ +\text{back} \\ +\text{round} \\ +\text{long} \end{bmatrix}$$

That the vowel is [+back, +round, –low] is evident from the phonetic forms of this root which all have these features. We deduce that it is [+long] in the underlying representation on the basis of the previous arguments that all roots whose vowels alternate in length have underlying long vowels. The only feature of (27) that does not appear in any of the phonetic forms of this root is [+high], since all the phonetic forms have [–high] vowels. The underlying representation differs *minimally* from the phonetic forms in being specified [+high], a choice dictated by its harmonic activity. Both its phonetic appearance as [–high] and the phonetic lack of long high vowels (except for those resulting from Contraction) are accounted for by the rule of Vowel Lowering, (28).

(28)   *Vowel Lowering (Yawelmani)*

$$\begin{bmatrix} +\text{syl} \\ +\text{long} \end{bmatrix} \rightarrow [-\text{high}]$$

Notice that Vowel Lowering is stated without a context. In section 2.8.1 of chapter 2 we discussed *neutralization,* the effect two or more underlying seg-

---

[7] Phonetic high long vowels appear only as the result of contraction, not from underlying forms with such vowels.

[8] The feature [ATR] is redundant in Yawelmani and so is omitted from the underlying representation.

ments having the same phonetic realization. Most often, neutralization is *con-textual*. That is, it is specified as occurring in a specific context. For example, in Russian, voiced and voiceless obstruents are neutralized in word-final position. The underlying /b/ of /xleb/ 'bread' is realized as [p], identical to the realization of the underlying /p/ of /xolop/ 'bondman.' In other contexts, however, underlying /b/ remains distinct from underlying /p/, and we have contrasts like *pa'ka* 'while' versus *ba'ka* 'sides.' Rule (28) is an example of *absolute neutralization:* in Yawelmani *all* instances of underlying /uː/ are merged with underlying /oː/. Whereas the Russian rule neutralizing voicing is stated in the context ____#, rule (28) is stated without a context and applies everywhere a long high vowel occurs. Actually, rule (28) is neutralizing only with /uː/. The rule also affects underlying /iː/, converting this to [eː], but such applications of (28) are not neutralizing because there are no instances of underlying /eː/.

The underlying representations of the roots in (26) are abstract in having one feature that appears in none of the phonetic forms of those roots. Our analysis of the future suffix with phonetic alternants *-en* and *-on* is slightly more abstract. We gave this morpheme the underlying representation /-iːn/, which contains two features, [+high, +long], that do not appear in any of the phonetic forms of this suffix. We justified this representation by showing that it accounts for the alternation without any additional rules. Under this analysis, this suffix undergoes harmonic alternation just like any other suffix with a high vowel, for example /-hin/ with its alternant [-hun]. However, unlike the latter, which has an underlying short vowel which undergoes no further changes, the vowel of /-iːn/, because it is long, is subject to further modification, to [-en] if it remains unround, or to [-on] if it is backed and rounded, by the rules of Vowel Lowering and Vowel Shortening that are needed independently for other alternations. If we did not have this abstract underlying representation, we would need additional rules to account for this one alternation, significantly complicating the grammar. The abstract analysis is justified by simplicity and by explanatory adequacy, because the seemingly unusual vowel alternation of the future suffix is explained by independently needed rules.

An underlying representation can be even more abstract than the Yawelmani future suffix if it contains a segment which is not realized in any phonetic realization of the morpheme. English provides an example. The word *sing*, [sɪŋ], is analyzed by Sapir (1925) and by *SPE* as having an underlying representation with a final stop: /sɪŋg/. The segment [ŋ] superficially contrasts with the nasals [m] and [n] in words like *whim, win, wing*, but not in word-initial position (*map, nap* but not **ŋap*) or after a consonant (*smear, snear,* but not **sŋeer*). In addition, the sequences [nk] and [ng] do not occur in English phonetic forms while the sequences [ŋk] and [ŋg] do, as in *sink, rank, finger, anger.* Also, the sequence [ŋg] does not occur word finally, whereas the simple segment [ŋ] does. These distributions can be accounted for by assuming a rule such as (29) that assimilates a nasal to the point of articulation of a following stop. Such rules are fairly common; we saw similar examples in chapter 4, section 4.6, from Spanish and Lumasaaba.

(29)   *Nasal Assimilation (English)*

$$\begin{bmatrix} +\text{cons} \\ +\text{nasal} \end{bmatrix} \rightarrow \begin{bmatrix} \alpha\text{anterior} \\ \beta\text{coronal} \end{bmatrix} \Big/ \underline{\quad\quad} \begin{bmatrix} -\text{syll} \\ \alpha\text{anterior} \\ \beta\text{coronal} \end{bmatrix}$$

We then require a rule that deletes [g] in word-final position after a nasal consonant, as in (30).

(30)   g-*Deletion (English)*

$$g \rightarrow \emptyset \Big/ \begin{bmatrix} +\text{cons} \\ +\text{nasal} \end{bmatrix} \underline{\quad\quad} \#$$

The formulation of this rule makes it possible to account for the deletion of /g/ in derived and inflected forms like *singer, sings, singing, ringed* as well. According to the *SPE* analysis, certain suffixes in English, including the agentive[9] *-er* and the regular inflectional suffixes *-s, -ed,* and *-ing,* are associated with a word boundary (#) rather than with the simple morpheme boundary (+).[10] Other suffixes in English are associated with the morpheme boundary and no deletion of /g/ occurs in these cases. The operation of these rules is illustrated in the derivations of (31).

---

[9] The agentive suffix *-er* forms a noun from a verb and indicates a person who performs the action designated by the verb.

[10] This idea will be developed further in the context of lexical phonology in section 7.4 of chapter 7.

(31)   /#sɪng#/   /#sɪng#əɹ#/   /#lɒng#/   /#lɒng+əɹ#/   underlying
                                                          representations

              ŋ   ŋ   ŋ   ŋ   Nasal
                                                          Assimilation (29)

              Ø   Ø   Ø   ——————   g-Deletion (30)

       [#sɪŋ#]   [#sɪŋəɹ#]   [#lɒŋ#]   [#lɒŋgəɹ#]   phonetic
                                                          representations

       'sing'   'singer'   'long'   'longer'

We have now motivated an underlying representation, /sɪng/ for *sing*, which
contains a segment /g/ which appears in none of the phonetic alternants of this
morpheme. This is more abstract than the underlying /uː/ in Yawelmani
t͡somhun or the underlying /iː/ in the future morpheme [-en]~[on].
Nevertheless, the underlying /g/ in *sing* appears to be well motivated on distributional grounds.

6.6.5   Limits on abstractness

Given that we have motivated relatively abstract analyses, the question arises
as to whether there are any limits to the degree of abstractness of underlying
representations, within the limits of the naturalness condition (16).
Bloomfield's (1939) analysis of Menomini may surpass the limits of desirable
abstractness.[11] In Menomini, some phonetic *n* alternate with *s* while others do
not. Where the alternation occurs, underlying /n/ is replaced by *s* when followed by a nonlow front vowel or glide; under the same conditions underlying /t/ is replaced by *č*. We can give the rule as (32).[12]

(32) $\begin{Bmatrix} n \to s \\ t \to č \end{Bmatrix}$ / ——— $\begin{bmatrix} -cons \\ -low \\ -back \end{bmatrix}$

This alternation is illustrated by the forms in (33).

---

[11] Bloomfield predates generative phonology by about a decade, but this paper is remark-
able in its sophisticated appeal to ordered rules.

[12] We give the inputs and structural changes somewhat informally here, since {n, t} is not
a particularly natural class. The rule would actually be quite complex to state in features.

(33) en-oːhnɛ   'if he walks hither'
      es-y-aː-t   'if he goes hither'

      w-eːn-owawan   'their heads'
      w-eːs ← /w-en-e/ 'his head'·

      oːn-an   'canoes'
      oːs ← /on-e/   'canoe'

Nonalternating *n* remains [n] under the same conditions, as illustrated in (34).

(34) o-taːn-an   'his daughter'
      o-taːn-ew   'he has a daughter'

      koːn   'snow'
      koːn-eːwew   'it is snowing'
      kuːny-ak   'lumps of snow'

Bloomfield accounts for this difference by assuming two underlying segments: /n/ underlies the alternation in (33), while nonalternating *n* are underlyingly /N/, in Bloomfield's notation. Bloomfield proposes a rule, ordered after (32), that neutralizes /N/ with /n/ absolutely. The problem is that Bloomfield's analysis has no phonetic properties specified for /N/, a fact that is somewhat disguised by its symbol, a capital /N/. In fact, it is completely arbitrary what phonetic properties are attributed to Bloomfield's /N/ in Menomini, as long as it is distinct from all other underlying segments in Menomini. The Menomini sound inventory is relatively restricted. The phonetic consonants are given in (35).

(35) glides: w   y   ʔ   h
      obstruents: p   t   s   č   k
      nasals   m   n

For example, /N/ could be identified with a nasal other than /m/, /n/, or an obstruent other than those listed. There is no clue from the alternation or from the phonetic realization what the underlying features of /N/ should be. This is in sharp contrast to Yawelmani /uː/, whose features are completely determined from the nature of the alternation and its phonetic realizations.

Bever (1967) reanalyzes the Menomini data in a more strictly generative phonological approach and sets up an underlying /θ/ for the [n]~[s] alternation and underlying /n/ for the nonalternating [n]. This permits a simpler version of the palatalization rule, which we give as (36).

(36) $\begin{bmatrix} -son \\ +cor \end{bmatrix} \rightarrow [+strid] / \underline{\qquad} \begin{bmatrix} -cons \\ -low \\ -back \end{bmatrix}$

A later rule in Bever's analysis merges /θ/ absolutely with /n/. Bever notes that this analysis involves minimal feature changes in the realizations of the underlying /θ/. It need change only in terms of [strident] to become [s] and in nasality, obstruency, and continuancy to become [n]. But this simplicity is of a mere formal nature: there is nothing in the alternation or in the phonetics that would suggest /θ/ rather than some other consonant that is absent from the Menomini inventory of (35) as the underlying segment that underlies the [n]~[s] alternation. For example, one of the liquids /l/ or /r/ might be an equally plausible candidate. Bever also tries to relate his analysis to the historical development of Menomini, since many of the *n* that palatalize are derived historically from Proto-Algonquian *θ.[13] While it is true that the historical development of a language can leave some residues in the synchronic grammar, it cannot be used as a justification for a synchronic analysis. The grammar that is constructed by a linguist is intended to represent the grammar that is internalized by a child in first language acquisition, and the child does not have access to historical data. Furthermore, on closer inspection, the historical data are more complex, and do not support Bever's analysis entirely (see Piggott 1971 for some discussion).

6.7   Corpus-external evidence

We have derived the bulk of our evidence for underlying representations and rules from normal language use, what has been referred to as *corpus-internal evidence*. This may be derived from written sources giving phonetic transcriptions of texts in the language together with some grammatical and semantic analysis, or from working actively within a speech community. In addition to such evidence, we can appeal to evidence from outside the language system proper, including such items as speech errors, second language acquisition, writing systems, poetic use of language, language games, language change, and native speaker intuitions about their language. We will have a brief look at each of these types of information in this section.

---

[13] The asterisk here refers to an historically reconstructed form rather than to an ungrammatical form.

6.7.1 Speech errors

We have examined speech errors in two contexts so far. In chapter 1, we pointed out that errors involving transposition and substitutions of segments provides evidence that the continuum of speech is correctly analyzed as a sequence of such segments. In chapter 3 we pointed out that such transpositions and substitutions can involve individual features as well, thus providing evidence for the analysis of segments into distinctive features. Speech errors may also provide evidence for more abstract phonological analyses. For example, in section 6.6.4 we showed that the English velar nasal [ŋ] can be analyzed as derived from an underlying representation /ng/, even in those cases where no [g] appears in any phonetic alternant of the morpheme in question, such as *sing*. Our evidence there was corpus internal; there is also some evidence from speech errors for this analysis (Fromkin 1971, 34), given in (37).

(37) a. Chuck Young   →   [čəŋk yəg]
         [čək yəŋ]

      b. cut the string   →   [kənt] the [strɪg]
         [kət]…[strɪŋ]

Under the abstract analysis of the English [ŋ], these errors can be interpreted as involving the transposition of an underlying segment /n/ from the second word to the first prior to the operation of rules (29) and (30). Nasal Assimilation (29) is then responsible for the appearance of [ŋ] in [čəŋk], but no such assimilation occurs in [kənt] because the stop following the transposed /n/ is alveolar rather than velar. In both cases, the transposition of the underlying /n/ allows the underlying /g/ to appear phonetically, since, after the transposition, this segment no longer meets the structural description of *g*-Deletion (30).

6.7.2 Second language acquisition

Adults learning a second language frequently make errors that can reasonably be attributed to aspects of the grammar of their first language. Native speakers of Russian learning English often devoice word-final obstruents in their English utterances. As we discussed in section 4.3 of chapter 4, Russian has a rule of word-final obstruent devoicing, and this pattern can be explained by the assumption that Russian speakers transfer their rule to their developing grammar of English. Similarly, English speakers learning French or Russian have a strong tendency to aspirate voiceless stops in word-initial position, characteristic of an English accent in speaking those languages. Conversely, speakers of French or Russian have an equally strong tendency not to aspirate voiceless stops in that position.

6.7.3   Writing systems

The orthography of a language may reveal aspects of its phonology as well. This is true both of languages with long-established orthographies, such as English or French, and languages for which orthographies are being developed. Sapir (1933) cites several examples of the latter from North American indigenous languages. In one case Alex Thomas, a native speaker of Nootka, wrote [sː] (a long [s]) in two different ways, either as *ss* or as *s*. He wrote *ss* when it was clear that the long consonant arose as a result of juxtaposition of two morphologically distinct consonants as in *tsiːqšitʼłassatłni* 'we went there only to speak,' but single *s* in *hisiːk* (not glossed), although both are pronounced with [sː]. The former is analyzed morphologically as *tsiːqšitłʼ+as+sa+(ʔa)tł+ni*, whereas the latter is apparently monomorphemic. There is a rule of Nootka that lengthens a consonant after a short vowel and before another vowel, resulting in neutralization of the underlying single /s/ of *hisiːk* and the underlying geminate /s+s/ at a morpheme boundary.

Similar phenomena appear in languages with long-established writing systems. French writes *petit* for [pəti] 'small (masculine)' and *petite* for [pətit] 'small (feminine).' The final orthographic *t* of the masculine form is not pronounced in this word in isolation, but appears in the feminine form, whose final orthographic *e* is not normally pronounced. In Schane's (1968) analysis, the underlying representation of the morpheme for 'small' is /pətit/ and /-ə/ is the feminine suffix. A rule deletes a word-final consonant unless it is followed in the same phrase by a vowel-initial word

The English writing system is notorious for its lack of correspondence to the phonetics of the language, and there have been numerous attempts to revise English spelling to make it more phonetically accurate. But all such attempts have failed. It would be easy to attribute these failures to mere conservatism, but there is probably more to it than this. In fact, Chomsky & Halle 1968, 49 regard "conventional orthography...a near optimal system for the lexical representation of English words." To be sure, English spelling has its quirks, such as multiple ways of writing the same sound ([i] as in *tea, tee, machine, people, amoeba*), multiple sounds for the same letter (<o> as in *woman, women, come, comb, port*), and silent letters (*debt, island, light, pneumatic*), to name a few. But English spelling is highly systematic nevertheless. The vowel alternations in (38) provide a striking illustration, where the italicized letter of each word is given a phonetic transcription.

(38) *"long" vowel*   *"short" vowel*   *reduced vowel*

harmonious	[ow]	harmonic	[ɒ]	harmony	[ə]
marginalia	[ey]	marginality	[æ]	marginal	[ə]
sane	[ey]	sanity	[æ]		
serene	[iy]	serenity	[ɛ]		
sublime	[ay]	sublimity	[ɪ]		

Although the phonetic value of each letter varies widely, the spelling preserves the appearance of each morpheme. The vowel alternations illustrated in (38) are systematically related to the stress and morphological form of the words. English vowels regularly have their "short" (lax) version before the suffixes *-ic* and *-ity*, their "long" (tense and diphthongized) versions before a C*i*V sequence or in a final syllable that ends with a silent *e*. English vowels are also reduced when unstressed. Because these are regular rules, there is no need to indicate these variations in spelling. As Chomsky & Halle say, "[t]he fundamental principle of orthography is that phonetic variation is not indicated where it is predictable by general rule" (1968, 49). English orthography is closely related to underlying representations, and, as such, supports the somewhat abstract analysis of English vowels that has been hinted at here.[14]

6.7.4 Language games

A language game is played by introducing a systematic distortion of the words of a language, often as a way of disguising speech. It operates by inserting some specified sound or sequence of sounds or rearranging the composition of a word, or some combination of these methods. While the rules of the game are not, strictly speaking, phonological rules, they may interact with phono-

---

[14] The arguments for the required underlying representations and phonological rules required for these English vowel alternations are somewhat complex. See Jensen (1993, chapter 7) for details.

logical rules, providing evidence for these, especially if the language rules
precede some phonological rules. An example from English is Pig Latin, produced from English words by moving the initial consonant or consonant cluster to the end of the word and then adding the diphthong [ey] at the end. For
example, the phrase *Pig Latin* is changed to ['ɪgpey 'æʔn̩ley]. This game rule
interacts with the rule, Diphthong Shortening, that produces shortened and
raised diphthongs before voiceless consonants. This rule was briefly introduced in section 2.7.9 of chapter 2, and has the effect of producing the diphthong [əy] in the words *write* and *writer.*

(39)	write	[ɹəyt]	ride	[ɹɑːyd]
	writer	[ɹəyɾəɹ]	rider	[ɹɑːyɾəɹ]

Two varieties of Pig Latin can be distinguished. In one, the Pig Latin rule
operates on phonetic representations, that is, after all the phonological rules of
English including Diphthong Shortening. In this variety, words like *ice* and
sigh remain distinct in Pig Latin, as shown in (40).

(40)	['əys]	['sɑy]	phonetic representation
			(after Diphthong Shortening)
	['əysey]	['ɑysey]	Pig Latin rule
	['əysey]	['ɑysey]	Pig Latin form
	'ice'	'sigh'	

In the other variety of Pig Latin, these words merge as ['əysey]. This can be
explained by saying that the Pig Latin rule applies before Diphthong
Shortening for these speakers. This is shown in the derivations of (41).

(41)	['ɑys]	['sɑy]	near-final representation
			(after other rules; before Diphthong Shortening)
	['ɑysey]	['ɑysey]	Pig Latin rule
	['əysey]	['əysey]	Diphthong Shortening; Pig Latin form
	'ice'	'sigh'	

These two varieties of Pig Latin support the idea of rule ordering and the rule
of Diphthong Shortening.

An example of a language game that supports a relatively abstract underlying representation is *sorsik sunmakke* ('talking backwards'), a language game of the Cuna Indians of the San Blas Islands in Panama (Sherzer 1970). Before turning to the game, we will describe some of the basic phonology of the language. In Cuna, there is a phonetic distinction between voiced and voiceless stops. There is fairly good evidence that this phonetic distinction should be derived from an underlying distinction between single and geminate stops, so that [d] is derived from /d/ while [t] is derived from /dd/, and similarly for the labial and velar stops. The evidence comes both from distribution and from alternations. In Cuna consonant clusters can contain at most two consonants and there can be no more than a single consonant at the beginning or end of a word. While voiced stops can appear in clusters and at the beginning and end of words, as shown in the first two columns of (42), voiceless stops cannot appear in these positions.

(42)   obsa   'bathed'   dage   'come'   sapan   'firewood'
       argan   'hand'   goe   'deer'   sate   'no'
       neg   'house'   biriga   'year'   dake   'see'

This is immediately explained if voiceless stops are underlying clusters. The underlying representation of *sapan* 'firewood' is thus /sabban/, and the phonetic form is derived via a rule of Reduction (43).

(43)   *Reduction (Cuna)*

$$\begin{bmatrix} -son \\ -cont \end{bmatrix} \quad \begin{bmatrix} -son \\ -cont \end{bmatrix}$$

          1   2
   $\Rightarrow$ Ø   2   where 1 = 2
                [-voice]

In addition to distribution, this rule accounts for alternations such as (44).

(44)   /#neg+gine#/ 'house' + 'inside'   underlying representation
       [#nekine#]   'inside the house'   Reduction; phonetic representation

Two other rules of Cuna are Syncope, which deletes a morpheme-final vowel before a suffix, and Cluster Simplification, which deletes the first of three consecutive consonants. Some derivations illustrating the interaction of these three rules are given in (45).

(45)

/#balimay-de#/	/#balimay-de-gu#/	underlying representations
_____	Ø	Syncope
_____	Ø	Cluster Simplification
_____	_____	Reduction
[#balimay-de#]	[#balimadgu#]	phonetic representation
'then he pursued'	'having then pursued'	

/#dubbu-dagge#/	/#dubbu#/	underlying representations
Ø	_____	Syncope
Ø	_____	Cluster Simplification
k	p	Reduction
[#dubdake#]	[#dupu#]	phonetic representation
'he sees the island'	'island'	

In *sorsik sunmakke,* the initial syllable of a word is moved to the end. A single consonant between vowels belongs to the syllable of the second vowel; two consonants between vowels are divided between the syllables. Some examples of the game are shown in (46).

(46)

Cuna	*sorsik sunmakke*	*gloss*
ina	nai	'medicine'
dage	geda	'come'
saban	bansa	'belly'
obsa	saob	'bathed'
argan	ganar	'hand'
inna	nain	'chicha'
goe	ego	'deer'

sapan	bansab	'firewood'	/sabban/
sate	desad	'no'	/sadde/
dake	gedag	'see'	/dagge/

The last three examples in (46), with a medial voiceless stop in Cuna, are the interesting ones. These appear in the game with a voiced stop initially and finally. These are easily explained if we assume that the rule of the game moving the initial syllable to the end operates on a stage of representation before Reduction has applied, that is, it operates on the underlying representations in the rightmost column, bleeding Reduction in these cases.

Sherzer identifies another variety of *sorsik sunmakke* in which the disguised form of 'firewood,' 'no,' and 'see' are pronounced *bansa, desa, geda,* that is, without the final voiced stop that appears in these forms in (46). The analysis of these forms is not entirely clear. Applying the *sorsik sunmakke* rule after reduction would result in forms *pansa, tesa, keda,* which are quite anomalous due to the exclusion of voiceless stops from word-initial position, as mentioned before. It is possible that a rule voicing initial stops operates in this form of the language.

6.7.5   Poetry

We mentioned poetic evidence briefly in section 3.3 of chapter 3 as part of the evidence for distinctive features of vowels. At that point we noted that German rhymes may disregard the feature [round] on vowels in determining rhyming words. There we were concerned only with the phonetic level, not with any more abstract representation. Poetic evidence has also been used to support more abstract representations in cases where a poetic convention can be shown to apply to a level before the application of certain phonological rules. One of the best cases of this type appears in the analysis of the Finnish folk epic, the Kalevala, discussed by Kiparsky (1968c).

Each line of the Kalevala is composed of eight syllables, arranged in four trochaic feet, that is, feet consisting of a downbeat followed by an upbeat. The downbeats of the verse pattern do not necessarily coincide with word stress, which is always on the first syllable of the word in Finnish. A fundamental rule concerning the alignment of words to the verse pattern is stated in (47).

(47)   A stressed syllable must be heavy on the downbeat and light on the upbeat.

A syllable is heavy if it contains a long vowel or diphthong or if it ends in a consonant. Finnish syllable structure allows a maximum of one consonant at the beginning of a syllable, so that a vowel followed by two (or more) consonants will belong to a long syllable. A vowel followed by a single consonant and another vowel belongs to a light syllable. Diphthongs are formed by various vowel sequences where the second is always the nonsyllabic element, indicated here by the nonsyllabic diacritic [̯]. Long vowels are indicated the same way, using an identical vowel in the nonsyllabic position. Kiparsky cites the lines in (48) as conforming to the metrical scheme.[15]

(48) a. luvan antoi̯ suu̯ri luo̯ya   'the great creator gave permission'
      b. selæssæ meren sinisen   'on the expanse of the blue sea'
      c. oi ukko üliyumala   'O Ukko, supreme god'

We have set out the alignment of line (48b) to the metrical scheme in (49). The numbers indicate the downbeats and the stars indicate the upbeats; feet are separated by vertical lines.

(49) | 1   * | 2   * | 3   * | 4   * |
            se   læs   sæ   me   ren   si   ni   sen

Rule (47) is enforced strictly in the fourth foot, and progressively less so as we move from there to the beginning of the line. In the first foot it is waived completely; notice that both (48a, b) begin with a stressed short syllable.

In addition to aligning to the metrical scheme, most lines of the Kalevala show alliteration, an identity between the beginning of two words. The most common type requires identity of the initial consonant, if any, and the immediately following vowel, which can be the first part of a long vowel or diphthong. The examples in (50) show this type of alliteration (alliterating elements are underlined).

(50) a. lappalainen laiha poika   'The Laplander, the lean boy'
      b. astu leski aitastasi   'Widow, step out of your storehouse!'

---

15   Finnish examples have been transcribed into our phonetic notation. The sym [i̯] should be considered phonetically equivalent; we write [y] as a syllable onset but [i̯] as the second element of a diphthong or long vowel. The rules below sometimes entail an interchange in these two functions of what is phonetically the same sound. I thank Irene Enright and Marja Kerttu Enright for help with the Finnish data.

However, some alliterations of this type have different vowels phonetically, as in (51)

(51) a. hie̯kkɑ, helkki — 'sand, jingled'
b. honkɑsessɑ huo̯nehessɑ — 'in their rooms of fir'
c. šæveltænæ šeæ̯telemmæ — 'we will pitch our tunes'
d. munɑ vie̯ræhti vetenæ — 'the egg rolled in the water'

Kiparsky attributes this pattern to a rule of Diphthongization. In Standard Finnish underlying long mid vowels become diphthongs whose first element is high; in Eastern Finnish dialects, in which the Kalevala was composed, low vowels also diphthongize. The effects of this rule are summarized in (52).

(52)

underlying	*by Diphthongization*	
/ee̯/	[ie̯]	(All dialects)
/oo̯/	[uo̯]	"
/öö̯/	[üö̯]	"
/ɑɑ̯/	[oɑ̯]	(Eastern Finnish only)
/ææ̯/	[eæ̯]	"

Diphthongization can be expressed formally using our notational conventions as in (53).

(53) *Diphthongization (Finnish)*

$$\begin{array}{lcc} & \begin{bmatrix} -\text{cons} \\ +\text{syll} \\ -\text{hi} \\ \alpha\text{low} \\ \langle +\text{back} \rangle \end{bmatrix} & \begin{bmatrix} -\text{cons} \\ -\text{syl} \\ -\text{hi} \end{bmatrix} \\ & 1 & 2 \\ \Rightarrow & 1 & 2 \\ & \begin{bmatrix} -\text{low} \\ -\alpha\text{hi} \\ \langle +\text{rd} \rangle \end{bmatrix} & \end{array}$$

The alliteration in (51), *hiekka helkki,* then fits the general requirements for alliteration on the assumption that alliteration operates on representations prior to the operation of Diphthongization (53), that is /heekka helkki/.

Diphthongization is also supported by internal evidence, from alternations. There is a general rule in Finnish that shortens a long vowel when another vowel immediately follows. For example, the plural of the oblique (nonnominative) cases are formed by adding the plural suffix *-i-* and then the case suffix, for example *-ssa, -ssæ* 'in.'[16] In (54a) we see some examples with overt long vowels in the uninflected (nominative singular) form, and in (54b) we see some examples with diphthongs derived in the uninflected form by Diphthongization (53).

(54)		*nom. sg.*	*'in' pl.*	*gloss*	*underlying*	
	a.	puu	puissa	'tree'		
		püü	püissæ	'hazel grouse'		
	b.	tie	teissæ	'road'	/tee/	
		moa	maissa	'land'	/maa/	(standard Finnish: *maa*)
		üö	öissæ	'night'	/öö/	

Kiparsky notes that there are many lines in the Kalevala that violate the metrical principle (47) if scanned in accordance with the phonetic representation. Two such lines are given in (55).

(55)	a.	vapa vaskinen keæyessæ	'bronze rod in hand'
	b.	otin oinon, toin kottiin	'I took a ram and brought it home'

Line (55a) has a long stressed (i.e., word-initial) syllable *keæ* in the upbeat of the third foot, where (47) requires a short syllable. Line (55b) likewise has a long syllable *kot* on the upbeat of the third foot and in addition contains only seven syllables, whereas the meter requires eight syllables in each line. Kiparsky attributes these apparent anomalies to the level of the phonological derivation where the metrical principle (47) is applicable. Kiparsky identifies a sequence of seven ordered rules, and shows that the metrical principle (47)

---

[16] This alternation is a form of vowel harmony, introduced in section 3.2 of chapter 3 (for Turkish), and this suffix in Finnish is discussed in section 4.8 of chapter 4. Since vowel harmony is not directly relevant to the metrical analysis, and introduces additional complications, we will simply assume it here rather than give a separate rule for it.

is enforced at the stage after the first two of these rules but before the remaining five rules. The first rule is Epenthesis (56).

(56)   *First rule: Epenthesis*

$$\text{V} \quad \begin{bmatrix} \text{C} \\ +\text{coronal} \end{bmatrix} \quad \text{i} \qquad \#$$

$$\begin{array}{ccccc}
 & 1 & 2 & 3 & 4 \\
\Rightarrow & 1 & 3 & 2 & 3 & 4 \\
 & & [-\text{syll}] & & &
\end{array}$$

An example of Epenthesis is /poįka-ni/ → /poįkaįni/ (further modified by Consonant Gradation, 57) 'my son.' Epenthesis has the effect of creating a long syllable, thereby feeding rule six (62), Gemination of Consonants, in certain cases. It also creates a closed syllable, that is, a syllable whose final segment is [–syllabic], thereby feeding the second rule, Consonant Gradation (57) in some cases. We have stated the change somewhat informally in (57). Essentially, geminate stops degeminate, while a simple /p/ turns to [v] and /t/ and /k/ are dropped. In the environment, recall that the symbol C stands for any nonsyllabic segment, so that it includes glides as well as true consonants.

(57)   *Second rule: Consonant Gradation*

$$\left\{ \begin{array}{l}
\text{pp} \rightarrow \text{p} \\
\text{tt} \rightarrow \text{t} \\
\text{kk} \rightarrow \text{k} \\
\text{p} \rightarrow \text{v} \\
\text{t} \rightarrow \text{Ø} \\
\text{k} \rightarrow \text{Ø}
\end{array} \right\} \quad / \underline{\quad} \text{VC} \left\{ \begin{array}{l} \text{C} \\ \# \end{array} \right\}$$

left-to-right iterative
Condition: word-initial consonants are not gradated

We can illustrate Consonant Gradation with the nominative and genitive singular forms of some nouns in (58), where the genitive singular suffix *-n* creates the environment for Gradation.

(58)   *nominative*   *genitive*   *gloss*

    pappi   papin   'priest'

    tüttö   tütön   'girl'

    kukka   kukan   'flower'

    apu   avun   'help'

    kæsi (/kæte/) keæ̣en   'hand'

    ạika   ạian   'time

Consonant gradation can apply more than once in a single word. For example, the suffix /-ttom/ '-less' itself undergoes gradation as well as inducing gradation in a stem like *pappi*. This comes from left to right iterative application of Gradation, in a counterbleeding direction. In the genitive the geminate *tt* of the suffix is retained, since here adding the genitive suffix creates an open syllable. We give the derivations of the nominative and genitive of 'priestless' in (59).[17]

(59)   *nominative*   *genitive*
    /#pappi-ttom#/   /#pappi-ttom-an#/   underlying representations

        p   p   Gradation (first iteration)

        t   ————   Gradation (second iteration)

   [#papiton#]   [#papittoman#]   other rules;
                                  phonetic representations

In the case of /poịkaịni/, derived from /poịka-ni/ by Epenthesis, we derive /poịaịni/ = /poyaịni/ by Consonant Gradation. This form is further modified by Gemination of Consonants (62).

Kiparsky's third rule geminates a vowel before another vowel. We give the rule in (60).

(60)   *Third rule: Gemination of Vowels*

$$\begin{array}{ccc} [+syll] & [+syll] \\ 1 & 2 \end{array}$$

$$\Rightarrow \quad \begin{array}{ccc} 1 & 1 & 2 \\ & [-syll] & \end{array}$$

---

[17] We assume the genitive suffix has the (phonologically unpredictable) allomorph *-an* in this context. In the nominative, word-final m is replaced by n, since m cannot occur in word-final position in Standard Finnish.

By Gemination of Vowels the intermediate form /kæessæ/, derived from underlying /kætessæ/ by Consonant Gradation, is converted to /kæ**æ**essæ/, which in turn is further modified to /ke**æ**essæ/ by Diphthongization (53).

The fourth rule in the ordering is Diphthongization, which we have already introduced and formalized in (53).[18]

The fifth rule is Contraction, which deletes *h* between vowels. We state this rule in (61).

(61)   *Fifth rule: Contraction*
        $h \rightarrow \emptyset / V \_\_\_\_ V$

Contraction converts /koti+hin/ to /kotiin/,[19] which is further modified by the sixth rule, Gemination of Consonants, which we state in (62).

(62)   *Sixth rule: Gemination of Consonants*

$$
\begin{array}{cccccc}
V & C & V & \begin{bmatrix} -\text{cons} \\ -\text{syll} \end{bmatrix} & \left\{ \begin{array}{c} C \\ \# \end{array} \right\} \\
1 & 2 & 3 & 4 & 5 \\
\Rightarrow \quad 1 & 2 & 2 & 3 & 4 & 5
\end{array}
$$

Consonants are geminated between a short vowel and a long vowel or diphthong. The form /kotiin/, derived by Contraction, is transformed into [kottiin] 'into the house.' This is the form in which this word appears in line (55b). Recall that that line was problematic in two respects: it has only seven syllables, and the upbeat of the third foot has a heavy syllable, contrary to (47). This line is seen to be entirely regular if the poetic conventions apply to a more abstract level of representation, that is where this word has the representation /kotihin/, with one more syllable than the phonetic form (so that the line as a whole has eight syllables) and where the first syllable of this word is light, in conformity with (47) where this syllable appears in the upbeat of the third foot.

---

[18] Kiparsky puts this rule last, after Apocopation. We have ordered it before Contraction, however, because Contraction does not feed Diphthongization in forms like *pakkoon* from /pɑkko+hon/ or /pɑko+hon/ (counterfeeding order). See discussion of these forms at the end of this subsection.

[19] We assume that a [+high] vowel becomes a glide (i.e., [–syllabic]), when it comes to follow another vowel directly as a result of any other rule.

Gemination of consonants affects glides as well as true consonants, since C stands for any nonsyllabic segment. Thus /poi̯ɑi̯ni/, as it emerges from Consonant Gradation, becomes /poi̯i̯ɑi̯ni/ = /poi̯yɑi̯ni/.

The seventh rule is an optional rule of Apocopation, that deletes a final short *i* after a consonant. We write it as in (63).

(63)   *Seventh rule: Apocopation*
        i → Ø / C ____#
        (optional)

By Apocopation, an alternative phonetic form for /poi̯yɑi̯ni/, derived by Gemination of Consonants, is /poi̯yɑi̯n/.

We explained the apparent anomaly of line (55b) by proposing that the line is scanned at a point in the derivation before the operation of Contraction (61) and Gemination of Consonants. The apparent anomaly of line (55a) is explained similarly by scanning the line before the operation of Gemination of Vowels. We give the derivation of keæyessæ in (64).

(64)   /#kæte-ssæ#/   underlying representation
            Ø   Consonant Gradation (57)
            æææ̯   Gemination of Vowels (60)
            eæ̯   Diphthongization (53)
        [#keæ̯yessæ#]   other rules;[20] phonetic representation

We see that, up to the operation of Gemination of Vowels (60), *keæyessæ* has a light first syllable, so that it conforms to (47) as a stressed light syllable in the upbeat of the third foot.

In both lines of (55) the underlying representation could serve as the metrically relevant level, but Kiparsky shows that in general this is not the case and that, where Consonant Gradation changes the weight of a syllable, the output of Consonant Gradation is the form scanned by the metre. For example in line (65), the first syllable of *kesellæ* is scanned as light (as in the phonetic representation) even though it is heavy underlyingly.

(65)   istuṳ voɑn kesellæ mertæ   'just sits in the middle of the sea'
        /keske-llæ/ 'in the middle'

---

[20] Kiparsky proposes that an "automatic glide insertion" inserts [y] here, although he does not formalize the rule.

Kiparsky concludes that, in all cases, the metrically relevant level is after Consonant Gradation but before Gemination of vowels. He gives two examples of lines containing a stressed syllable that must be scanned as metrically light, even though that syllable is heavy at both the underlying and phonetic level. We give the lines in (66).

(66)   a. peælle sulkkuse sukkαin   'on my silk stockings'

     b. αnnαn αinuvαn poiyαini   'I give my only son'

The last word in each of these lines are the ones of interest. We give their complete derivations in (67).

(67)   /#sukkα-ni#/   /#poikα-ni#/   underlying representations

       i̯   i   Epenthesis (56)

       k   Ø   Consonant Gradation (57)

    sukαini   poiαini   —Metrically relevant level—

    ———   ———   Gemination of Vowels (60)

    ———   ———   Diphthongization (53)

    ———   ———   Contraction (61)

     kk   ii   Gemination of Consonants (62)

     Ø   ———   Apocopation (63)

  [#sukkαin#]   [#poiyαini#]   phonetic representations

After Consonant Gradation we have written each form in full to show the metrically relevant level. This level is actually identical to the previous line that shows the result of applying Consonant Gradation. At this level, the first syllable of each word is light, as required by (47). In addition line (66a) has only seven syllables—compare (55b)—but this results from the optional application of Apocopation (63). At the metrically relevant level the word *sukkαin* has an additional syllable, so that at that level the line as a whole contains the required eight syllables.

   A further consequence is that there can be words that are phonetically identical but metrically distinct. Kiparsky points out that the underlying representations /pαkko+hon/ 'into compulsion' and /pαko+hon/ 'into flight' merge phonetically as [pαkkoon]. Both forms are subject to Contraction (61), which deletes *h,* and 'into flight' is further subject to Gemination of

Consonants, which turns the underlying single *k* into a geminate. They remain distinct at the metrically relevant level, and are treated as metrically distinct, so that *pakkoon* 'into compulsion' almost invariably begins on a downbeat, while *pakkoon* 'into flight' almost invariably begins on a upbeat, in accordance with (47). "These, then, are word pairs which are always homonymous but never metrically equivalent" (Kiparsky 1968c, 144).

This discussion of metrics has provided strong corpus-external support for a somewhat abstract phonological analysis of Finnish along with a rather complex set of ordered rules. Perhaps the most surprising result is that the metrical analysis relies on a representation which is neither underlying nor phonetic, but intermediate between the two, the result of applying certain rules but before the application of other rules. This in turn supports the theory of grammar, specifically phonology, that makes use of abstract underlying representations and ordered rules to derive their phonetic realizations.

6.7.6   Language change

Language change is another means of gaining a window on a grammatical system. Languages change in a variety of ways, for example, by gaining or losing vocabulary items. We are concerned here with language change as a change in the grammar. Possible changes in grammar include adding a rule, losing a rule, or reordering existing rules.

A common type of sound change is for a rule to be added to the grammar. In Old High German voiced and voiceless obstruents contrasted in word-final position as well as in other positions, so that the word <tag> 'day' was pronounced [tɑg].[21] Its plural is <taga> [tɑgɑ]. In Middle High German the singular of 'day' was pronounced [tɑk], as indicated by spellings like <tac>. The plural retained the voiced stop [tɑgə] (the reduction of unstressed vowels to [ə] was an independent development in Middle High German). The phonological system changed by adding a rule devoicing obstruents in word-final position. The underlying representations of such words remained the same, retaining the stem-final voiced stop. This situation continues in modern Standard German. However, some Yiddish and Swiss dialects have undergone a further change that restores final voiced stops in words like [tɑg] and in other words like [bund] 'league,' whose plural is [bundə]. The singular of 'league' is [bunt] in Standard German. However, the final voiceless stop of [bunt] 'motley,' with the plural [buntə], underwent no such change, retaining the

---

[21] We use angled brackets <> here to enclose orthographic representations.

voiceless stop in all forms. Furthermore, certain adverbial forms that had final voiced obstruents in word-final position in Old High German, such as <ab> [ɑb] 'away,' and <enwec> 'away,' which also underwent final devoicing in Middle High German, retain their voiceless stops in these dialects. These developments are explained by saying that these dialects lost the final devoicing rule. The retention of the final voiceless stop in adverbial forms like [ɑp] and [vɛk] in these dialects is the result of *restructuring* their underlying representations. An abstract underlying representation can be learned only on the basis of evidence, generally from alternations. From alternations like [bunt] ~ [bundə] 'league, sg. and pl.' a language learner can extract the underlying representation /bund/ as well as the underlying representation /bunt/ for nonalternating forms like 'motley.' However, when the adverbial form [ɑb] in Old High German undergoes devoicing in Middle High German, the first generation of speakers may retain the underlying representation /ab/, but later generations are unable to reconstruct this abstract underlying representation because it doesn't alternate with anything. In accordance with the Naturalness Condition (16) they construct the more concrete underlying representation /ɑp/. When, at a subsequent stage, the final devoicing rule is lost, alternating [bunt] 'league' can revert to its form with an final voiced obstruent [bund], but [ɑp] remains with its final voiceless stop because its underlying representation has been changed. These stages are summarized in (68).

(68)

	underlying representations	rules	phonetic representations
a.	Old High German		
	/tɑg/ 'day'	No final devoicing	[tɑg, tɑgɑ]
	/bund/ 'league'		
	/bunt/ 'motley'		
	/ɑb/ 'away from'		[ɑb]
b.	Middle High German (first generation)		
	/tɑg/ 'day'	Final Devoicing	[tɑk], [tɑgə]
	/bund/ 'league'	rule added	[bunt], [bundə]
	/bunt/ 'motley'		[bunt], [buntə]
	/ɑb/ 'away from'		[ɑp]

c. Middle High German
    (later generations)
    /tɑg/ 'day'   [tɑk], [tɑgə]
    /bund/ 'league'   [bunt], [bundə]
    /bunt/ 'motley'   [bunt], [buntə]
    /ɑp/   [ɑp]

Same

d. Swiss, Yiddish dialects
    /tɑg/ 'day'   Final Devoicing   [tɑg], [tɑgə]
    /bund/ 'league'   rule lost   [bund], [bundə]
    /bunt/ 'motley'   [bunt], [buntə]
    /ɑp/   [ɑp]

BS

A third way in which grammars can change is by reordering existing rules. We noted in section 2.7.9 of chapter 2 that, in English, vowels are shortened before voiceless consonants. In section 2.3 of that chapter we observed that English /t/ and /d/ are merged into the flap [ɾ] before a stressless vowel. These processes are illustrated in the forms of (69).

(69)   write   [ɹəyt]   ride   [ɹɑːyd]
        writer   [ɹəyɾəɹ]   rider   [ɹɑːyɾəɹ]

These facts can be explained by two rules, Diphthong Shortening and Flapping, in that order (counterbleeding). We give a preliminary formulation of these rules in (70).

(70)   a.   *Diphthong Shortening*

        $$V \rightarrow \begin{bmatrix} -low \\ -tense \end{bmatrix} / \underline{\hspace{1cm}} \begin{bmatrix} -cons \\ -syll \end{bmatrix} [-voice]$$

        Condition: applies within a phonological word

        b.   *Flapping*[22]

        $$\begin{bmatrix} +cor \\ -strid \\ -cont \end{bmatrix} \rightarrow ɾ / [-cons] \underline{\hspace{1cm}} \begin{bmatrix} +syll \\ -stress \end{bmatrix}$$

---

[22] Flapping is reformulated in (40) of section 7.2.3 in terms of the phonological utterance, with no reference to stress.

With these rules we have derivations like those in (71).

(71)   /#ɹɑyt#/   /#ɹɑyd#/   /#ɹɑyt + əɹ#/   /#ɹɑyd + əɹ#/   underlying
                                                                representations

        ə   ─────   ə   ─────   Diphthong
                                                              Shortening

        ─────   ─────   ɾ   ɾ   Flapping

       [#ɹəyt#]   [#ɹɑyd#]   [#ɹəyɾəɹ#]   [#ɹɑyɾəɹ#]   phonetic
                                                              representations

       'write'   'ride'   'writer'   'rider'

In some dialects the order of these two rules is reversed, so that 'writer' and 'rider' are homophonous. In the derivation of 'writer' in (71) these rules are in a counterbleeding order. In dialects that reverse the two rules, the order is bleeding in this word, as illustrated in (72).

(72)   /#ɹɑyt#/   /#ɹɑyd#/   /#ɹɑyt + əɹ#/   /#ɹɑyd + əɹ#/   underlying
                                                                representations

        ─────   ─────   ɾ   ɾ   Flapping

        ə   ─────   ─────   ─────   Diphthong
                                                              Shortening

       [#ɹəyt#]   [#ɹɑyd#]   [#ɹɑyɾəɹ#]   [#ɹɑyɾəɹ#]   phonetic
                                                              representations

       'write'   'ride'   'writer'   'rider'

In our discussion of rule addition, we tacitly assumed that the new rule is ordered after phonological rules already in the grammar. Another possibility is for a rule to be added at an earlier point in the grammar, before one or more existing phonological rules. This has been called *rule insertion* (King 1973). An example is Old English palatalization. The velar stops in Old English are palatalized before front vowels by rule (73).

(73)   *Palatalization (Old English)*

$$\begin{Bmatrix} k \rightarrow \check{c} \\ g \rightarrow y \end{Bmatrix} / \underline{\hspace{1cm}} \begin{bmatrix} +syll \\ -back \end{bmatrix}$$

This rule is illustrated in (74). The modern English development is given where it differs from the gloss of the Old English word, and German cognates[23] are given to show that this rule does not operate in German.

(74)

Old English spelling	phonetic	gloss	Modern English development	German	gloss
ceorl	čeǫrl	'peasant'	churl	Kerl	'fellow'
cirice	čiriče	'church'		Kirche	
geolu	yeǫlu	'yellow'		gelb	

There are paradigmatic alternations between [k] and [č] in some verbs, as in (75).

(75)

spelling	phonetic	gloss
cēosan	čeːǫzɑn	'to choose'
cēas	čæːǫs	'I chose'
curon	kuron	'we, they chose'
coren	koren	'chosen'

However, Palatalization does not take place before front vowels that result from the rule of I-Umlaut. This rule makes back vowels front if they are followed in the next syllable by the high front vowel [i] or the corresponding glide [y]. (In some cases the vowel is raised from low to mid as well, but this does not concern us here.) This is illustrated in (76)

(76)

Old English spelling	phonetic	gloss	Modern English development	pre–Old English source
cyning	küninɡ	'king'		*kuni
cȳ	küː	'cows'	kine	*kūiz
cemban	kembɑn	'to comb'	unkempt	*kɑmbiɑn
cennan	kennɑn	'to know'	ken (dial.)	*kɑnniɑn
gēs	geːs	'geese'	geese	*gōsi
gǣst	gæːst	'goest'		*gāis

---

[23] Related words in related languages that are derived from a common source in the ancestor language are called *cognates*. The ancestor language in this case is Proto-Germanic.

This situation is explained by ordering Palatalization before I-Umlaut in the synchronic grammar of Old English. However, the chronological order is the reverse. I-Umlaut is an old feature of North and West Germanic languages; in fact, all the Germanic languages except Gothic have this rule in basically the same form in their grammars. Palatalization is a much later innovation in Anglo-Frisian (Old English and Frisian); it does not exist in Old High German or Old Saxon or the early Nordic languages. Thus it appears that Palatalization was added to the Grammar of Old English, but not at the end of the ordered rules but rather before the existing rule of I-Umlaut.

King (1973, 564) disputes this as an example of rule insertion, and in fact claims that all cases that have been analyzed as rule insertion should be reanalyzed as rule addition at the end of the ordering followed by reordering. Kiparsky (1968b) proposed that rule reordering is governed by a principle according to which rules move into an order that maximizes their utilization in the grammar. According to this principle, counterfeeding orders tend to change into feeding orders and bleeding orders tend to change into counterbleeding orders. Kiparsky's principle would not predict reordering in the Old English case because the synchronic ordering, in the derivations under discussion, is counterfeeding. King discusses another possible principle governing reordering according to which rules tend to reorder in such a way as to minimize paradigmatic alternation. He applies this idea to the Old English case. With I-Umlaut ordered before Palatalization, a feeding order, a word like [goːs] 'goose' would have a plural [yeːs], showing an alternation in the initial consonant. In the counterfeeding order, Palatalization before I-Umlaut, we have a paradigm that includes [goːs] and [gēs], where both forms begin with the velar stop. This order minimizes paradigmatic alternation. The problem with King's approach is that the theory of generative phonology has no formal way of expressing the concept of paradigm uniformity. A derivation begins with an underlying representation and ends with a phonetic representation after the the operation of all relevant phonological rules. But a derivation cannot compare its result to that of another derivation, nor can it be influenced by another derivation. Such *transderivational constraints* are clearly a powerful device that must be given a formal interpretation that limits their power and even then used with caution.

It is clearly difficult to tell these two types of historical analysis apart, but King's analysis, with rule addition at the end followed by reordering, predicts that there should be a stage where the synchronic order corresponds to the historical order, that is where the Old English forms in (76) had palatalized velars. Such a stage does not exist,[24] so Old English Palatalization is a likely candidate for rule insertion.

Regardless of whether rule insertion is possible or not, the types of historical change that are describable as rule addition, rule loss, and rule reordering provide corpus-external support for the concept of grammar as a set of ordered rules that convert underlying representations to phonetic forms.

6.7.7 Maori

In exercise 4.2 of chapter 4 we considered some forms of Maori, some of which were discussed in section 5.4 of chapter 5. We repeat the examples in (77).

(77)	*active*	*passive*	*gerundive*	*gloss*
	awhi	awhitia	awhitaŋa	'embrace'
	hopu	hopukia	hopukaŋa	'catch'
	mau	mauria	mauraŋa	'carry'
	inu	inumia	inumaŋa	'drink'
	aru	arumia	arumaŋa	'follow'
	tohu	tohuŋia	tohuŋaŋa	'point out'
	kimi	kimihia	kimihaŋa	'seek'
	wero	werohia	werohaŋa	'stab'
	patu	patua	patuŋa	'strike, kill'
	kite	kitea	kiteŋa	'see, find'

The solution in terms of the criteria of phonological analysis introduced in (5) chapter 4 includes the underlying representations and rules in (78). Call this the *phonological solution.*

---

[24] There is a single instance of a spelling that may indicate a palatalized /k/ (i.e., [č]), the word *chūn* 'cows' in the Lindisfarne Gospels. However, this may be a scribal error, and in any case little follows from a single example.

(78) *stems*   *affixes*

/awhit/   'embrace'   /-ia/   'passive'

/hopuk/   'catch'   /-aŋa/ 'gerundive'

/maur/   'carry

/inum/   'drink'   *rules*

/arum/   'follow   *Consonant Deletion*

/tohuŋ/   'point out'   C → Ø / ____ #

/kimih/   'seek'

/weroh/   'stab'   *Vowel Deletion*

/patu/   'strike, kill'   V → Ø / V+____

/kite/   'see, find'

Obviously, an alternative solution, that can be called the *morphological solution,* in which the underlying representations of the stems were the same as the active forms in the left column of (77), and in which there were multiple forms for the affixes (passive: /-tia, kia, -ria, -mia, -ŋia, -hia, a/ and gerundive /-taŋa, -kaŋa, -raŋa, maŋa, haŋa, -ŋa/) would be far more complex. Each stem would have to be marked for which passive suffix it takes, and it would be a complete accident that the same initial consonant appears in the gerundive suffix as well for each of those stems. Furthermore it would fail to link the C~Ø alternation with the fact that no word ends in a consonant in Maori.

However, Hale (1973) proposes that the morphological solution is correct in this case, and offers corpus-external support for the position that *-tia* is actually the productive, regular passive suffix. (1) Nominal stems used verbally in spontaneous discourse take the passive suffix *-tia.* (2) Derived causatives take *-tia* in the passive even though their basic stem may take a different suffix in the noncausative. For example, the passive of *fakahopu* 'cause to catch' is *fakahoputia* even though the passive of *hopu* is *hopukia.* (3) Certain adverbials agree in voice with the verb by taking the suffix *-tia* in the passive regardless of the passive ending on the verb itself. (4) English loanwords, even if they are so unassimilated that they retain a final consonant, form passives in *-tia.* (5) Compound verbs formed by the incorporation of an adverbial phrase regularly form the passive in *-tia.* (6) The suffix *-tia* can be used on any verb if the conventional passive form is forgotten. These six facts would not be predictable on the phonological analysis. Under the phonological analysis it would be a mystery why verb stems that end in a consonant should replace that consonant by /t/ in derived causatives or when a speaker forgets the passive form. Hale proposes that speakers take the fact that all words end in a vowel as something that should be represented in underlying representations. So in this case, corpus-external evidence supports a less abstract analysis of the data. However, it is not so clear how general this conclusion is. It is still preferable to have a phonological analysis that conforms to the criteria of predictability, naturalness, and simplicity, unless there is strong corpus-external evidence to the contrary.

6.8   Exercises

6.1   Nupe (Hyman 1970)

Nupe has five vowels phonetically: [i, e, ɑ, o, u]. Palatalization and labialization are predictable on consonants before nonlow vowels. Write a rule to account for this.

èdʸé	'cloth'	yèkʷó	'road'
ēgʸē	'beer'	ēgʷó	'grass'
ēgʸī	'child'	ēgʷū̄	'mud'

Palatalized and labialized consonants appear to contrast with plain consonants before the low vowel [ɑ]. Propose underlying representations that allow these forms to be predicted by your rule (adjust your rule if necessary). A second rule will also be required.

ēgʸā	'blood'	ēgʷā	'hand'
ètʸā	'is/are mild'	étʷá	'is/are trimming'
ēgā	'stranger'	tá	'to tell'

Nupe has a reduplication process that forms nominalizations from verbs. State the reduplication as a morphological process using features and show how it fits into your phonological analysis.

gʸí	'to eat'	gʸīgʸí	'eating'
gʸē	'to be good'	gʸīgʸē	'goodness'
gʷú	'to puncture'	gʷūgʷú	'puncturing'

(Continued)

gʷò	'to receive'	gʷūgʷò	'receiving'
tʷá	'to trim'	tʷūtʷá	'trimming'
tʸá	'to be mild'	tʸɪtʸá	'mildness'
tá	'to tell'	tʸītá	'telling'

Nupe has borrowed a number of words from Yoruba. How do these examples bear on your analysis?

Yoruba	Nupe	gloss
kèké	kʸàkʸá	'bicycle'
èg͡bè	èg͡bʸà	a Yoruba town
tɔ̄rē	tʷārʸā	'to give a gift'
kɔ́bɔ̀	kʷábʷà	'penny'

6.2 Hungarian (Jensen 1972; Vago 1980)

nom.	'to' dative	'from' 'ablative	'by' adessive	'from off'	gloss
haːz	haːznɒk	haːstoːl	haːznaːl	haːzroːl	'house'
vaːroš	vaːrošnɒk	vaːroštoːl	vaːrošnaːl	vaːrošroːl	'city'
moːkuš	moːkušnɒk	moːkuštoːl	moːkušnaːl	moːkušroːl	'squirrel'
öröm	örömnɛk	örömtöːl	örömneːl	örömröːl	'joy'
tömɛg	tömɛgnɛk	tömɛgtöːl	tömɛgneːl	tömɛgröːl	'crowd'
idöː	idöːnɛk	idöːtöːl	idöːneːl	idöːröl	'time'
siːn	siːnnɛk	siːntöːl	siːnneːl	siːnröːl	'colour'
sɛgeːɲ	sɛgeːɲnɛk	sɛgeːɲtöːl	sɛgeːɲneːl	sɛgeːɲröːl	'poor'
kɛrt	kɛrtnɛk	kɛrttöːl	kɛrtneːl	kɛrtröːl	'garden'
rɒdiːr	rɒdiːrnɒk	rɒdiːrtoːl	rɒdiːrnaːl	rɒdiːrroːl	'eraser'
hiːd	hiːdnɒk	hiːttoːl	hiːdnaːl	hiːdroːl	'bridge'
ɲiːl	ɲiːlnɒk	ɲiːltoːl	ɲiːlnaːl	ɲiːlroːl	'arrow'
t͡seːl	t͡seːlnɒk	t͡seːltoːl	t͡seːlnaːl	t͡seːlroːl	'goal'
	nɛkɛm	töːlɛm	naːlɒm	roːlɒm	'me'
	nɛkɛd	töːlɛd	naːlɒd	roːlɒd	'you sg.'

6.3   Okpe (Hoffmann 1973)

Okpe distinguishes tense [+ATR] and lax [−ATR] vowels, and has vowel harmony involving this feature, but this distinction is *phonetically* apparent only in the case of mid vowels. Assume that all roots are monosyllabic in the underlying representation and that all glides alternating with vowels are derived by rule. Give the underlying representation of all morphemes and write a set of ordered rules to account for the alternations.

imperative	infinitive	3 sg. past	1 sg. past	3 sg. contin.	Gloss
ti	etyo	o tiri	mi tiri	o tyɛ	'pull'
ru	erwo	o ruru	mi ruru	o rwɛ	'do'
sĩ	esyõ	o sĩrĩ	mi sĩrĩ	o syẽ	'bury'
zũ	ezwõ	o zũrũ	mi zũrũ	o zwẽ	'fan'
se	ese	oseri	mi seri	o se	'fill'
kpe	ekpe	o kperi	mi kperi	o kpe	'beat'
nẽ	enẽ	o nẽrĩ	mi nẽrĩ	o nẽ	'defecate'
so	eso	o sori	mi sori	o so	'steal'
gbõ	egbõ	o gbõrĩ	mi gbõrĩ	o gbõ	'rot'
zɛ	ɛzɛ	ɔ zɛre	me zɛre	ɔ zɛ	'run'
dɛ	ɛde	ɔ dɛre	me dɛre	ɔ dɛ	'buy'
lɔ	ɛlɔ	ɔ lɔre	me lɔre	ɔ lɔ	'grind'
wɔ	ɛwɔ	ɔ wɔre	me wɔre	ɔ wɔ	'bathe'
tõ	ɛtõ	ɔ tõrẽ	me tõrẽ	ɔ tõ	'dig'
da	ɛda	ɔ dare	me dare	ɔ da	'drink'
dã	ɛdã	ɔ dãrẽ	me dãrẽ	ɔ dã	'fly'
re	ɛryɔ	ɔ rere	me rere	ɔ rya	'eat'
rhe	ɛrhyɔ	ɔ rhere	me rhere	ɔ rhya	'come'
tẽ	ɛtyõ	ɔ tẽrẽ	me tẽrẽ	ɔ tyã	'refuse'
so	ɛswɔ	ɔ soro	me soro	ɔ swa	'sing'

6.4   Ukrainian (Struk 1978, Andruyshen 1985)

Ukrainian has a contrast between palatalized and nonpalatalized coronals, as shown by minimal pairs such as the following:

test	'test'	test^y	'father in law'
pyat	'heel (gen. pl.)	pyat^y	'five'
povid	'bridle'	povid^y	'high water'
grud	'clod (gen. pl.)'	grud^y	'breast'
trus	'search (n.)'	trus^y	'rabbit'
os	'wasp (gen. pl.)'	os^y	'here'
vyɑz	'elm tree'	vyɑz^y	'band'
stɑn	'state, condition'	stɑn^y	'stable (gen. pl.)'
kil	'stake'	kil^y	'keel'

In addition, there is a rule palatalizing coronal consonants before the vowel /i/, and a rule depalatalizing coronal consonants before the vowel /e/. Another rule is needed to account for the alternations between the vowels /o/ and /e/ in some forms and /i/ in other forms. A fourth rule converts underlying /l/ and /v/ to /w/. On the basis of the data below, based on Western dialects, determine the underlying representations of all roots and suffixes and formulate the four rules and determine their ordering. You should be able to account for the distribution of palatalized and nonpalatalized coronals in the underlying representations. Note that the variation between -*a* and -*u* in the genitive singular of masculine nouns and the variation between -*o* and -*e* in the nominative singular of neuter nouns is morphologically determined. In masculine nouns referring to persons the morpheme -*ov~-ev* appears between the root and the case morpheme for the locative singular, again morphologically determined. You should not try to account for this morphological variation with phonological rules.

Masculine nouns

nom. sg.	*gen. sg.*	*loc. sg.*	*gen. pl.*	*dat. pl.*	*gloss*
brat	brata	bratovi	brat^{y}iw	bratam	'brother'
xl^{y}ib	xl^{y}iba	xl^{y}ibi	xl^{y}ibiw	xl^{y}ibam	'bread'

(Continued)

list	lista	list^{y}i	list^{y}iw	listam	'letter'
svit	svitu	svit^{y}i	svit^{y}iw	svitam	'world'
mis^{y}at͡s^y	mis^{y}at͡s^{y}a	mistat͡s^{y}i	mistat͡s^{y}iw	mistat͡s^{y}am	'month'
od^{y}ah	od^{y}ahu	od^{y}ahi	od^{y}ahiw	od^{y}aham	'clothing'
dim	domu	domi	domiw	domam	'home'
stiw	stola	stol^{y}i	stol^{y}iw	stolam	'table'
nis	nosa	nos^{y}i	nos^{y}iw	nosam	'nose'
kɨyiw	kɨyeva	kɨyevi			'Kiev'
korin^y	koren^{y}a	koren^{y}i	koren^{y}iw	koren^{y}am	'root'
kol^{y}ir	kol^{y}oru	kol^{y}ori	kol^{y}oriw	kol^{y}oram	'colour'
učitel^y	učitel^{y}a	učitelevi	učitel^{y}iw	učitel^{y}am	'teacher'

Neuter nouns

nom. sg.	*gen. sg.*	*dat. sg.*	*loc. sg.*	*gen. pl.*	*gloss*
l^{y}ito	l^{y}ita	l^{y}itu	l^{y}it^{y}i	l^{y}it	'summer'
lit͡se	lit͡s^{y}a	lit͡s^{y}u	lit͡s^{y}i	lit͡s^y	'face'
pole	pol^{y}a	pol^{y}u	pol^{y}i	pil^y	'field'
d^{y}ilo	d^{y}ila	d^{y}ilu	d^{y}il^{y}i	d^{y}iw	'affair'
ozero	ozera	ozeru	ozeri	oz^{y}ir	'lake'
selo	sela	selu	sel^{y}i	s^{y}iw	'village'
slovo	slova	slovu	slovi	sliw	'word'

What difficulties are encountered if you try to account for the same data by means of the morpheme alternant theory? In most Eastern dialects, the rule palatalizing coronals before /i/ is true phonetically; that is, we have the forms below for nominative singular of 'home' and 'nose' rather the ones in the table above.

d^{y}im   'home'
n^{y}is   'nose'

Explain the Eastern dialects in terms of your analysis. Which dialect is likely to be the innovative one, and why?

6.5   Land Dayak (Scott 1964; Kenstowicz & Kisseberth 1979, 146ff.)

a. Formulate rules to account for the distribution of nasal vowels and
    voiced stop–nasal clusters in the following data. Note that *nũʔãːn*
    and *mɔ̃ʔãn* are derived from the same bases as *tuʔaːdn* and *pəʔadn*
    by a morphological process that converts the initial voiceless stop
    to the corresponding nasal. This morphological process takes place
    before all phonological rules.

mãlu	'strike'	sampɛː	'extending to'
umɔ̃	'water'	int͡seh	'is'
nãbur	'sow'	suntɔk	'in need of'
ənãk	'child'	suŋkoi	'cooked rice'
siŋãũ	'cat'	mpɑhit	'send'
ntakɑdn	'taste'	kiñãm	'feeling'
pəlabm	'mango'	pimãĩn	'a game'
kaidn	'cloth'	pəmĩŋ	'dizzy'
pɑdɑgŋ	'field'	tanĩn	'story'
tuʔaːdn	'open'	nũʔãːn	'open'
pəʔadn	'feed'	mɔ̃ʔãn	'eat'

b. Although voiced and voiceless stops contrast in other positions,
    voiced stops do not appear after a nasal, although voiceless stops
    do appear in this position. Formulate an additional rule along with
    appropriate underlying representations that both explain this dis-
    tributional gap and account for some apparent exceptions to the
    vowel nasalization rule.

əmudn	'dew'	bɑnugŋ	'tapioca'
mɔ̃nabm	'sickness'	girunugŋ	'a small bell'
ənaːgŋ	'prawn'	kənãŋ	'posterior'

6.6   Estonian (Oinas 1968, Tauli 1973)

Assume that the case suffixes have the following underlying representations:

Nominative singular: Ø
Genitive singular: -h
Partitive singular: -tɑ
Inessive singular: -s

Determine the underlying representations of all stems and formulate ordered rules to account for the phonetic forms given. Note any difficulties that are encountered with a less abstract solution. Your rules should account for alternations in length of both consonants and vowels. One of your rules deletes a word-final vowel; this rule is blocked if its output would consist solely of the sequence (C)VC. Note that diphthongs may have the second (nonsyllabic) element lengthened, and that traditionally overlong vowels are represented as diphthongs of two identical vowels, of which the second is marked long. Similarly, overlong consonants are represented as clusters of two identical consonants, with the first marked long.

nom. sg.	gen. sg.	part. sg.	inessive sg.	gloss
mɑkːs	mɑksɑ	mɑkːsɑ	mɑksɑs	'liver'
linːn	linnɑ	linːnɑ	linnɑs	'city'
nukːk	nukkɑ	nukːkɑ	nukkɑs	'corner'
lɑẹːv	lɑẹvɑ	lɑẹːvɑ	lɑẹvɑs	'ship'
isɑ	isɑ	isɑ	isɑs	'father'
mɑkːs	mɑksu	mɑkːsu	mɑksus	'payment'
nukːk	nukku	nukːku	nukkus	'doll'
lɑu̯ːl	lɑu̯lu	lɑu̯ːlu	lɑu̯lus	'song'
tɑlu	tɑlu	tɑlu	tɑlus	'farm'
lilːl	lille	lilːle	lilles	'song'
nimi	nime	nime	nimes	'name'
kɑsʸːsʸ	kɑsʸsʸi	kɑsʸːsʸi	kɑsʸsʸis	'cat'
roŋːg	roŋgi	roŋːgi	roŋgis	'train'

(Continued)

koo̰ːlʸ	koo̰lʸi	koo̰ːlʸi	koo̰lʸis	'school'
kivi	kivi	kivi	kivis	'stone'
tupɑ	toɑ̰ː	tupɑ	toɑ̰ːs	'room'
leḭːp	leḭva	leḭːpɑ	leḭvas	'bread'
raṵːt	raṵwa	raṵːta	raṵwas	'iron'
silːt	sillɑ	silːtɑ	sillɑs	'bridge'
ləṵːk	ləṵwa	ləṵːka	ləṵwas	'chin'
yalːk	yalɑ	yalːkɑ	yalɑs	'leg'
orp	orvu	orːpu	orvus	'orphan'
itu	eo̰ː	itu	eo̰ːs	'germ'
mɑtu	mɑo̰ː	mɑtu	mɑo̰ːs	'snake'
linːt	linnu	linːtu	linnus	'bird'
oḭːt	oḭyu	oḭːtu	oḭyus	'intelligence'

7 Multilinear phonology

Up to this point we have been assuming that phonological representations consist strictly of a linear sequence of segments and boundaries, as proposed in *SPE*. While this linear theory accounts for a great many phonological phenomena, as we have seen, its shortcomings became apparent shortly after the appearance of *SPE*. These difficulties have led to proposals for a "nonlinear" approach to phonology, although "multilinear" is a more appropriate term, since these approaches add additional lines to phonological representations. The principal proposals along these lines are *autosegmental* phonology, in which certain features are extracted from the representations of individual segments and given a line of their own, and *metrical* and *prosodic* phonology, in which the line of segments is organized into higher-level units, such as syllables and feet. We will also discuss a third revision of *SPE* theory that arose in the context of autosegmental and metrical and prosodic approaches, but is essentially independent of these: underspecification theory. Finally, we will look briefly at the theory of lexical phonology, which provides a means of organizing the phonology in relation to other components of grammar: semantics, syntax, and morphology.

7.1 Autosegmental phonology

7.1.1 Tone

SPE did not propose features for tone. Wang (1967) proposed a set of seven features for tone. These are given in (1) along with some of the tone contours distinguished by these features, in the tone-letter notation of Chao (1930), which also appears in the IPA chart on page 3. The tone letters distinguish up to five level pitches and various contours, as shown.

(1)

	1	2	3	4	5	6	7	8	9	10	11	12	13
	˥	˩	˦	˧	˧	˩˥	˧˥	˥˩	˧˩	˦˩	˩˦	˩˥˩	˥˩˥
[Contour]	–	–	–	–	–	+	+	+	+	+	+	+	+
[High]	+	–	+	–	–	+	–	+	–	+	–	+	–
[Central]	–	–	+	+	+	–	–	–	–	–	–	–	–
[Mid]	–	–	–	–	+	–	–	–	–	–	–	–	–
[Rising]	–	–	–	–	–	+	+	–	–	+	+	+	+
[Falling]	–	–	–	–	–	–	–	+	+	+	+	+	+
[Convex]	–	–	–	–	–	–	–	–	–	–	–	+	+

However, there are a number of ways in which tonal features act quite unlike the segmental features we discussed in chapter 3. One is that a contour tone often behaves like a sequence of level tones: a falling tone acts like a sequence of a high tone and a low tone, and so on. A striking example occurs in Mende (Leben 1973). Mende nouns may be one, two, or three syllables long. A short vowel can appear in one of five tone patterns: *high, low, falling, rising,* and *rising–falling.* But these tonal patterns cannot appear freely on the vowels of a word; in fact, the tone patterns of morphemes are restricted to these same five patterns. The same five tonal patterns can appear on morphemes of up to three syllables, as shown in (2).

(2)

syllables	*one*		*two*	
high tone	kɔ́	'war'	pɛ́lɛ́	'house'
low tone	kpà	'debt'	bÈlÈ	'trousers'
falling tone	mbû	'owl'	kényà	'uncle'
rising tone	mbǎ	'rice'	nìká	'cow'
rising–falling tone	mbã̌	'companion'	nyàhâ	'woman'
	(three syllables)		nìkílì	'groundnut'

So a word with a high tone pattern has high tone on each syllable, whether the word has one, two, or three syllables. A low tone pattern works the same way. With contour tones, the entire contour is realized on a single vowel on a word of one syllable, but spread out over two or three syllables when words are of that size. It would be difficult to express the equivalence of the falling tone on *mbû* (Wang's tone 8) with the sequence of high and low on *kényà* (Wang's 1 and 2). In autosegmental theory this is expressed by assigning tone to a tier separate from the segmental features. A given morpheme in (2) would then consist of a sequence of segments plus one of the five tonal patterns, expressed as H (high tone), L (low tone), HL (high–low, i.e., falling), LH (low–high), or LHL. Initially, the tones would not be associated to the segments. Association is achieved by the association conventions in (3) (Goldsmith 1976).

(3) a. Associate free autosegments to appropriate segments one to one, left to right.
   b. All appropriate segments must be linked to an autosegment.
   c. All autosegments must be linked to an appropriate segment.
   d. Association lines may not cross.

Some sample derivations of words from (2) are given in (4). While Goldsmith regarded the statements in (3) as purely well-formedness conditions, Pulleyblank (1986) has demonstrated the need for rules of autosegmental association, and that such association cannot simply be the result of conditions. We will thus continue to regard (3a), at least, as a rule.

(4) a. H   H
                                     |
        /kɔ/   →   ·kɔ

     b. H   H
                                    ╱╲
        /pɛlɛ/   →   pɛ   lɛ

     c. HL   H   L
                                   ╲ ╱
        /mbu/   →   mbu

     d. HL   H L
                                   | |
        /kenya/   →   kenya

     e. LHL   L H L
                                    ╲ |╱
        /mba/   →   mba

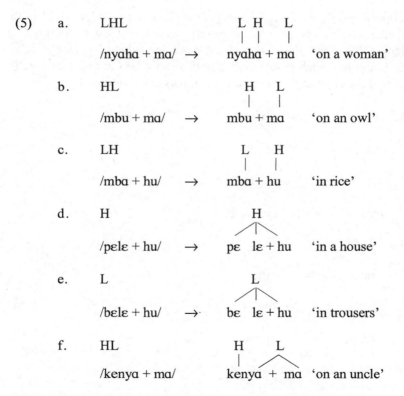

f. LHL   L H L
    /nyaha/   →   nyaha

g. LHL   L H L
    /nikili/   →   ni ki li

When the words in (2) are combined with underlyingly toneless suffixes, the
entire word is treated as the domain for the spreading of the underlying tone
pattern of the root, as shown in (5). This again shows the indpendence of the
tone pattern from the segment sequence, and further justifies treating tone
autosegmentally (Leben 1973).

(5)   a.   LHL   L H   L
             /nyaha + ma/ →   nyaha + ma   'on a woman'

       b.   HL   H   L
             /mbu + ma/   →   mbu + ma   'on an owl'

       c.   LH   L   H
             /mba + hu/   →   mba + hu   'in rice'

       d.   H   H
             /pεlε + hu/   →   pε lε + hu   'in a house'

       e.   L   L
             /bεlε + hu/   →·   bε lε + hu   'in trousers'

       f.   HL   H   L
             /kenya + ma/   kenya + ma   'on an uncle'

When *nyàhâ* 'woman' occurs in isolation, the second and third underlying tones (HL) both associate with the final vowel, producing a falling tone on this syllable. But when this same word has the toneless suffix *ma* 'on' attached, the underlying tone melody of the root (LHL) has three syllables to spread over, and so the final L of the underlying melody attaches to the suffix rather than to the final vowel of the root. Conversely, when the underlying tone melody has fewer tones than there are syllables available, the last available tone spreads over as many syllables as remain. These representations are all predicted by the association conventions (3), which require one-to-one association from left to right, with additional associations as necessary to ensure that all tones are associated and that all vowels are associated to some tone.

A particularly striking example of the independence of tone from the segments occurs in Kikuyu (Goldsmith 1990, 13–14). Here, each morpheme is associated with a tone in its underlying representation, but a morpheme may be realized phonetically with quite a different tone. In this language a verb form can consist of a subject marker followed by an object marker, a root, and a tense suffix, in that order. Some of these morphemes are given in (6).

(6)   a. $\begin{bmatrix} L \\ to \end{bmatrix}$ 'we' (subject marker)

       b. $\begin{bmatrix} H \\ ma \end{bmatrix}$ 'them' (objrct marker)

       c. $\begin{bmatrix} L \\ rɔr \end{bmatrix}$ 'look at' (root)

       d. $\begin{bmatrix} H \\ irɛ \end{bmatrix}$ 'past'

These morphemes can be concatenated in that order to give the verb in (7).

(7) $\begin{bmatrix} L & H & L & H \\ to & ma & rɔr & irɛ \end{bmatrix}$

Kikuyu has a rule that requires that the first tone in a construction such as (7) be associated with the second vowel of the sequence. In the notation commonly used for autosegmental rules, this rule is given in (8). This rule is ordered before the association conventions (3).

(8)
$$
\begin{bmatrix} T_{\text{---------}} \\ C_0 \quad V \quad C_0 \quad \bar{V} \end{bmatrix}
$$

A dotted line in an autosegmental rule says "add this association line." The result of applying rule (8) to the underlying representation (7) is given in (9).

(9)   L   H   L   H

to   ma   rɔr   irɛ

Subsequently, the association conventions (3) apply, resulting in the representation (10). The result of this sequence of events is that each tone ends up on a vowel to the right of the one it was initially associated with, except that the first tone is ultimately associated with both the vowel it was associated with and with the one to its right.

(10)   L   H   L   H

to   ma   rɔr   i   rɛ

Without the resources of autosegmental phonology, especially the ability to represent tone on a separate tier from the segmental features, it would be difficult to capture the appropriate generalizations of tone systems such as Mende and Kikuyu. Such independence of tones from other features is very common in tone languages, and so autosegmental theory is appropriate for the description of such systems.

7.1.2   Vowel harmony

A second area where autosegmental theory is invoked is in the description of vowel harmony. In chapter 3 we observed that Turkish vowels harmonize, or assimilate, within a word, in terms of the features [back] and [round]. Any vowel assumes the same value for [back] as the preceding vowel, which has the effect of making all the vowels in a word the same for this feature, either [+back] or [−back]. In addition, vowels that are [+high] assimilate to the value of [round] of the preceding vowel. In (54) of chapter 4 we provided a left-to-right iterative rule that performs the appropriate assimilation in both [back] and [round]. We repeat this rule here as (11).

(11)   *Vowel Harmony (Turkish)*

$$\begin{bmatrix} +\text{syll} \\ \langle +\text{high} \rangle \end{bmatrix} \rightarrow \begin{bmatrix} \alpha\text{back} \\ \langle \beta\text{round} \rangle \end{bmatrix} / \begin{bmatrix} +\text{syll} \\ \alpha\text{back} \\ \beta\text{round} \end{bmatrix} C_0 \underline{\quad} \text{(left to right iterative)}$$

Clements & Sezer (1982) analyze this system autosegmentally by assigning the features [back] and [round] each to their own autosegmental tier. Root morphemes are associated with autosegments for these features (analogous to the morphemic tone patterns in Mende), while all other features are represented on individual segments, including [high] for vowels. Autosegments [back] and [round] then spread to suffix vowels that are unspecified for these features, similar to the tone spreading in Mende. This can be illustrated in (12) with some representative forms from chapter 3. (B abbreviates [back]; R abbreviates [round].)

(12)   a.   −B

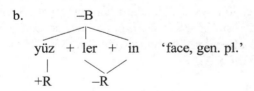

             yüz + ün   'face, gen. sg.'

                  +R

        b.   −B

             yüz + ler + in   'face, gen. pl.'

              | _/
             +R   −R

        c.   +B

             sap + in   'stalk, gen. sg.'

                  −R

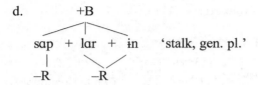

d.   +B

sɑp + lɑr + ɪn   'stalk, gen. pl.'

—R   —R

As with tone, we assume that suffix vowels may be unspecified for the har-monic features in underlying representation. The genitive suffix is specified with an underlying segmental [+high] vowel, but it has no underlying autoseg-ments for [back] or [round]. The plural suffix is segmentally specified for [−high] and autosegmentally specified with a [−round] autosegment. Vowels in root morphemes are segmentally specified for [±high]. If [+high] they carry no autosegments for either [back] or [round]; if [−high] they are specified autosegmentally for [−round]. Suffix vowels are therefore *archiphonemes,* as hinted in chapter 3, where we used the notation [I] for the natural class [+syll, +high] and A for [+syll, +high, −round]. The autosegments [+back] or [−back], [+round] or [−round] spread to suffixes, as shown in (12). In (12b), the autosegment [−round] on the plural suffix prevents spreading of the root specification [+round], and itself spreads to the genitive vowel in this form. We assume a similar derivation in (12d), although it is possible that the sequence of two [−round] autosegments in this form is simplified to a single specification, linked to all three vowels.[1]

Clements & Sezer discuss a number of other aspects of Turkish harmony in terms of this framework. One is disharmonic suffixes, such as *-Iyor* 'pro-gressive,' whose first vowel follows the standard harmonic pattern of high vowels (just like the genitive suffix *-In* in (12), but whose second vowel is invariably *o,* which in turn affects following vowels harmonically. We give some examples of this suffix in (13).

(13)   a. gel-iyor-um   'I am coming'

        b. koš-uyor-um   'I am running'

        c. gül-üyou-um   'I am laughing'

        d. bɑk-ɪyor-um   'I am looking'

This is handled rather straightforwardly by associating the second vowel of the suffix *-Iyor* wth the autosegments [+back] and [+round]. The association

---

[1] This is referred to as the Obligatory Contour Principle or OCP. The term is due to Leben (1973). The idea is that a sequence of autosegments should not be identical.

conventions in (3) are interpreted in such a way that only previously unlinked segments receive a value by autosegmental spreading. The lexical specification of [+round] on the second vowel of *-Iyor* both prevents spreading of [−round] to this vowel in cases like (13a, c) and ensures that the vowel of the following suffix *-Im* harmonizes to the *o* of *-Iyor*. Clause (3d) of the association conventions prevents spreading of the features [back] and [round] from the vowels preceding this *o* to the vowels following it.

7.1.3 Stability

Some phonological features are sufficiently independent of their segments to remain in place even when the segment they started off on are deleted. This is especially the case with tone. Goldsmith (1990, 28–29) gives the example from KiRundi in (14).

(14)

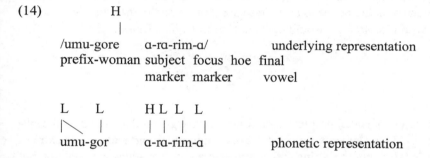

/umu-gore	a-ra-rim-a/	underlying representation
prefix-woman	subject focus hoe	final
	marker marker	vowel

From Goldsmith's discussion we assume that only high tone is marked underlyingly, with low tone inserted by default on all vowels unspecified at the end of the derivation. KiRundi has a rule that deletes a word-final vowel when the following word begins with a vowel. This rule affects the final vowel of *goré* 'woman.' The high tone underlyingly associated with this vowel does not delete; rather, it remains phonetically, but associated with the first vowel of the following word, which otherwise would appear with a low tone. Such stability effects are observed frequently with tone, but less frequently with other phonological features. In general, autosegmental analyses are best motivated by tone systems but less so in other areas of phonology. It is difficult to find examples of contours, for example, with features other than tone. The vowel harmony analysis we examined in section 7.1.2 depends more on underspecification theory, that is, the claim that certain features are unspecified in underlying representation (see section 7.3) than on autosegmental representations. Another area that has been treated autosegmentally is syllable structure, but this turns out to be better analyzed in metrical theory, to which we turn in the next section.

7.2   Metrical and prosodic phonology

SPE did not include the syllable in their discussion. They could have done so only by means of a syllable boundary, such as we introduced in section 1.1.3, either a period (.) or a dollar sign ($). We have also adopted the IPA convention of indicating stress by a raised tick (for primary) or a lower tick (for secondary), since the IPA uses accent marks for tone, another of their conventions that we have adopted. The use of such ticks implies a knowledge of the location of syllable breaks, but we have not yet discussed any general method of determining such breaks. The first discussion of syllable structure in generative phonology is Kahn (1976), who appeals to autosegmental representations, assigning syllable nodes to a separate tier. For example, the syllable structure of a word like *Atlantic* would be as in (15) in Kahn's framework.[2]

(15)

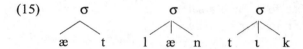

There is a conceptual problem with Kahn's autosegmental approach to the syllable, in that the syllable is not a *feature* of individual segments that is extracted from the segmental string and assigned to a separate autosegmental tier, but rather an *organization* of segments. In this way syllable structure differs fundamentally from the tonal and vowel harmony systems that originally motivated autosegmental treatments. Besides this conceptual difficulty there is evidence that the syllable does not group the segments directly but is composed of smaller constituents that group the segments. In the treatment we adopt here these constituents are called *moras*. Finally, syllables themselves are grouped into larger units called *feet*, where each foot contains a stressed syllable along with optionally one or more unstressed syllables. These considerations require a somewhat different approach to the syllable—the metrical approach. The prosodic approach extends the metrical approach into a whole hierarchy of prosodic categories, as we shall see shortly.

---

[2] Kahn used S for syllable. We adopt the more usual convention of using the Greek lower-case sigma (σ) for this purpose.

Because Kahn used an autosegmental formalism, he could make use of the autosegmental device of multiple linking that we saw with tone and vowel harmony systems. In particular, he proposed that certain consonants in English are *ambisyllabic,* that is, they belong to two syllables at once. For example, the word *butter* would appear as in (16) in Kahn's analysis.

(16)

Kahn uses this approach to account for the flap /ɾ/ that occurs as the allophone of /t/ in this context. However, all the allophonic effects that Kahn accounts for using ambisyllabicity can be accounted for in other ways using the prosodic categories, such as feet, that are independently required to account for stress.[3] Therefore we conclude that a metrical rather than an autosegmental approach is correct for syllable structure and stress, and that there is no ambisyllabicity.[4]

7.2.1 Metrical syllable structure

Many languages, including English, make a distinction between heavy and light syllables, for example, in the assignment of stress. English stress is quite complex, but a fairly straighforward example comes from nouns, where main stress is generally on the penultimate (second from last) syllable if this is a heavy syllable, otherwise stress falls on the antepenult (third syllable from last). The examples in (17) are typical. The words are transcribed phonetically, with syllable boundaries indicated by periods or by stress ticks.

---

[3] For a detailed analysis, including a number of cases that cannot be handled with ambisyllabicity, see Jensen (2000).

[4] In general, however, both types of representation are necessary. For example, syllables in a tone language would be represented metrically while tone would be autosegmental.

(17) a. *light penult*   b. *heavy penult*   c. *heavy penult*
          stress on   *tense vowel*   *consonant final*
          antepenult   *(diphthong)*   *stress on penult*
                                      stress on penult

America	Manitoba	agenda
[ə'mɛ.ɹɪ.kə]	[ˌmæ.nɪ'tow.bə]	[ə'jɛn.də]
Canada	citation	Alberta
['kæ.nə.də]	[ˌsəy'tey.šən]	[ˌæl'bɹ.rə]
labyrinth	amoeba	appendix
['læ.bɪ.ɹɪnθ]	[ə'miy.bə]	[ə'pɛn.dɪks]
continuity	appliance	amalgam
[ˌkɒn.tɪ'nyuw.ɪ.ɾi]	[ə'plɑy.əns]	[ə'mæl.gəm]

There are two ways that a syllable in English can be heavy. It may contain a
tense ([+ATR]) vowel, which is usually realized phonetically as a diphthong,
as in (17b), or it may end in a consonant, as in (17c).[5] In both these columns
the penultimate syllable is heavy and is stressed. If the penultimate syllable
ends in a lax vowel, as in (17a), stress is on the antepenult (as long as the word
has at least three syllables). We say that a heavy syllable consists of two
moras, while a light syllable contains only one mora. A light syllable, like the
penultimate syllable of *Canada,* has the structure in (18), where σ stands for
syllable and m stands for mora.[6]

(18)   σ
           |
           m
          /\
         n   ə

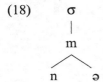

A heavy syllable, like the penultimate syllable in *agenda,* has the structure in
(19). As is customary in metrical trees we label the syllable branches s(trong)

---

[5] The phonetic syllabic [ɹ] in *Alberta* is derived from a phonetic sequence vowel plus [ɹ].
This sequence is present at the time that stress is assigned.

[6] Some authors use μ for mora, but this is more correctly used for morpheme (McCarthy
1981).

and w(eak); in this case the strong branch is on the left. We also assume that metrical branching is normally binary; that is, that a node ordinarily has at most two daughter nodes.

(19)

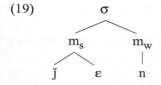

The situation is slightly more complex in (17b), where we have a diphthong consisting of a tense vowel followed by a glide. Following *SPE,* most analysts agree that English diphthongs are derived from underlying tense monophthongs by rules that are ordered after the rules assigning stress. (For a review of the relevant literature see Jensen 1993.) Therefore, at the time that stress is assigned, the penultimate syllable of *Manitoba* looks like (20), where the underlying tense /ɒ/ is linked to two moras.

(20)

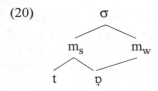

The arguments for the underlying low vowel quality in /ɒ/ are somewhat complex and beyond the scope of our present concerns. However, the principles of syllabification in English are fairly straightforward once we clarify certain aspects of our feature system. The phonological features we introduced in chapter 3 included the feature [syllabic] among the major class features. We used [+syllabic] as a feature of syllable *peaks,* most commonly vowels, distinguishing these from segments at the *margins* of syllables, that is segments preceding or following the peak. We noted in chapter 3 that segments other than vowels can function as syllable peaks, such as sonorants in English, and even obstruents in Berber. Since we are now enriching phonological structure with the metrical organization of segments into syllables, it should be possible to dispense with the feature [syllabic]. We noted in chapter 3 that speech exhibits a constant rising and falling of sonority, with the points of highest sonority identified as syllable peaks. This idea can be formalized in terms of the *sonority hierarchy,* which correlates with the relative openness of the vocal tract. The least sonorous segments are the oral stops and the most

sonorous segment is the open back vowel [ɑ], with other segments arranged
between according to the scale in (21) (Kiparsky 1979).

(21)   stops, fricatives, nasals, l, ɹ, w, y, u. i, o, e, ɑ
        w←————————————————————————————→s

Kiparsky observes that the syllable is normally composed of a peak preceded
in the *onset* by segments less sonorous than the peak in an order of rising
sonority and followed in the *coda* by segments less sonorous than the peak in
an order of decreasing sonority. Selkirk (1984b) refers to this as the *Sonority
Sequencing Generalization (SSG)*. In a word like *plant,* the most sonorous
segment is the vowel [æ]. The onset contains the stop [p] followed by the
more sonorous liquid [l] while the coda contains the nasal [n] followed by the
less sonorous stop [t]. The sonority hierarchy explains why the word *harm* can
be a single syllable: its coda contains the segments [ɹ] and [m] in that order,
which is a decrease in sonority, while the word *hammer* cannot be a single syllable, since here the segments [m] and [ɹ] increase in sonority after the peak
vowel, so it must be [ˈhæ.mɹ], not *[ˈhæmɹ].

    There are some additional provisions to English syllable structure that are
required in addition to the SSG. One is that a sequence of a stop followed by
a nasal is not permitted in an onset, even though this would be permitted by
the SSG. No word like *bnick* is possible in English, for example. Kiparsky
proposes the constraint in (22) to rule these out.

(22)   *[$_\sigma$ [–cont] [–cont]...

Another restriction in English is that the liquid *l* cannot be preceded in the
onset by the coronals [t], [d], or [θ]. Since [l] can be preceded in an onset by
noncoronal stops, as in *plant, crank* or by coronal stridents as in *slip,* Kiparsky
proposes the constraint (23).

(23)   *[$_\sigma$ $\begin{bmatrix} +cor \\ -strid \end{bmatrix}$ [l]

A third restriction is that sonorants do not appear before other consonants in
the onset. A sequence of a sonorant plus obstruent is ruled out by the SSG, but
a sequence of a nasal followed by a liquid might be expected to be possible
by the SSG. We rule these out by the constraint in (24).

(24) $*[_\sigma \text{ [+son] C } \ldots$

English does not allow onset sequences of a stop plus a fricative, which can be excluded by the constraint in (25).

(25) $*[_\sigma \text{ [--cont] } \begin{bmatrix} -\text{son} \\ +\text{cont} \end{bmatrix} \ldots$

But English does allow the reverse sequence with the fricative [s] followed by a voiceless stop, [p], [t], or [k] in an onset, even though this sequence is contrary to the SSG. Kiparsky states this as a *dispensation,* given in (26).

(26) $[_\sigma \text{ s} \begin{bmatrix} -\text{son} \\ -\text{cont} \\ -\text{voice} \end{bmatrix} \ldots \text{ is OK}$

Since syllabification in English is predictable, we do not specify it in underlying representations, but predict it by rules. An important principle of syllabification, which appears to operate in all languages, says that syllables have onsets whenever possible. This means that, within a word, if a single consonant appears between vowels, it will syllabify with the following vowel as an onset rather than with the preceding vowel as a coda. Thus *Ma.ni.to.ba* in (17b) is syllabified as shown. More generally, at least in English, when a string of consonants appears between vowels, the maximal substring of that string that forms a possible onset will syllabify with the following vowel and form an onset. Thus, in the word *mon.strous,* the syllable division is between the *n* and the *s,* as shown, since *str-* is a possible onset by the SSG and the dispensation in (26), and indeed appears word initially as in *strip.* Similarly, in *ma.ttress,* the syllable division is between the vowel *a* and *t,* since *tr-* is a possible onset, but in *at.las* the syllable division is between *t* and *l,* since *tl-* is not a possible onset by (23). It is only after onsets have been maximized that leftover consonants can be syllabified as codas. This is the case with the *n* of *mon.strous* and the *t* of *at.las.*

To summarize this subsection, we present the rules for syllabification in English in (27) (Jensen 1993, 64).

(27)   1.   Assign a mora to a string C_0V, where V is a local sonority max-
             imum according to the sonority hierarchy (21) and C_0 is a pos-
             sible (maximal) onset according to the sonority hierarchy and
             the restrictions and dispensations on onsets (22)–(26).

        2.   If V in 1 is tense, assign a second mora to it.

        3.   A string C_1 which does not belong to an onset must be a coda.
             Assign such a string to the second mora of a bimoraic vowel;
             assign it a mora on its own after a monomoraic vowel.

7.2.2   Metrical stress

In chapter 3 we tentatively proposed a feature [stress] that appears in the
matrix of vowels such that [+stress] characterizes the vowel of a stressed syllable and [–stress] characterizes the vowel of an unstressed syllable. We noted
there, however, that stress is more properly regarded as a property of syllables
than of vowels, and indicates a relation between the syllables of a word. This
is expressed in metrical theory by grouping syllables into *feet*. A foot is
defined as a unit containing one and only one stressed syllable. A monosyllabic word like *cat* has a single (stressed) syllable and a single foot, and can
be metrically represented as in (28), where we use F for foot. We will also use
the symbol ω for the word, or prosodic word, explained more fully in the next
subsection.

(28)

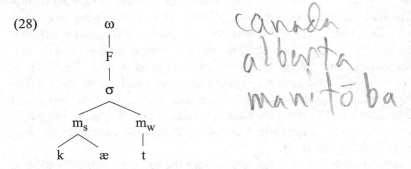

A disyllabic word like *butter* also has a single foot. As with the moras that
comprise a syllable, we label the syllables within a foot as strong and weak,
where the syllable labelled strong is interpreted as stressed. The metrical rep-

resentation of this word is given in (29), which avoids the ambisyllabic representation of (16).

(29)

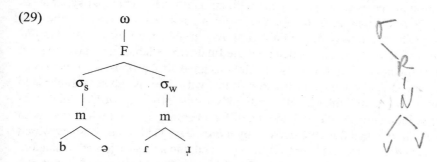

With a longer word, like *Manitoba,* we have one foot for each stress, in this case two feet. We label the feet strong and weak also, with the strongest foot containing the primary word stress. A metrical representation of *Manitoba* is given in (30).

(30)

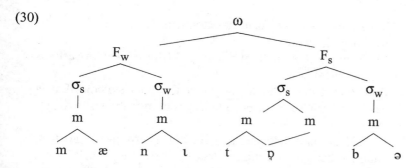

We have now introduced four prosodic units: the mora, the syllable, the foot, and the prosodic word. The relation of these units so far is quite straightforward. Each unit is contained within the next higher unit, and each unit groups together one or more of the next lower units. This is known as the *Strict Layer Hypothesis* (Selkirk 1984a; Nespor & Vogel 1986). The only exception to this hypothesis in the representation of (30) is the tense vowel [ɒ] in the third syllable, which belongs simultaneously to two moras, a consequence of the rule of English that assigns two moras to underlying tense vowels. Other violations of strict layering may be introduced by other rules of the language. In English a foot typically consists of two syllables, as is the case with the two feet in (30). Each of these binary feet, with the strong (stressed) syllable first, is called a *trochee,* or *trochaic foot.* English also has feet of one syllable, as in *cat* (28) or the first syllable of *Alberta,* which bears a secondary stress. The question arises as to what happens with an additional unstressed syllable, as in *Canada* or *appliance.* In *Canada,* we can construct a trochee on the first two syllables and have one syllable left over at the end of the word; in *appliance* we can construct a trochee over the final two syllables and have one left over at the beginning. A variety of solutions have been proposed for this problem. One is to allow the construction of feet with three syllables, another is to allow left-over syllables to attach directly to the prosodic word (which violates strict layering). We will adopt a different solution, under which feet with more than two syllables are derived by *adjunction.* This is a process by which a *stray syllable* (a syllable not yet incorporated into a foot) is joined to an adjacent foot. A complete discussion of English stress would take us too far afield, but the basic outline of the system can be given briefly in (31). The system of English stress makes much use of the concept *extrametricality,* by which certain parts of a word are rendered temporarily invisible to some of the procedures, to be reintroduced into the structure at a later stage.

(31) a. Mark a word-final consonant extrametrical
      b. Syllabify the word
      c. Mark the final syllable of nouns and adjectives with suffixes extrametrical.
      d. Construct a one-syllable foot over the final syllable if it is heavy; otherwise construct a binary foot over the last two syllables.
      e. If there are still syllables that are not incorporated into feet, continue constructing binary feet from right to left. Where a single syllable remains at the left edge of the word, construct a one-syllable foot.
      f. Construct a word tree
      g. Certain syllables are destressed by removing the foot dominating them
      h. Adjoin stray syllables (either originally extrametrical or by destressing) to an adjacent foot.

The provision of final consonant extrametricality (31a) allows us to account for the fact that verbs and unsuffixed adjectives are stressed on the final syllable if that syllable contains a tense vowel or if it ends in two consonants, but not if the final syllable consists of a lax vowel followed by a single consonant. In other words, the final syllable of such words is stressed if it is heavy, with the proviso that a final consonant does not contribute to weight. This predicts the pattern of stresses in (32).

(32)

		tense vowel in final syllable	two or more final consonants	lax vowel before one final consonant
a.	verbs	obéy	molést	astónish
		atóne	usúrp	devélop
b.	adjectives	divíne	robúst	cómmon
		discreét	overt	illícit

The provision of final syllable extrametricality (31c) allows us to account for the stress pattern of (17). Here, the position of primary stress is determined by the weight of the penultimate syllable. If we disregard the final syllable, provision (31d) will construct a one-syllable foot over the penultimate syllable if it is heavy (as in *Manitoba*), or a binary foot over the antepenultimate and penultimate if the penultimate is light (as in *America*). If the word is long enough, (31e) ensures that additional feet are constructed from right to left until the beginning of the word is reached. This provides an additional binary foot over the first two syllables of *Manitoba*. In *America,* a second foot is constructed over the first syllable, but this syllable is destressed by a rule known as Prestress Destressing that removes the foot over a light syllable immediately preceding a stressed syllable. Extrametrical and destressed syllables are incorporated into adjacent feet by the process of Stray Syllable Adjunction (31g), which operates as in (33). Adjunction creates a new foot which comes to dominate both the original foot and the formerly stray syllable. In (33a) we illustrate adjunction of a stray syllable to a foot on its left, and in (33b) we illustrate adjunction of a stray syllable to a foot on its right.

(33)   a.

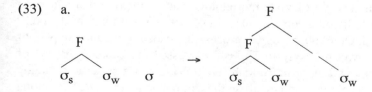

b.

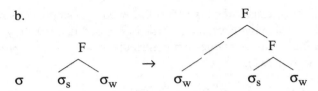

As a result of stray adjunction, all syllables are incorporated into feet, but strict layering is violated in another respect: the top foot that results from (33a, b) dominates another foot in addition to a syllable. Under strict layering a foot should dominate syllables only. However, we allow violations of strict layering when they are derived by rules.

Although the foot was originally designed to capture stress facts, it turns out to have implications for the segmental phonology as well. In chapter 2 we discussed the allophones of English voiceless stop consonants, pointing out that an aspirated allophone appears in two positions: at the beginning of a word and at the beginning of a stressed syllable. In this statement, the two environments do not form a natural class. However, with metrical structure, we can say that voiceless stops are aspirated at the beginning of a foot. Thus, in a word like *potato,* the word-initial /p/ and the first /t/ are both initial in a foot. The first /t/ is initial in the foot constructed over the last two syllables, and the /p/ is foot initial by virtue of adjunction of its syllable by (33b) to the following foot. Thus these two stops are both aspirated. The second /t/, by contrast, is not foot initial, and it undergoes Flapping.

7.2.3 Higher metrical units

Above the prosodic word, prosodic units are constructed with reference to syntactic structure. In contrast to *SPE,* prosodic phonology proposes that syntactic structure does not influence phonology directly, but rather forms the basis for the construction of prosodic units. Indeed, the prosodic word is not necessarily identical to the syntactic word. In English a compound word like *light ray* can be considered to consist of two prosodic words. Each prosodic word is a separate domain for the assignment of stress, for example. Indeed, according to the theory of lexical morphology and phonology word stress is assigned to the individual components of a compound word before the compound is formed. Other phonological processes are also limited to the phonological word. Vowel harmony in Turkish, discussed in chapter 3, is one of these. In a compound word in Turkish, each element is a separate harmony domain. Suffixes belong semantically to the compound as a whole, but belong phonologically only to the last element of the compound, participating in its harmonic requirements. We can therefore define a prosodic word both for English and Turkish as consisting of a stem together with any linearly adjacent string of affixes. The prosodic word is the domain for the operation of Diphthong Shortening in certain dialects of English. This rule affects the diphthongs [ɑy] and [ɑw], converting them to [əy] and [əw] respectively when they appear before a voiceless consonant. Both the diphthong and the voiceless consonant must appear in the same prosodic word. The diphthong in the word *light* is affected by this rule but not the diphthong in the word *lye*. The same is true when these words appear in compounds. The diphthong in *light ray* is shortened but not that in *lye tray,* where the voiceless consonant [t] following the diphthong [ɑy] appears in a distinct phonological word, under our assumption that compounded elements are separate prosodic words, even if they form a single unit syntactically. The diphthong is also shortened in *nitrate,* which is a single prosodic word consisting of two stressed syllables, and hence of two feet. By the principles of the previous section, the syllable (and foot) boundary falls between the diphthong and the following voiceless consonant, so that the rule would not be expected to operate in this word if either the syllable or the foot were the relevant unit.

The phonological phrase, for which we use the symbol φ, groups one or more phonological words.[7] These phrases are constructed on the basis of a syntactic representation by first isolating lexical heads, that is nouns, verbs, adjectives, and adverbs, but not prepositions, articles, or auxiliary verbs, and then grouping all the prosodic words to the left of that head into a single phonological phrase up to but not including the next such lexical head outside the maximal projection of the first head. The maximal projection of a head is the phrase defined by that head, so that a noun phrase is the maximal projection of a noun, for example. Binary branching within the phonological phrase is labelled with the strong on the right. In (34) we give an example from

---

[7] Nespor & Vogel (1986) recognize the clitic group (C) as a unit intermediate between the prosodic word and the phonological phrases. This unit is problematic in that clitics are by definition unstressed, but would have to be considered prosodic words included in a clitic group in a system that recognizes this unit. Since each prosodic word includes one or more feet, each of which contains a stressed syllable, we arrive at the contradiction that the clitic must be stressed. Therefore, most recent phonological treatments of clitics include them as part of an adjacent prosodic word. We might also countenance a prosodic word that includes two or more prosodic words within it, say in a compound. This again violates strict layering, but provides the appropriate groupings for certain operations of the Rhythm Rule, discussed later in this subsection.

Nespor & Vogel (1986, 178). the syntactic structure is in (43a) while the prosodic structure is in (34b).

(34)   a.   [[More than fifteen carpenters]$_{NP}$ [are working [in [the house]$_{NP}$]$_{PP}$]$_{VP}$]$_S$

        b.   [More than fifteen carpenters]$_\phi$ [are working]$_\phi$ [in the house]$_\phi$

The phonological phrases are defined by the heads *carpenters, working,* and *house.* The auxiliary verb *are* and the preposition *in* do not count as lexical heads, and so do not define phonological phrases. The result is that the prosodic structure in (34b) is not isomorphic to the syntactic structure (34a). It is the prosodic structure rather than the syntactic structure that forms the domain for phonological rules. The phonological phrase serves as the domain for at least two phonological rules in English. One is the Rhythm Rule, which reverses the prominence of two stresses in a weak–strong relationship when they stand before a stronger stress. This can be represented schematically in (35).

(35)

For example, the word *fifteen,* in isolation or at the end of a phrase, has primary stress on the last syllable and secondary stress on the first syllable. However, in the phrase *fifteen carpenters,* in (34) these relative prominences are reversed, so that the strongest stress in the word *fifteen* is on the first syllable. The Rhythm rule is responsible for this reversal due to the presence of the strongest stress of the phrase on its final element, *carpenters.* However, this reversal of stress does not occur every time these two words appear adjacent to each other in a sentence, as shown by (36), where the phonological phrases are shown.

(36)   [When she was fifteen]$_\phi$, [carpenters]$_\phi$ [rebuilt]$_\phi$ [the house]$_\phi$

This shows that no reversal of prominence occurs on the word *fifteen* when followed by the same word *carpenters* but in a different phonological phrase.

    The other phonological process in English that has the phonological phrase as its domain is the Monosyllable Rule (Selkirk 1978). This rule reduces monosyllabic words that are not members of the major lexical categories (noun, adjective, verb) when they are labelled weak within the phonological phrase. Since the constituents of the phonological phrase are labelled strong on the right, it follows that such words are unreduced when they are rightmost in a phonological phrase; otherwise they are reduced. Selkirk's examples (with prosodic labelling provided by Nespor & Vogel 1986, 179) shows the contrast.

(37) a. [The sluggers]$_\phi$ [boxed]$_\phi$ [in the crowd]$_\phi$ (reduced *in*)

b. [The cops]$_\phi$ [boxed in]$_\phi$ [the crowd]$_\phi$ (unreduced *in*)

Above the phonological phrase, the next prosodic category is the intonation phrase (I). The intonation phrase is the domain for the intonation contour, often on a fairly steady pitch until the end of the phrase, then exhibiting a sharp fall (or in some cases a rise) in pitch. The intonation phrase can comprise a whole sentence, but cannot be longer than a root sentence, in the sense of Emonds (1976), that is, a matrix clause and any subordinate clauses embedded within it. Conjoined sentences and certain elements external to a clause that they appear in form separate intonation phrases. These external elements include parentheticals, nonrestrictive relative clauses, tag questions, vocatives, expletives, dislocated elements, and appositives. The material before and after such obligatory intonation phrases also constitute intonation phrases, allowing the utterance to be exhaustively divided into such phrases. We give some examples in (38).

(38) a. [More than fifteen carpenters are working in the house]$_I$

b. [When she was fifteen, carpenters rebuilt the house]$_I$

c. [Paul is an artist]$_I$ [and Paula is a musician]$_I$

d. [Lions are dangerous]$_I$, [as you know]$_I$

e. [Lions]$_I$, [as you know]$_I$ [are dangerous]$_I$

f. [My brother]$_I$, [who absolutely loves animals]$_I$, [just bought
    himself an exotic tropical bird]$_I$

g. [That's Theodore's cat]$_I$, [isn't it]$_I$

h. [Clarence]$_I$, [I'd like you to meet Mr Smith]$_I$

i. [Good heavens]$_I$, [there's a bear in the back yard]$_I$

j. [They're so cute]$_I$, [those Australian koalas]$_I$

k. [Paul and Paula]$_I$, [our new neighbours]$_I$, [had an open house
   last week]$_I$

Sentence (38a) consists of a single intonation phrase which comprises three phonological phrases, as we saw in (34b). In (38b) we also have a single intonation phrase, here with four phonological phrases (36). In (38c) we have a coordinate structure, hence two intonation phrases. In (38d, e) the phrase *as you know* is a parenthetical and so is required to have an intonation phrase to itself. In (38d) the remainder of the sentence comprises an intonation phrase; in (38e) the material before the parenthetical *(lions)* and the material after the parenthetical *(are dangerous)* each comprise an intonation phrase in order to parse the sentence exhaustively into intonation phrases. In (38f) the phrase *who absolutely loves animals* is a nonrestrictive relative clause, another case that requires a separate intonation phrase. The phrase *isn't it* in (38g) is a tag question and a separate intonation phrase. The phrase *Clarence* in (38h) is a vocative and an intonation phrase. *Good heavens* in (38i) is an expletive and an intonation phrase. In (38j) the phrase *those Australian koalas* is a right dislocated subject that requires a separate intonation phrase, the syntactic subject position being occupied by the pronoun *they*. Finally in (38k) the phrase *our new neighbours* is an appositive, semantically equivalent to a nonrestrictive relative clause, and so requiring a separate intonation phrase. These items that appear outside the root sentence are often set off by commas in writing, but orthographic commas are not an infallible guide to intonation phrases, as seen in (38b) where the comma signals a phonological phrase boundary but not an intonation phrase boundary. However, Nespor & Vogel (1986, 193ff) suggest that intonation phrases may be *restructured* so that long intonation phrases are converted to a series of shorter ones. Such restructuring necessarily follows the boundaries of the phonological phrases owing to the nature of the prosodic hierarchy. For example, it would be possible to restructure (38b) into two intonation phrases, separated at the orthographic comma.

The final prosodic category is the phonological utterance (U). This groups all the intonation phrases that belong to the highest node in the syntactic tree, ordinarily a sentence, but which may be some other syntactic constituent when the utterance is not actually a sentence. Each of the sentences in (38) constitutes a single U. Nespor & Vogel (1986, 223ff) identify the utterance as the domain of Flapping in English. In chapter 2 we observed that flap [ɾ] is an allophone of /t/ in English. There we gave the environment as word internally after a vowel before a stressed vowel. We can now formulate the environment more precisely. Actually, much of the work is already done for us if we assume that the Aspiration rule, discussed at the end of section 7.2.2, is ordered before Flapping, a bleeding relationship. We will find that Flapping can affect both voiced and voiceless alveolar stops, that is /d/ as well as /t/ can be flapped. To simplify still further, following Nespor & Vogel 1986, 224), I assume that there is a rule that marks all consonants [+tense] when they occur at the beginning of a foot. All consonants not marked [+tense] by this rule are [–tense] by default. Voiceless stops and affricates of all points of articulation, /p/, /t/, /č/, and /k/, undergo Aspiration if they are tense. Alveolar stops /t/ and /d/ undergo Flapping if they are [–tense] and in the appropriate segmental environment, that is after a [–consonantal] segment and before a vowel, anywhere within the phonological utterance.

The first point to notice is that the vowel following /t/ or /d/ need not always be unstressed for Flapping to occur. A selection of flapping contexts is given in (39), based on Nespor & Vogel 1986, 225), where the segment that is flapped is given in boldface.

(39) a. water
      b. wri**t**er
      c. whi**t**ish
      d. hea**d**ache
      e. nigh**t** owl
      f. a hundre**d** eggs
      g. the whi**t**e owl
      h. I me**t** Ann
      i. My brother bough**t** a parrot last week.
      j. A very dangerous wild ca**t** escaped from the zoo.
      k. [Ichabo**d**]$_I$, [our pet crane]$_I$, [usually hides when geusts come]$_I$

Word internally, it is usually the case that the following vowel is unstressed, whether the word is monomorphemic (39a) or contains a vowel-initial suffix after the alveolar stop (39b, c). In compounds (39d, e) the vowel following the alveolar stop can bear (secondary) stress, and in phrases (39f, g, h) the following syllable can bear the main stress of the phrase. Flapping can also occur at the boundaries of various syntactic phrases (39i, j, k), including the case where the alveolar stop appears at an I boundary (39k), where the phrase *our pet crane,* being an appositive, defines an obligatory intonation phrase. The rule of Flapping is given in (40).

(40)   *Flapping (English)*

$$\begin{bmatrix} +\text{cor} \\ -\text{strid} \\ -\text{cont} \\ -\text{tense} \end{bmatrix} \rightarrow [\text{ɾ}] \ / \ [\ldots[-\text{consonantal}] \_\_\_\_ \ V \ldots]_U$$

The environment preceding the alveolar stop is given as [–consonantal] rather than as V to allow for the case of Flapping after /ɹ/, as in *article.*

Nespor & Vogel also provide evidence that Flapping can occur across sentence boundaries under certain conditions. Some examples are in (41).

(41)   a.   Have a sea**t**. I'll be right back.
         b.   It's la**t**e. I'm leaving.
         c.   That's a nice ca**t**. Is it yours?
         d.   Turn up the hea**t**. I'm freezing.

Since we have defined the utterance in terms of the highest node in the syntactic tree, normally a sentence, Flapping is unexpected in the indicated positions of (41). Nespor & Vogel attribute Flapping in these contexts to the possibility of restructuring the utterance. A sequence of two U can be restructured into a single U under fairly specific conditions. Among these conditions are the pragmatic requirements that the sentences must be uttered by the same speaker and addressed to the same interlocutors, and the phonological conditions that the sentences must be relatively short and must not have a pause between them. In addition, the sentences must be linked either syntactically or semantically. A syntactic link is made if the interpretation of the second sentence depends on material from the first sentence by either ellipsis or anaphora, illustrated by (42a, b) respectively. The boldfaced alveolar stops of (42) can be flapped, since the two sentences in each example can be restructured into a single utterance.

(42)   a.   Martha didn't invite To**dd**. I did.
         b.   Where's Pa**t**? I need him.

Ellipsis is illustrated in (42a) because the interpretation of the second sentence

I did includes the phrase *invite Todd,* which appears in the first sentence. Anaphora in (42b) refers to the pronoun him which is understood as referring to Pat from the first sentence. A semantic link is made between the sentences if they are implicitly related by one of the "logico-semantic connectors" *and, therefore,* or *because.* These are illustrated in (43a, b, c) respectively. Again the boldfaced alveolar stops can be flapped in (43).

(43)   a.   You invite Charlotte. I'll invite Joan.

        b.   It's late. I'm leaving. (= 41b)

        c.   Take your coat. It's cold out.

The examples in (44) show that restructuring doesn't take place when neither the syntactic nor the semantic conditions are met, even though the pragmatic and phonological conditions are. In (44) the boldfaced alveolar stops cannot be flapped.

(44)   a.   Have a seat. It's warm in here.

        b.   It's late. I'm Larry.

        c.   That's a nice cat. Is it after eight already?

        d.   Turn up the heat. I'm Frances.

In this section we have given a brief survey of the prosodic categories above the word, illustrating each with the phonological rules of English that have been shown to apply within each domain. It also shows how the principles of phonology which we developed in chapters 1–6 can be extended to phrasal phonology. We will discuss the organization of phonology in relation to other components of grammar in section 7.4 when we introduce the theory of lexical phonology. In the next section we develop one further post-*SPE* development that contributes to the overall model of phonology, the theory of underspecification.

7.3   Underspecification

In *SPE* the assumption was made that all phonological rules operate on fully specified phonological matrices. However, as we observed in chapter 3, many of the features specified in a given segment in a given language are redundant, since languages do not make full use of all possible oppositions. For example, in Turkish, the eight vowels of the system can be distinguished by the three features [high], [back], and [round]. In Turkish there is no need for the features [low] and [ATR] to distinguish among the vowels, although these features play a role in distinguishing the vowels of other languages. Therefore, we introduced the notion of redundancy rules. In Turkish, redundancy rules specify [ɑ] as [+low] and [–ATR] and all the other vowels as [–low] and [+ATR].

Actually, much of the work in generative phonology that preceded *SPE* assumed that phonological rules operate on incompletely specified matrices, under our assumption that grammars are maximally *simple* (recall the criteria of phonological analysis listed in (5) of chapter 4, section 4.3). The reason that *SPE* abandoned this assumption is the possibility that an unspecified feature could be interpreted as a third value, different from both plus and minus. This is obviously unacceptable: if the blank feature value is indeed redundant, it cannot be used in such a way as to contrast with both plus and minus, but the following demonstration shows that such a situation can arise.

Let us suppose that a language like Turkish has the three vowels in (45) with the indicated feature specifications, leaving [low] and [ATR] out of consideration.

(45)

	X	Y	Z
[high]	–	–	–
[back]	–	–	–
[round]	+		–
phonetic:	[ö]	?	[e]

It is clear that X = [ö] and Z = [e], but what is Y? With [round] not specified, Y could be equal to either X or Z. Actually, Y is an archisegment, or natural class, containing both X and Z, but we are interested in the situation where Y is ultimately realized as a single, fully specified vowel.

Let us introduce some terminology at this point. We will say that two segments A and B are *distinct* just in case there is some feature F such that one of the two segments is specified [+F] and the other is specified [–F]. If there is no such feature, we say that A and B are *nondistinct*. In the matrix of (45) X is distinct from Z because X is specified [+round] and Z is specified [–round]. However, Y is nondistinct from both X and Z because there is no feature for which Y has a specification opposite to that of X or Z. Y is specified the same as X and Z for the features [high] and [back]. Since Y is not specified for [round] this feature cannot make Y distinct from either X or Z.

Now suppose we have the rules in (46) in the order given, where (46c) is a redundancy rule, in which the empty brackets on the left of the arrow signify "any segment so far unspecified for [round]."

(46)   a.   [+round] → [+high]
       b.   [−round] → [+back]
       c.   R: [] → [−round]

Applying these rules in this order to the matrix of (45) gives the result in (47).

(47)

	X	Y	Z
[high]	+	−	−
[back]	−	−	+
[round]	+	−	−
phonetic:	[ü]	[e]	[ɑ]

In (47) all three segments are distinct. X is distinct from Y and Z in terms of [high] or [round], Y is distinct from Z in terms of [back], and X is distinct from Z in terms of all three features. This is an undesirable result, because initially Y was not distinct from either X or Z. The nonspecification of Y for [round] has covertly turned into a value distinct from both plus and minus, which is not allowed in a binary system. Clearly, this problem can be solved, as it was in *SPE*, by assuming that all redundant values are filled in before the operation of any phonological rules. But this is not the only possibility. The culprit is obviously (46b), which is an instruction to change segments which are specified [−round]. This rule applies to Z of (45), but not to X, which is specified [+round], and crucially also not to Y, which is not specified for [round]. Rather than insist on all redundant values being filled in before any phonological rules, as in *SPE*, it suffices to require any redundant value to be filled in before any phonological rule can apply which refers to that value. Archangeli (1984, 85) calls this the Redundancy Rule Ordering Constraint. We state it in (48).

(48)   *Redundancy Rule Ordering Constraint*
       A redundancy rule assigning α to F, where a is + or −, is automatically ordered prior to the first rule referring to [αF] in its structural description.

By (48), rule (46c) must be ordered before (46b), since (46c) is a redundancy rule assigning minus to [round] and (46b) refers to [–round] in its structural description. But rule (46c) need not be ordered before (46a), since (46a) does not refer to [–round] in its structural description. With this ordering, the result of applying the rules gives (49) instead of (47).

(49)

	X	Y	Z
[high]	+	–	–
[back]	–	+	+
[round]	+	–	–
	[ü]	[ɑ]	[ɑ]

Inserting the feature [–round] on Y by (46c) prior to the operation of (46b) ensures that Y and Z are treated identically from that point on. Thus both Y and Z emerge with the phonetic value [ɑ], as shown in (49). There is no danger of a blank feature value behaving as distinct from both plus and minus as long as any redundant feature must be filled in before that value can be referred to by a phonological rule.

In fact, if [–round] is redundant in Y of (45), it should also be redundant for Z. Of several proposals for underspecified underlying representations, the most interesting is one which removes as many feature specifications as possible from underlying representations, a position which is known as "radical underspecification." Under this proposal, if some feature [F] is specified as [+F] in underlying representations, there will not be any underlying specifications of [–F].[8]

In order to exemplify this theory we return to our discussion of Yawelmani from chapter 5. A central rule of Yawelmani phonology is Vowel Harmony, which we formulated in chapter 5 as in (50).

---

[8] At least not in the same environment (Kiparsky 1982). In some vowel harmony systems there are disharmonic underlying representations, such as Hungarian [šofőːr] 'driver.' The first vowel is [+back] and the second is [–back] in underlying representation, since otherwise the [+back] specification of the first vowel would spread to the second vowel. In normal harmonic forms of Hungarian only [+back] needs to be specified, with [–back] as default. In the ensuing discussion we will ignore this complication.

(50)   *Vowel Harmony (Yawelmani)*

$$\begin{bmatrix} +\text{syl} \\ \alpha\text{high} \end{bmatrix} \rightarrow \begin{bmatrix} +\text{round} \\ +\text{back} \\ -\text{low} \end{bmatrix} / \begin{bmatrix} +\text{syl} \\ +\text{round} \\ \alpha\text{high} \end{bmatrix} C_0 \underline{\qquad}$$

(left-to-right iterative)

This is a fairly complex rule. We will now show that it can be simplified considerably by appealing to underspecified underlying representations (following Archangeli 1984).

In chapter 5 we demonstrated that Yawelmani has four vowels at the underlying level, although there are five phonetically. In chapter 3 we stated that these four underlying vowels can be distinguished by two distinctive features, [high] and [round], and we gave a matrix, repeated in (51), that shows that the four underlying vowels are all distinct in terms of these features.

(51)   i   ɑ   o   u
    high   +   −   −   +
    round   −   −   +   +

No redundancies can be extracted from this matrix by the method developed in chapter 3. But under radical underspecification we should specify only one value for high and one value for round. For reasons that will become apparent as we proceed, we specify [−high] and [+round], removing the reverse values of these features. The result is the underspecified vowel matrix in (52).

(52)   i   ɑ   o   u
    high   −   −
    round   +   +

We now need redundancy rules to provide values for the remaining vowel features, [back], [low], and [ATR] for these vowels and for the vowel [e] which results from Vowel Lowering (rule 52 of chapter 5 and 56 below). A number of the phonological rules we discussed in chapter 5 are simplified by assuming that these redundancy rules mostly apply after the phonological rules rather than before them. Let us take the rule of Epenthesis, which we formulated in chapter 5 as (53).

(53)   *Epenthesis (Yawelmani)*

$$\emptyset \rightarrow i \,/\, C\underline{\quad\quad} C \left\{ \begin{array}{c} \# \\ C \end{array} \right\}$$

Recall that writing a phonetic symbol like [i] in a rule is actually a shorthand for the appropriate phonological features, in this case [+syllabic, +high, −low, −back, −round, +ATR]. With underspecification we can simplify this rule by removing all the features except for [syllabic]. That is, the rule can simply insert a vowel. A striking point about the vowel representations in (52) is that the vowel /i/ is represented underlyingly with no articulatory features at all. The redundancy rules of Yawelmani will specify any vowel with no features as [i]: this will be true of the epenthetic vowel as well as the underlying vowel if the redundancy rules are ordered after Epenthesis.

The epenthetic vowel can also appear as [u] when it is affected by Vowel Harmony. A major source of complexity in Vowel Harmony as formulated in (50) is the need to specify three features in the output of the rule. However, the core of Vowel Harmony is an assimilation in the feature [round] of vowels that agree in the feature [high]. This essence can be captured with under-specification by reformulating Vowel Harmony as in (54) (Archangeli 1984, 79), which also employs the autosegmental spreading notation that we saw in section 7.1.1.

(54)   *Vowel Harmony (Yawelmani, revised)*

$$
[+\text{round}] \\
\begin{bmatrix} +\text{syllabic} \\ \alpha\text{high} \end{bmatrix} C_0 \begin{bmatrix} +\text{syllabic} \\ \alpha\text{high} \end{bmatrix}
$$

(left-to-right iterative)

This notation states that the feature [+round] that is linked to a vowel with a specification for [high], either plus or minus, is spread to the right to another vowel with the same specification for high. The use of the Greek-letter variable α here implies that *both* values of [high] have to be specified at the time Vowel Harmony applies, due to the Redundancy Rule Ordering Constraint (48). The redundancy rule that specifies the redundant value of [high] is (55). As in chapter 3, we prefix redundancy rules by *R:* to indicate that such rules can fill in features but not change features.

(55)   R: [] → [+high]

The next two redundancy rules specify the value of [low]. These are ordered
before Vowel Lowering. These orderings must be stipulated, since they do not
follow from the Redundancy Rule Ordering Constraint.

(56)   a.   R: $\begin{bmatrix} +\text{round} \\ -\text{high} \end{bmatrix}$ → [–low]

        b.   R: [αhigh] → [–αlow]

Vowel Lowering can be reformulated by employing the syllabic notation of
section 7.2.1. As formulated in (57), Vowel Lowering changes the value of
[high] to minus on a vowel which is linked to two moras. This allows us to
eliminate the feature [long] from our inventory of segments, at least for
Yawelmani.

(57)   *Vowel Lowering (Yawelmani, revised)*
        m   m
         \   /
          V → [–high]

The remaining three redundancy rules can all apply after the rest of the phonological rules. They are given in (58).

(58)   a.   R: [+low] → $\begin{bmatrix} +\text{back} \\ -\text{round} \end{bmatrix}$

        b.   R: [] → [–round]

        c.   R: $\begin{bmatrix} -\text{low} \\ \alpha\text{round} \end{bmatrix}$ → [αback]

The chart in (59; next page) illustrates the operation of the redundancy rules
in conjunction with the rules of Epenthesis, Vowel Harmony, and Vowel
Lowering.
    The heading segment for each column indicates the vowel that is derived
by the operation of the rules. The underlying representation under each seg-

(59)

segment	[i]	[a]	[o]	[u]	[e]
underlying representation	[]	[–high]	$\begin{bmatrix}\text{–high}\\\text{+round}\end{bmatrix}$	[+round]	[]
rule					
Redundant [+high] (55)	[+high]	——	——	$\begin{bmatrix}\text{+round}\\\text{+high}\end{bmatrix}$	[+high]
Vowel Harmony (54)					
Redundant [–low] (56a)	——	——	$\begin{bmatrix}\text{–high}\\\text{+round}\\\text{–low}\end{bmatrix}$	——	——
Redundant [–αlow] (56b)	$\begin{bmatrix}\text{+high}\\\text{–low}\end{bmatrix}$	$\begin{bmatrix}\text{–high}\\\text{+low}\end{bmatrix}$	——	$\begin{bmatrix}\text{+round}\\\text{+high}\\\text{–low}\end{bmatrix}$	$\begin{bmatrix}\text{+high}\\\text{–low}\end{bmatrix}$
Vowel Lowering (57)	——	——	——	——	$\begin{bmatrix}\text{–high}\\\text{–low}\end{bmatrix}$
Redundant Back/round (58a)	——	$\begin{bmatrix}\text{–high}\\\text{+low}\\\text{+back}\\\text{–round}\end{bmatrix}$	——	——	——
Redundant [–round] (58b)	$\begin{bmatrix}\text{+high}\\\text{–low}\\\text{–round}\end{bmatrix}$	——	——	——	$\begin{bmatrix}\text{–high}\\\text{–low}\\\text{–round}\end{bmatrix}$
Redundant [αback] (58c)	$\begin{bmatrix}\text{+high}\\\text{–low}\\\text{–round}\\\text{–back}\end{bmatrix}$	——	$\begin{bmatrix}\text{–high}\\\text{+round}\\\text{–low}\\\text{+back}\end{bmatrix}$	$\begin{bmatrix}\text{+round}\\\text{+high}\\\text{–low}\\\text{+back}\end{bmatrix}$	$\begin{bmatrix}\text{–high}\\\text{–low}\\\text{–round}\\\text{–back}\end{bmatrix}$

ment indicates the features that are present initially, assuming radical underspecification. Then the rules are listed in the order of application. For each rule the resulting specifications for each segment are indicated, including specifications underlyingly present or assigned by previous rules. No specific outputs are listed for Vowel Harmony. If Vowel Harmony applies to /i/, it spreads [+round] to it, at which point it falls together with the derivation given for /u/. If Vowel Harmony applies to /a/, it spreads [+round] to it, and the derivation falls together with that of /o/. Recall from chapter 5 that all phonetic [e] in Yawelmani are derived from underlying long /i/. Therefore the column for [e] has the same underlying representation as [i]. The derivation in this column assumes a representation to which Vowel Lowering is applicable, and shows this rule as applying, specifying the vowel as [–high]. Since this is a phonological rule, it can change feature values. The column under [i] assumes a representation to which Vowel Lowering cannot apply. Recall also that Vowel Lowering also affects underlying long /u/. This possibility is not shown in the chart. If Vowel Lowering affects /u/, assigning the feature [–high] to it, its representation becomes identical to that of underlying /o/ and follows the rest of the derivation leading to a phonetic [o].

The use of radically underspecified representations allows us to simplify the underlying representations and several of the phonological rules of Yawelmani. More than that, it allows rules to express the core of the process more clearly, without having to deal with features extraneous to the basic generalizations expressed by the rules.

7.4   Lexical phonology

In chapter 4, section 4.7, we developed a series of steps for phonological analysis. The first step is to make a preliminary morphological analysis of the data. This step raises the question of the relation of phonology to morphology, and more generally to other components of grammar such as syntax and semantics. The theory of lexical phonology addresses these issues by proposing a formal model of the lexicon, replacing the somewhat simplistic view in *SPE,* where morphology had no formal place at all. In *SPE* the syntax was seen as generating surface structures which were the input to phonological rules. *SPE* did allow for certain "readjustment rules" to intervene between syntax and phonology, and some of these rules were essentially morphological spell-outs of syntactic elements. As we have seen in section 7.2.3, syntactic structure as such is not an appropriate form for phonological rules to operate on. In a similar vein, lexical phonology proposes that phonology up to the word level does not depend on syntax, but rather that word-internal phonology applies in the lexicon prior to the insertion of words into syntactic representations. Lexical phonology also provides for the possibility that the rules of the lexicon may occupy distinct strata (sometimes called "levels"), each with their own particular properties. Each stratum is also associated with certain morphological operations. For English the consensus has emerged that there are two strata of lexical morphology and phonology, which together define the words of the language that are inserted into syntactic structures. On the basis of these structures a prosodic structure is formed, which in turn serves as the input to the rules of the postlexical phonology. A diagram of the basic model (for English) is given in Figure 1 (next page).

The large box titled "lexicon" encloses a number of submodules. The box titled "underived lexical items" includes a *list* of all the morphemes of the language (recall the discussion of list versus rule in section 2.9 of chapter 2 and

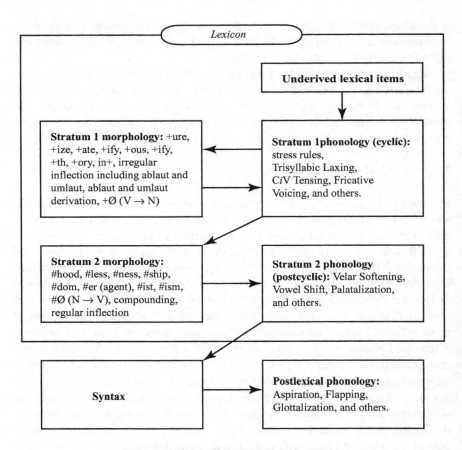

Figure 1. The model of Lexical Phonology

6.2 of chapter 6). Each morpheme includes a phonological underlying representation and syntactic and semantic information, as suggested in section 6.2 of chapter 6. These items undergo the phonology of stratum 1, and then enter the morphology of stratum 1, where they may undergo affixation or other modifications. They then reenter stratum 1 phonology where the rules apply again. Though each stage of affixation is optional, this process continues until no more affixation takes place, at which point the form enters the morphology of stratum 2. The reapplication of stratum 1 phonology at each stage of affixation is called *cyclic* application. This cyclic mode is indicated by the back-and-forth arrows linking the stratum 1 morphology and stratum 1 phonology boxes in Figure 1. For example, stress is assigned cyclically in English. On the first cycle, stress is assigned to the first syllable of *órigin*. If the suffix *-al* is attached, a second cycle of stress produces *oríginal*. If further affixation adds *-ity*, a third stress cycle produces *originálity*, with a secondary stress on the second syllable, preserving the position of stress of *oríginal*. This can be contrasted with *spìrituálity*, with secondary stress on the first syllable, preserving the position of stress in *spíritual*.

On stratum 2 the phonological rules do not apply cyclically, but rather all in a block after all stratum 2 affixation. This then forms the input to syntax on the basis of which prosodic categories (above the prosodic word) are formed. The postlexical phonology then applies, producing finished utterances.

This model makes a number of predictions about the interaction of morphology and phonology. One is that affixation may be sensitive to derived phonological properties such as stress. Indeed, the noun-forming suffix *-al* in English can be added to verbs that are stressed on the final syllable, such as *deny, try, withdraw, renew, betray,* but not to verbs that are stressed elsewhere, such as *promise, abandon, develop, edit.* This implies that stress is assigned to verbs before affixation of *-al* is attempted.

Another prediction is that affixes from stratum 2 can appear outside of affixes from stratum 1 but not vice versa. This prediction is borne out by the suffixes *+ian* and *#ism*, where we encode the stratum by means of the boundary symbol, + for stratum 1 and # for stratum 2. Either affix can be added alone to a root, as shown by *Mendelian* and *Mendelism*, but if both affixes are added they can only be in one order: *Mendelianism* but not **Mendelismian*. The model does not permit a form from stratum 2 to reenter stratum 1, allowing precisely this result.

In the concept of the morpheme discussed in chapter 6 the possibiliy exists for morphemes whose phonological underlying representations are null, known as *zero morphemes,* which nevertheless have syntactic and semantic content. Kiparsky (1982) discusses two zero morphemes. One is at stratum 1 and derives nouns from verbs, as in the examples of (60).

(60)   *basic verb*   *derived noun*
       protést   prótèst
       conflíct   cónflìct
       increáse   íncreàse
       permít   pérmìt

Since no overt morpheme distinguishes the nouns from the verbs in (60), how can we tell whether the verb or the noun is basic? We do observe a shift in stress, which has sometimes been taken as the marker of the morphological categories here. However, the stress patterns of these words can be predicted on the assumptions that the verb is basic, the noun is derived from it by the affixation of zero on stratum 1, and the stress rules apply cyclically on stratum 1, as we saw in words like *originality*. According to the stress rules in (31) of section 7.2.2, nouns, but not verbs, mark a final syllable extrametrical and assign stress on the basis of what remains. But the nouns in (60) retain the verb stress, reduced to secondary, with the assignment of stress by the noun rules to the first syllable. Notice also that there is a semantic relation between the noun and the verb in (60) such that the noun is paraphrasable as 'that which Vs or is Ved' (where V stands for the verb). An *increase* is 'that which increases,' a *conflict* is 'a situation where people or things conflict,' etc.

A second zero morpheme that Kiparsky examines converts nouns into verbs on stratum 2, and is illustrated in (61).

(61)   *basic noun*   *derived verb*

      páttern   páttern

      cómfort   cómfort

      poíson   poíson

      pícture   pícture

In (61) there is no change of stress, and semantically the verb is paraphrasable in terms of the noun, as 'to do something with N.' So *to pattern* is 'to do something after a pattern,' *to poison* is 'to use poison (to kill or injure),' etc. Since the stress patterns are established on stratum 1, these assumptions lead to the retention of the noun's stress pattern on the derived verb.

Since there is a zero affix on stratum 1 converting verbs to nouns and another zero affix on stratum 2 converting nouns to verbs, we might expect words to exist in which both zero affixes have been attached, since, as in the case of *Mendelianism,* we have seen that stratum 2 affixes can be attached to words derived by affixation at stratum 1. This possibility is indeed realized, as in (62).

(62)   *basic verb*   *derived noun*   *derived verb*

      protèst   prótèst   prótèst   'to stage a protest'

      discoúnt   díscoùnt   díscoùnt   'to sell at a discount'

compoúnd	cómpoùnd	cómpoùnd	'to join in a compound'
digést	dígèst	dígèst	'to make a digest'

In each case the derived verb does not mean the same thing as the basic verb. As Kiparsky puts it, "demonstrators may *prótèst* but a child can only *protést*" (Kiparsky 1982, 13). This is parallel to overt derivations. For example, the noun *originality* does not mean the same as the noun *origin*.

While stacking of several overt affixes at the same stratum is possible, as shown be examples like *originality*, Kiparsky argues that zero affixes are not added to words derived by the attachment of overt affixes on the same stratum. For example, the verbs in (63) derived by the stratum 1 suffixes *-ize, -ate, -ify*, do not permit zero derivation of nouns, which is also on stratum 1.

(63) publicize   *a publicize
      demonstrate   *a demonstrate
      clarify   *a clarify

Similarly, nouns derived by overt stratum 2 affixes do not permit zero derivation to verbs, which is also on stratum 2, as shown in (64).

(64) singer   *to singer
      beating   *to beating
      freedom   *to freedom
      promptness   *to promptness
      chanpionship   *to championship
      alcoholism   *to alcoholism
      nationalist   *to nationalist
      sisterhood   *to sisterhood

This prompts Kiparsky to propose a rather ad hoc constraint on zero derivation, stated in (65).

(65) *Constraint on Zero Derivation*
      *] X] Ø]
      where] is a morphological bracket and X≠Ø

However, nouns derived by an overt affix on stratum 1 do undergo zero derivation to verbs, as shown in (66).

(66)   *verb*   *derived noun*   *zero derived verb*
        or stem   *stratum 1*   *stratum 2*

        press   press+ure   to pressure

        pict-   pict+ure   to picture

        commit   commiss+ion   to commission

        propose   propos+ition   to proposition

        requis-   requis+ition   to requisition

        try   tri+al   to trial

        engine   engin+eer   to engineer

        revere   rever+ence   to reverence

        refer   refer+ence   to reference

To account for this Kiparsky proposes a general principle of Bracket Erasure, stated in (67).

(67)   *Bracket Erasure*
        Erase all internal brackets at the end of a stratum.

Under this principle, pressure is derived as in (68). Since brackets are erased at the end of stratum 1, the zero affixation deriving verbs on stratum 2 does not "know" that the noun pressure is derived with a suffix; i.e., constraint (65) does not prevent zero affixation.

(68)   underlying
        (underived lexical item) $[press]_V$
        stratum 1 phonology: stress $[préss]_V$
        stratum 1 morphology: -*ure* $[[préss]_V \text{ ure}]_N$
        stratum 1 phonology   ———
        exit stratum 1: bracket erasure $[préssure]_N$
        stratum 2 morphology: Ø-derivation $[[préssure]_N \text{ Ø }]_V$
        stratum 2 phonology   ———
        exit stratum 2: bracket erasure $[préssure]_V$

In the derivation of (68) we use outlined brackets to indicate both the edges of morphological constituents and morpheme boundaries. This distinguishes constituent brackets from the normal brackets that enclose distinctive feature matrices. Bracket erasure also interacts with certain rules that apply at the edges of words. In (4) of chapter 4 we proposed a rule of Final Devoicing for Russian, which we gave as (69).

(69)   *Final Devoicing (Russian)*
        [–sonorant] → [–voice] / _____ #

We would now express that rule as in (70).

(70)   *Final Devoicing (Russian, revised)*
        [–sonorant → [–voice] / _____]

English has a rule that simplifies clusters of nasals at the end of a word. The rule in (71) deletes the nasal *n* when it is preceded by another nasal (always *m* in these examples) at the end of a word or before a stratum 2 suffix. The nasal *n* is retained before a stratum 1 suffix.

(71)   n-*Deletion (English)*
        n → Ø / [+nasal] _____]

This rule is responsible for the alternations shown in (72).

(72)

n retained before stratum 1 suffix	*n deleted before stratum 2 suffix or compound*	*n deleted at end of word*	*underlying representation of root*
damn + ation	damn # ing	damn	/dæmn/
damn + able			
hymn + al	hymn # ing	hymn	/hɪmn/
hymn + ology	hymn ## index		
solemn + ity		solemn	/sɒlɛmn/
solemn + ize			
autumn + al		autumn	/ɔːtəmn/
column + ar		column	/kɒləmn/
condemn + ation	condemn # ing	condemn	/kɒndɛmn/

These alternations are accounted for by situating rule (71) at stratum 2. If the root emerges from the stratum 2 morphology unaffixed, or affixed at stratum 2, the bracket is present at the end of the root and *n*-Deletion is applicable. If the root is affixed at stratum 1, the bracket at the end of the root is erased by Bracket Erasure before stratum 2 phonology is applicable, and so the rule cannot apply. These possibilities are illustrated in the derivations of (73).

(73)	*stratum 1 suffix*	*stratum 2 suffix*	*no suffix*	
	/dæmn/	/dæmn/	/dæmn/	underived item
				stratum 1 phonology:
	['dæmn]	['dæmn]	['dæmn]	stress (1st cycle)
	[['dæmn] ætyən]	———	———	stratum 1 morphology
				stratum 1 phonology:
	[[ˌdæm'n] ætyən]			stress (2nd cycle)
	[ˌdæm'nætyən]			Bracket Erasure
	———	[['dæmn] ɪng]		stratum 2 morphology
				stratum 2 phonology:
	(cannot apply)	[['dæm] ɪng]	['dæm]	(71)
	[ˌdæm'neyšən]			other rules
		['dæmɪng]		Bracket Erasure
	[ˌdæm'neyšən]	['dæmɪng]	['dæm]	output of lexicon

This very brief introduction to lexical phonology should give some idea of the architecture of the theory, though many details have necessarily been omitted. A selection of the affixes associated with each of the lexical strata in English were given in the sketch of the model in Figure 1. The phonology of English requires approximately 20 rules on stratum 1, 30 rules on stratum 2, and ten postlexical rules. For more complete discussion of the details of the model in English, see Jensen (1993) and the literature cited there.

7.5   Exercises

7.1   Tiv (Pulleyblank 1986)

Tiv verbs may have either a high-toned or a low-toned stem. We will
illustrate two of the several tenses in which verbs appear, the general
past, characterized by a low tone, and the recent past, characterized by
a high tone. Pulleyblank makes the following assumptions:

1. Tone association is cyclic, as in lexical phonology.
2. Prefixes and suffixes may consist exclusively of tone.
3. Morphemes may have floating (underlyingly usassociated)
   tones.
4. Spreading is not automatic.
5. Vowels may receive a default tone (Low in Tiv) if not assigned
   tone by other rules.
6. Downstep (a high tone realized on a somewhat lower pitch
   than other high tones, indicated by a raised !) may result
   from a floating (unassociated) low tone.

Show how the following verb forms receive their tone patterns. The
recent past is also characterized by ablaut (vowel change), which you
can disregard.

	High tone stem		*Low tone stem*	
General past	ˈvá	'came'	d͡zà	'went'
	ˈúŋ͡gwà	'heard'	vèndè	'refused'
	ˈyévèsè	'fled'	ŋgòhòrò (→ ŋgòhòr)	'accepted'
Recent past	vé	'came (recently)'	d͡zé	'went (recently)'
	óŋgó	'heard (recently)'	vèndé	'refused (recently)'
	yévésè	'fled (recently)'	ŋgòhórò (→ ŋgòhôr)	'accepted (recently)'

7.2   Hungarian

        Reconsider the Hungarian data from exercise 6.2. How can an
        autosegmental solution avoid the appeal to abstract underlying repre-
        sentations for the stems of 'bridge,' 'arrow,' and 'goal'?

7.3   Transcribe the following English words phonetically, then divide the
        words into syllables and give the metrical syllable structure for each
        syllable according to the procedures discussed in section 7.2.1

        acknowledges
        appearance
        appliance
        metronome
        Atlantic
        erudition
        irreparable
        potato
        pterodactyl
        helicopter
        phonologist

        Do the same with your full name, your birthplace, and your favourite
        singer, actor, or other person.

7.4 Recall the Pulaar data from section 4.5 of chapter 4 illustrating ATR harmony.

a. sof+ru   'chick (singular)'
b. ser+du   'rifle butt (singular)'
c. m͡beːl+u   'shadow (singular)'
d. peːc+i   'slit (singular)'
e. beːl+i   'puddle (singular)'
f. dog-oː+ru   'runner (singular)'
g. cɔf-ɔn   'chick (diminutive plural)'
h. cɛr-kɔn   'rifle butt (diminutive plural)'
i. m͡beːl-ɔn   'shadow (diminutive plural)'
j. peːc-ɔn   'slit (diminutive plural)'
k. m͡beːl-ɔn   'puddle'
l. n͡dɔg-ɔ-w-ɔn   'runner (diminutive plural)'
m. fɑyi   'fat'
n. lɑmmi   'salted'
o. bɔːt-ɑː-ri   'to dine'
p. pɔːf-ɑː-li   'respirations'
q. nɔdd-ɑː-li   'call'
r. ŋ͡gɔr-ɑː-gu   'courage'

Reanalyze the vowel patterns of these data in an underspecification framework. Construct the maximally underspecified matrix for the underlying representations of the vowels and analyze the ATR harmony as an autosegmental spreading.

References

Andruyshen, C.H. (1985) *Ukrainian-English Dictionary* (third printing), Toronto: University of Toronto Press.

Archangeli, Diana (1984) *Underspecification in Yawelmani Phonology and Morphology,* Ph.D. dissertation, MIT.

Archangeli, Diana & D. Terence Langendoen (1997) *Optimality Theory: An Overview,* Malden, MA.: Blackwell.

Archangeli, Diana & Douglas Pulleyblank (1989) "Yoruba vowel harmony," *Linguistic Inquiry* 20, 173–217.

Archangeli, Diana & Douglas Pulleyblank (1994) *Grounded Phonology,* Cambridge, MA.: MIT Press.

Aronoff, Mark (1976) *Word Formation in Generative Grammar,* Cambridge, MA.: MIT Press.

Backus, John (1969) *The Acoustical Foundations of Music,* New York.: W.W. Norton & Co.

Bever, Thomas (1967) *Leonard Bloomfield and the Phonology of the Menomini Language,* Ph.D. dissertation, MIT.

Bloch, Bernard (1953) "Contrast," *Language* 29, 59–61. Reprinted in Makkai (1972), 224–225.

Bloomfield, Leonard (1939) "Menomini morphophonemics," *Traveaux du Cercle linguistique de Prague* 8, 105–115. Reprinted in Makkai (1972), 58–64.

Braune, Wilhelm (1975) *Althochdeutsche Grammatik* (13. Auflage bearbeitet von Hans Eggers), Tübingen: Max Niemeyer.

Bright, William (1957) *The Karok Language,* University of California Publications in Linguistics 13. Berkeley & Los Angeles.: University of California Press.

Brown, Gillian (1972) *Phonological Rules and Dialect Variation: A Study of the Phonology of Lumasaaba,* Cambridge University Press.

Budiṇa-Lazdiṇa (1966) *Teach Yourself Latvian,* London: The English Universities Press.

Burrow, T. (1970) *The Pengo Language,* Oxford.: The Clarendon Press.

Carr, Philip (1993) *Phonology,* London.: MacMillan.

Chao, Yuan Ren (1930) "A system of tone letters," *Le maître phonétique* 45, 24–47.

Chiba, T. & J. Kajiyama (1941) *The Vowel: its Nature and Structure,* Tokyo: Tokyo Kaiseikan Publishing Company.

Chomsky, Noam & Morris Halle (1968) *The Sound Pattern of English,* New York.: Harper & Row.

Clements, George N. & Engin Sezer (1982) "Vowel and consonant disharmony in Turkish," in Harry van der Hulst & Norval Smith (eds.) *The Structure of Phonological Representations, Part II),* Dordrecht: Foris, 213–255.

Corbridge-Patkaniowska, M. (1964) *Polish* (revised and enlarged edition), London: Hodder and Stoughton.

Dell, François & Mohamed Elmedlaoui (1985) "Syllabic consonants and syllabification in Imdlawn Tashlhiyt Berber," *Journal of African Languages and Linguistics* 7, 105–130.

Dell, François & Mohamed Elmedlaoui (1988) "Syllabic consonants in Berber: Some new evidence," *Journal of African Languages and Linguistics* 10, 1–17.

Dell, François & Mohamed Elmedlaoui (1989) "Quantitative transfer in the nonconcatenative morphology of Imdlawn Tashlhiyt Berber," *Journal of Afroasiatic languages.*

de Rijk, Rudolf (1970) "Vowel interaction in Bizcayan Basque," *Fontes Linguae Vasconum* 2:5, 149–167.

Doke, Clement M. (1926) *The Phonetics of the Zulu Language,* Johannesburg: Witwatersrand University Press (Special number of *Bantu Studies*). Kraus Reprint, Nedeln/Liechtenstein, 1969.

Doke, Clement M. (1938) *Text Book of Lamba Grammar,* Johannesburg: Witwatersrand University Press.

Elson, Ben (1947) "Sierra Popoluca syllable structure," *International Journal of American Linguistics* 13, 13–17.

Emonds, Joseph E. (1976) *A Transformational Approach to English Syntax: Root, Structure Preserving, and Local Transformations,* New York: Academic Press.

Freeland, L.S. (1951) *Language of the Sierra Miwok,* Indiana University Publications in Anthropology and Linguistics.

Fromkin, Victoria A., ed. (1971) "The non-anomalous nature of anomalous utterances," *Language* 47, 27–52.Fudge, Eric C. (1967) "The nature of phonological primes," *Journal of Linguistics* 3, 1–36.

Geytenbeek, Brian and Helen Geytenbeek (1971) *Gidabal Grammar and Dictionary*, Australian Institute of Aboriginal Studies, no. 43, Canberra.

Gleason, Henry Allan, Jr (1955) *Workbook in Descriptive Linguistics*, New York: Holt, Rinehart and Winston.

Goldsmith, John A. (1976) *Autosegmental Phonology*, Ph.D. dissertation, MIT.

Goldsmith, John A. (1990) *Autosegmental and Metrical Phonology*, Oxford: Blackwell.

Gordon, E.V. (1957) *An Introduction to Old Norse* (second edition revised by A.R. Taylor), Oxford: Oxford University Press.

Gussenhoven, Carlos & Heike Jacobs (1998) *Understanding Phonology*, London: Arnold.

Gussmann, Edmund (1980) *Studies in Abstract Phonology*, Cambridge, MA: MIT Press.

Hagège, Claude (1986) *La langue Palau: une curiosité typologique*, München: Wilhelm Fink Verlag.

Hale, Kenneth (1973) "Deep-surface canonical disparities in relation to analogy and change: an Australian example," *Current Trends in Linguistics* 11, 401–458.

Halle, Morris & William J. Idsardi (1997) "*r*, hypercorrection, and the Elsewhere Condition." Iggy Roca (ed.) *Derivations and Constraints in Phonology*, Oxford: Clarendon Press.

Halle, Morris & Kenneth N. Stevens (1971) "A note on laryngeal features," *Quarterly Progress Reports* 101, 198–213, Research Laboratory of Electronics, MIT.

Halle, Morris (1959) *The Sound Pattern of Russian*, The Hague: Mouton.

Harris, James W. (1983) *Syllable structure and stress in Spanish*, Cambridge, MA: MIT Press.

Harris, Katerina (1976) *Colloquial Greek*, London: Routledge & Kegan Paul.

Hayes, Bruce (1989) "Compensatory lengthening in moraic phonology," *Linguistic Inquiry* 20, 253–306.

Hoijer, Harry (1933) *Tonkawa: An Indian Language of Texas*. Handbook of American Indian Languages 3, New York.

Hoijer, Harry (1946) "Tonkawa," in Cornelius Osgood (ed.) *Linguistic Structures of Native America* (Viking Fund Publications in Anthropology

6, 289–311), New York: The Viking Fund, Inc.

Hoijer, Harry (1949) *An Analytical Dictionary of the Tonkawa Language*, University of California Publications in Linguistics 5, University of California Press, Berkeley & Los Angeles.

Hoffmann, Carl (1963) *A Grammar of the Margi Language*, Oxford: Oxford University Press.

Hoffmann, Carl (1973) "The vowel system of the Okpe monosyllabic verb," *Research Notes* 6, nos. 1–3, Department of Linguistics, University of Ibadan, Nigeria, 79–112.

Householder, Fred W. (1965) "On some recent claims in phonological theory," *Journal of Linguistics* 1, 13–34.

Hualde, José Ignacio (1991) *Basque Phonology*, London: Routledge.

Hyman, Larry M. (1970) "How concrete is phonology?" *Language* 46, 58–76.

Ipola, Rosa Nahuys de & Lygia Fonesca de Ras (1962) *Lições de português*, Buenos Aires, Argentina: Editorial Kapelusz.

Itô, Junko & Ralf-Armin Mester (1986) "The phonology of voicing in Japanese: Theoretical consequences for morphological accessibility," *Linguistic Inquiry* 17, 49–73.

Ivanić, Josef (1926) *Serbokroatische Sprachlehre: Regeln und Übungen*, Wien: Österreicher Bundesverlag für Unterricht, Wissenschaft, und Kunst.

Jensen, John T. (1972) *Hungarian Phonology and Constraints on Phonological Theory*, Ph.D. dissertation, McGill University.

Jensen, John T. (1993) *English Phonology*, Amsterdam: Benjamins.

Jensen, John T. (2000) "Against ambisyllabicity," *Phonology* 17, 187–235.

Jones, Daniel (1966) *The Pronunciation of English (fourth edition)*, Cambridge, UK: Cambridge University Press.

Josephs, Lewis S. (1975) *Palauan Reference Grammar*, Honolulu: University Press of Hawaii.

Kager, René (1999) *Optimality Theory: A Textbook*, Cambridge: Cambridge University Press.

Kahn, Daniel (1976) *Syllable-based Generalizations in English Phonology*, Ph.D. dissertation, MIT.

Kaye, Jonathan (1981) "Recoverability, abstractness and phonotactic constraints," D.L. Goyvaerts (ed.) *Phonology in the 1980s*, Ghent: Storia Scientia, 469–81.

Kenstowicz, Michael J. (1972) "Lithuanian phonology," *Studies in the Linguistic Sciences (Working Papers)*, Department of Linguistics, University of Illinois, Urbana, 1–85.

Kenstowicz, Michael J. (1994) *Phonology in Generative Grammar,* Oxford: Blackwell.

Kenstowicz, Michael J. & Charles W. Kisseberth (1979) *Generative Phonology: Description and Theory,* New York: Academic Press.

King, Robert D. (1973) "Rule insertion," *Language* 49, 551–578.

Kiparsky, Paul (1968a) "How abstract is phonology?" Paul Kiparsky (ed.) *Explanation in Phonology,* Dordrecht: Foris, 119–163.

Kiparsky, Paul (1968b) "Linguistic universals and language change," Emmon Bach & Robert T. Harms (eds.) *Universals in Linguistic Theory,* New York: Holt, Rinehart, & Winston.

Kiparsky, Paul (1968c) "Metrics and morphophonemics in the Kalevala," Charles E. Gribble (ed.) *Studies Presented to Professor Roman Jakobson by his Students,* Cambridge, MA: Slavica Publishers, 137–148.

Kiparsky, Paul (1973) "Abstractness, opacity, and global rules," O. Fujimura (ed.) *Three Dimensions of Linguistic Theory,* TEC, Tokyo, 57–86. Also in Andreas Koutsoudas (ed.) *The Application and Ordering of Grammatical Rules,* The Hague: Mouton, 160–186.

Kiparsky, Paul (1979) "Metrical structure assignment is cyclic," *Linguistic Inquiry* 10, 421–441.

Kiparsky, Paul (1982) "Lexical morphology and phonology," I.S. Yang (ed.) *Linguistics in the Morning Calm,* Seoul: Hanshin, 3–91.

Kjellin, Olle (1975) "How to explain the 'tones' in Tibetan," *Annual Bulletin of the Research Institute of Logopedics and Phoniatrics,* Tokyo, 9: 151–166.

Kleinschmidt, Samuel (1851) *Grammatik der grönländischen Sprache,* Berlin: Walter de Gruyter [reprinted 1968, Georg Olms, Hildesheim].

Koutsoudas, Andreas, Gerald Sanders, and Craig Noll (1974) "The application of phonological rules," *Language* 50, 1–28.

Kwee, John B. (1976) *Indonesian* (second edition), London: Hodder and Stoughton.

Kuroda, S.-Y. (1967) *Yawelmani Phonology,* Cambridge, MA: MIT Press.

Ladefoged, Peter (1962) *Elements of Acoustic Phonetics,* Chicago: University of Chicago Press.

Ladefoged, Peter (1964) *A Phonetic Study of West African Languages,* Cambridge: Cambridge Univesity Press.

Ladefoged, Peter (1971) *Preliminaries to Linguistic Phonetics,* Chicago: The University of Chicago Press.

Ladefoged, Peter (1990) "The Revised International Phonetic Alphabet," *Language* 66, 550–552.

Ladefoged, Peter (2001) *A Course in Phonetics* (fourth edition), Fort Worth: Harcourt College Publishers.

Ladefoged, Peter & Ian Maddieson (1996) *The Sounds of the World's Languages,* Oxford: Blackwell.

Lamb, Sidney (1966) "Prolegomena to a theory of phonology," *Language* 42, 536–73. Reprinted in Makkai (1972), 606–633.

Lane, George M. (1903) *A Latin Grammar for Schools and Colleges* (revised edition), New York: American Book Company.

Lange, Roland A. (1971) *201 Japanese Verbs, Fully Described in All Inflections, Moods, Aspects, and Formality Levels,* Woodbury, N.Y.: Barron's Educational Series.

Leben, William (1973) *Suprasegmental Phonology,* Ph.D. dissertation, MIT.

Li, F.K. (1946) "Chipewyan," *Linguistic Structures of of Native America* (Viking Fund Publications in Anthropology 6), New York, 398–423.

Lieberman, Philip (1984) *The Biology and Evolution of Language,* Cambridge, MA.: Harvard University Press.

MacKay, Ian R.A. (1987) *Phonetics: the Science of Speech Production (second edition),* Austin, Texas: Pro-Ed.

Makkai, Valerie Becker, ed. (1972) *Phonological Theory: Evolution and Current Practice,* New York: Holt, Rinehart, and Winston.

Marsack, C.C. (1962) *Teach Yourself Samoan,* London: The English Universities Press.

Malécot, André (1960) "Vowel nasality as a distinctive feature in American English," *Language* 36, 222–229.

McCarthy, John J. (1981) "A prododic theory of nonconcatenative morphology," *Linguistic Inquiry* 12, 373–418.

McCarthy, John J. (1993) "A case of surface constraint violation," *Canadian Journal of Linguistics* 38, 169–195.

Navarro, Tomás (1967) *Manual de pronunciación española* (sixth edition), New York: Hafner.

Nespor, Marina & Irene Vogel (1986) *Prosodic Phonology,* Dordrecht: Foris.

Newman, Stanley (1944) *Yokuts Language of California,* Viking Fund Publications in Anthropology, No. 2, New York.

Oinas, Felix J. (1968) *Basic Course in Estonian,* third edition, The Hague: Mouton.

Pandit, P.B. (1957) "Nasalisation, aspiration and murmur in Gujarati," *Indian Linguistics* 17, 165–172.

Paradis, Carole (1986) *Phonologie et morphologie lexicales: les classes nominales en pulaar (Fula),* Ph.D. dissertation, University of Montreal. English version, Garland Press, New York, 1992.

Piggott, Glyne (1971) "Some implications of Algonquian palatalization," *Odawa Language Project, Anthropological Series* 9. University of Toronto, Department of Anthropology. Also in E.D. Cook and Jonathan Kaye (eds.) *Linguistic Studies of Native Canada,* Vancouver: University of British Columbia Press, 1978.

Postal, Paul M. (1968) *Aspects of Phonological Theory,* New York: Harper and Row.

Pulkina, Ilza & Ekaterina Zakhava-Nekrasova (1988) *Russian: A Practical Grammar with Exercises,* Moscow: Russky Yazyk Publishers.

Prince, Alan S. & Paul Smolensky (1993) *Optimality Theory: Constraint Interaction in Generative Grammar,* ms., Rutgers University and University of Colorado, Boulder.

The Principles of the International Phonetic Association (1949), The International Phonetic Association, London.

Pulleyblank, Douglas (1986) *Tone in Lexical Phonology,* Dordrecht: Reidel.

Pullum, Geoffrey & William Ladusaw (1986) *Phonetic Symbol Guide,* Chicago: University of Chicago Press.

Robins, R.H. & Natalie Waterson (1952) "Notes on the phonetics of the Georgian word," *Bulletin of the School of Oriental and African Studies* 14, 55–72, University of London.

Rubach, Jerzy (1984) *Cyclic and Lexical Phonology: The Structure of Polish,* Dordrecht: Foris.

Sanders, Gerald (1990) "On the analysis and implications of Maori verb alternations," *Lingua* 80, 149–96.

Sapir, Edward (1925) "Sound patterns in Language," *Language* 1, 37–51. Reprinted in Makkai (1972), 13–21.

Sapir, Edward (1933) "La réalité psychologique des phonèmes," *Journal de Psychologie Normale et Pathologique* 30, 247–265. English translation "The psychological reality of phonemes" in D.G, Mandelbaum (ed.) *Selected Writings of Edward Sapir in Language, Culture, and Personality,* Berkeley & Los Angeles: University of California Press, 46–60. Reprinted in Makkai 1972, 22–31.

Schane, Sanford A. (1968) *French Phonology and Morphology,* Cambridge, MA.: MIT Press.

Schane, Sanford A. (1973) *Generative Phonology,* Englewood Cliffs, N.J.: Prentice-Hall.

Schane, Sanford A. & Birgette Bendixen (1978) *Workbook in Generative Phonology,* Englewood Cliffs, N.J.: Prentice-Hall.

Scott, N.C. (1964) "Nasal consonants in Land Dayak (Bukar-Sadong)," in David Abercrombie (ed.) *In Honour of Daniel Jones,* 432–436, London: Longman.

Selkirk, Elisabeth O. (1978) "On prosodic structure and its relation to syntactic structure," Fretheim (ed. 1981) *Nordic Prosody II,* TAPIR, Trondheim, 111–140.

Selkirk, Elisabeth O. (1984a) *Phonology and Syntax: the Relation between Sound and Structure,* Cambridge, MA.: MIT Press.

Selkirk, Elisabeth O. (1984b) "On the major class features and syllable theory," in Mark Aronoff & Richard T. Oehrle (eds.) *Language Sound Structure,* Cambridge, MA.: MIT Press, 107–136.

Shaw, Patricia A. (1995) "On syllabic obstruents," presented at Canadian Linguistic Association annual meeting, Université du Québec à Montréal, June 2–5, 1995.

Sherzer, Joel (1970) "Talking backwards in Cuna: the sociological reality of phonological descriptions," *Southwestern Journal of Anthropology* 26, 343–353.

Sofroniou, S.A. (1962) *Modern Greek,* Teach Yourself Books, London: Hodder and Stoughton.

Spencer, Andrew (1996) *Phonology: Theory and Description,* Oxford: Blackwell.

Srruk, Danylo Husar (1978) *Ukrainian for Undergraduates,* Oakville, ON: Mosaic Press.

Tauli, Valter (1973) *Standard Estonian Grammar. Part I: Phonology, Morphology, Word-Formation,* Uppsala: Almqvist & Wiksell.

Topping, Donald (1968) "Chamorro vowel harmony," *Oceanic Linguistics* 7, 67–79.

Tsujimura, Natsuko (1996) *An Introduction to Japanese Linguistics,* Cambridge, MA.: Blackwell.

Underhill, Robert (1976) *Turkish Grammar* Cambridge, MA.: MIT Press.

Vago, Robert M. (1980) *The Sound Pattern of Hungarian,* Washington: Georgetown University Press.

Vance, Timothy J. (1987) *An Introduction to Japanese Phonology,* Albany: State University of New York Press.

Walker, Douglas C. (1984) *The Pronunciation of Canadian French,* Ottawa: University of Ottawa Press.

Wang, William S-Y. (1967) "Phonological features of tone," *International Journal of American Linguistics* 33, 93–105.

Waterhouse, V. (1949) "Learning a second language first," *International Journal of American Linguistics* 15, 106–109.

Wolfart, H. Christoph & Janet F. Carroll (1973) *Meet Cree: A Practical Guide to the Cree Language,* Edmonton: University of Alberta Press.

Index

corpus-external evidence 88, 230
corpus-internal evidence 88, 230
counterbleeding order 166, 194, 251
counterfeeding order 166, 192, 251
Cree 73
criteria of phonological analysis 117
cross classification 80
Cuna
    Reduction 235
curly braces 134
Czech 97

D

deletion 57
derivation 54
devoicing 115
diacritics chart 32
diphthong 15
    falling 15
    rising 15
disjunctive application 136
dissimilation 55, 138
distinctive features 79
distinctness 290
distribution
    coincident 44
    complementary 37
    overlapping 45

E

ejective consonants 12
encoding of speech 17, 24
English 6, 10, 15, 34, 37, 45, 47, 50, 51, 52, 56, 57, 59, 66, 88, 96, 110, 208, 210, 226, 231, 232, 273, 297, 306
    aspiration 217
    Diphthong Shortening 248
    Eastern New England 58
    Flapping 217, 248, 288
    g-Deletion 227
    Lowland Scots 41
    n-Deletion 303
    Nasal Assimilation 227
    RP 58
    stress 136, 273

    Velar Softening 140
environment 37, 53
epenthesis 57
Eskimo
    Greenlandic 69, 97
Estonian 16, 111, 260
Ewe 96
extrametricality 280

F

falling diphthong 15
Farsi 43, 113
    r-Devoicing 53
    r-Flapping 54
feeding order 190, 251
Finnish 131, 237
    Apocopation 244
    Consonant Gradation 241
    Contraction 243
    Diphthongization 239
    Epenthesis 241
    Gemination of Consonants 243
    Gemination of Vowels 242
flaps 6
focus 119
foot 272
formant frequency extraction 24
formants 20
fortition 57, 116
Fourier's theorem 18
free variation 50
French 10, 37, 40, 57, 87, 232
    Canadian 67, 72
frequency 18
fricatives 4, 90, 93
fundamental frequency 21, 24

G

geminate 16
generative phonology 60
Georgian 66
German 37, 88, 110, 146
Gidabal 164
    Vowel Shortening 166
glides 6, 15, 90

CURRENT ISSUES IN LINGUISTIC THEORY

E. F. K. Koerner
Zentrum für Allgemeine Sprachwissenschaft, Typologie
und Universalienforschung, Berlin

The *Current Issues in Linguistic Theory* (CILT) series is a theory-oriented series which welcomes contributions from scholars who have significant proposals to make towards the advancement of our understanding of language, its structure, functioning and development. CILT has been established in order to provide a forum for the presentation and discussion of linguistic opinions of scholars who do not necessarily accept the prevailing mode of thought in linguistic science. It offers an alternative outlet for meaningful contributions to the current linguistic debate, and furnishes the diversity of opinion which a healthy discipline must have. A complete list of titles in this series can be found on the publishers website, **www.benjamins.com**

233 WEIJER, Jeroen van de, Vincent J. van HEUVEN and Harry van der HULST (eds.): The Phonological Spectrum. Volume I: Segmental structure. 2003. x, 308 pp.

234 WEIJER, Jeroen van de, Vincent J. van HEUVEN and Harry van der HULST (eds.): The Phonological Spectrum. Volume II: Suprasegmental structure. 2003. x, 264 pp.

235 LINN, Andrew R. and Nicola McLELLAND (eds.): Standardization. Studies from the Germanic languages. 2002. xii, 258 pp.

236 SIMON-VANDENBERGEN, Anne-Marie, Miriam TAVERNIERS and Louise J. RAVELLI (eds.): Grammatical Metaphor. Views from systemic functional linguistics. 2003. vi, 453 pp.

237 BLAKE, Barry J. and Kate BURRIDGE (eds.): Historical Linguistics 2001. Selected papers from the 15th International Conference on Historical Linguistics, Melbourne, 13–17 August 2001. Editorial Assistant: Jo Taylor. 2003. x, 444 pp.

238 NÚÑEZ-CEDEÑO, Rafael, Luis LÓPEZ and Richard CAMERON (eds.): A Romance Perspective on Language Knowledge and Use. Selected papers from the 31st Linguistic Symposium on Romance Languages (LSRL), Chicago, 19–22 April 2001. 2003. xvi, 386 pp.

239 ANDERSEN, Henning (ed.): Language Contacts in Prehistory. Studies in Stratigraphy. Papers from the Workshop on Linguistic Stratigraphy and Prehistory at the Fifteenth International Conference on Historical Linguistics, Melbourne, 17 August 2001. 2003. viii, 292 pp.

240 JANSE, Mark and Sijmen TOL (eds.): Language Death and Language Maintenance. Theoretical, practical and descriptive approaches. With the assistance of Vincent Hendriks. 2003. xviii, 244 pp.

241 LECARME, Jacqueline (ed.): Research in Afroasiatic Grammar II. Selected papers from the Fifth Conference on Afroasiatic Languages, Paris, 2000. 2003. viii, 550 pp.

242 SEUREN, Pieter A.M. and Gerard KEMPEN (eds.): Verb Constructions in German and Dutch. 2003. vi, 316 pp.

243 CUYCKENS, Hubert, Thomas BERG, René DIRVEN and Klaus-Uwe PANTHER (eds.): Motivation in Language. Studies in honor of Günter Radden. 2003. xxvi, 403 pp.

244 PÉREZ-LEROUX, Ana Teresa and Yves ROBERGE (eds.): Romance Linguistics. Theory and Acquisition. Selected papers from the 32nd Linguistic Symposium on Romance Languages (LSRL), Toronto, April 2002. 2003. viii, 388 pp.

245 QUER, Josep, Jan SCHROTEN, Mauro SCORRETTI, Petra SLEEMAN and Els VERHEUGD (eds.): Romance Languages and Linguistic Theory 2001. Selected papers from 'Going Romance', Amsterdam, 6–8 December 2001. 2003. viii, 355 pp.

246 HOLISKY, Dee Ann and Kevin TUITE (eds.): Current Trends in Caucasian, East European and Inner Asian Linguistics. Papers in honor of Howard I. Aronson. 2003. xxviii, 426 pp.

247 PARKINSON, Dilworth B. and Samira FARWANEH (eds.): Perspectives on Arabic Linguistics XV. Papers from the Fifteenth Annual Symposium on Arabic Linguistics, Salt Lake City 2001. 2003. x, 214 pp.

248 WEIGAND, Edda (ed.): Emotion in Dialogic Interaction. Advances in the complex. 2004 vi, 284 pp.

249 BOWERN, Claire and Harold KOCH (eds.): Australian Languages. Classification and the comparative method. 2004. xii, 377 pp. (incl. CD-Rom).

250 JENSEN, JOHN T.: Principles of Generative Phonology. An introduction. 2004. xi, 324 pp.

251 KAY, Christian, Simon HOROBIN and Jeremy SMITH (eds.): New Perspectives on English Historical Linguistics. Selected papers from 12 ICEHL, Glasgow, 21–26 August 2002. Volume I: Syntax and Morphology. 2004. x, 264 pp.

252 KAY, Christian, Carole HOUGH and Irené WOTHERSPOON (eds.): New Perspectives on English Historical Linguistics. Selected papers from 12 ICEHL, Glasgow, 21–26 August 2002. Volume II: Lexis and Transmission. 2004. xii, 273 pp.

253 CAFFAREL, ALICE, J.R. MARTIN AND CHRISTIAN M.I.M. MATTHIESSEN (EDS.): Language Typology. A functional perspective. 2004. xiii, 690 pp. + index.

254 BALDI, PHILIP AND PIETRO U. DINI (EDS.): Studies in Baltic and Indo-European Linguistics. In honor of William R. Schmalstieg. 2004. xxx, 294 pp.

255 MEULEN, ALICE TER AND WERNER ABRAHAM (EDS.): The Composition of Meaning. From lexeme to discourse. 2004. vi, 225 pp. + index.

256 BOK-BENNEMA, REINEKE, BART HOLLEBRANDSE, BRIGITTE KAMPERS-MANHE AND PETRA SLEEMAN (EDS.): Romance Languages and Linguistic Theory 2002. Selected papers from 'Going Romance', Groningen, 28-30 November 2002. 2004. viii, 275 pp.

257 FORTESCUE, MICHAEL, EVA SKAFTE JENSEN, JENS ERIK MOGENSEN AND LENE SCHØSLER (EDS.): Historical Linguistics 2003. Selected papers from the 16th International Conference on Historical Linguistics, Copenhagen, 11-15 August 2003. 2004. *Expected Fall 2004.*